The Ten Commandments
of Career Indie Authors

1. Thou shall write!

2. Thou shall read widely

3. Thou shall continue thy self-education

4. Thou shall organize thy paperwork

5. Thou shall not covet thy fellow authors' successes

6. Thou shall resist the temptations of FOMO,
Imposture syndrome, Perfection syndrome,
and other mental storms

7. Thou shall engage socially with authors

8. Thou shall pay it forward

9. Thou shall chart thy progress

10. Thou shall enjoy thy creativity,
whether in a story, an ad or an email

THIS BOOK BELONGS TO

Career Indie Author

Tell your stories
& build a business
that will last a lifetime

BOOKS FROM PESCHEL PRESS

Career Indie Author

Tell your stories
& build a business
that will last a lifetime

Bill Peschel & Teresa Peschel

PESCHEL PRESS ~ HERSHEY, PA.

Cover and interior design by Bill Peschel.

Illustration on page 212 courtesy of Jeff Bacon and Broadside Cartoons, www.navybroadside.com/.

www.peschelpress.com
www.careerindieauthor.com

ISBN-13: 978-1-950347-24-7

Library of Congress Control Number: 2020917279

Second printing: October 2020, version 1.1

Table of Contents

Foreword

Indie publishing is for everyone who wants to publish a book, whether it's a collection of your grandmother's prized jam recipes or the next thriller to be picked up by Hollywood.

We're at a unique moment in history where the barriers to starting your publishing career are low. You can write and publish a book in a few weeks for free, or take years writing your opus, spending money on quality editing and covers, and formatting the ebook and trade paperback. Whether it'll be a book worth reading is another question. Getting there — striking that balance between the cost of production and making a profit from it — is what *Career Indie Author* is about.

When a writer begins a story, there are two ways to go. Pantsers start with the first sentence and go on from there. Plotters know where they're going before they write the first word. With your business, you can't afford to be a pantser. Before you press [Publish] on your first story, take time to think about your business. Figure out what you can do and who you should hire to do what you can't. Decide how much money you want to invest, and what your goals are.

We wrote *Career Indie Author* because the business supporting the writer is just as important as being able to tell a story. That wonderful story will not earn you that beach house in Kauai, fund your retirement, or even buy you coffee, if you don't make good decisions about how you will spend the money needed to create and market your books.

Before you panic, let me assure you that it's possible to get better while you're publishing. Failure is not final. If you're willing to change and accept criticism, you can learn on the job and get better at it. This isn't the presidency, brain surgery or even rocket science!

So let's begin. Unless you're a published writer with the rights to your backlist, or an unpublished writer with finished books in your trunk, you'll start with writing and publishing one book. Don't worry about making mistakes. Failure is never final. You'll get better with each subsequent book.

Successful indie publishing that can support you and your family is not for everyone. It requires you to develop the artistic skill to write good books and the entrepreneurial skills to run the business. It requires understanding the range of jobs that need to be done, either by yourself or someone you hire. It requires making decisions that can literally change your life, for better or for worse. To succeed, you need the business mindset. Good luck!

Bill and Teresa Peschel,
Peschel Press, Hershey Pa.

Preparation

The publisher thought
[*Little Women*] FLAT,
and so did I
and neither hoped much for or from it.
We found out our mistake,
and since then,
though I do not enjoy
writing "moral tales"
for the young,
I do it because
it pays well.

Louisa May Alcott

Chapter 1
The Business Mindset

Key Points to Remember
- Best-selling writers succeeded because they had marketing support.
- Many successful writers came from an advertising or marketing background.
- You too can learn how to promote and market your work.

I have a saying. If you want to write for yourself, get a diary. If you want to write for a few friends, get a blog. But if you want to write for a lot of people, think about them a little bit. What do they like? What are their needs? A lot of people in this country go through their days numb. They need to be entertained. They need to feel something.

James Patterson

Real artists ship.

Steve Jobs

"There are two types of manga artist who succeed in this world ... One is the type of person who draws what they want to draw. To put it in rather negative terms they're the ones who rely on natural instinct ... or in positive terms, they're the "genius" types. And the other is the type of manga artist like you, Takagi, who creates a hit through calculation. And the one who has the potential of creating a smash hit is by far the non-calculating person."

Akira Hattori, *Bakuman*

What does it take to succeed in the world of indie publishing? Is it through natural instinct? Is it through calculation, looking at the market and feeding it what it wants? Or both, as the fictional Akira Hattori, an editor at the popular Japanese manga magazine *Shogun Jump* implies?

That's a question that will always be argued and never settled to everyone's satisfaction. The path to success is never easy. Worse, some people get lucky. They're in the right place at the right time with the right book, and they catch the literary equivalent of lightning in a bottle:

- Lauren Weisberger turned her brief job as an assistant to Anna Wintour at *Vogue* into a *roman à clef* best-seller. *The Devil Wears Prada* received a critical pasting — *The New York Times* refused to identify the magazine it parodied in its coverage — but the novel was turned into a successful movie starring Meryl Streep and a Broadway musical is in the works with Elton John writing the music.
- John Grisham self-published his first novel, but sold his second book to a New York publishing house. *The Firm* rocketed up the best-seller list and was turned into a popular movie starring Tom Cruise.
- Robert James Waller, at 53, published his first novel, *The Bridges of Madison County*. The book sold 9.5 million copies worldwide and was

turned into a popular movie starring Clint Eastwood and Meryl Streep.

Looking at each of these books, the key to their success was not that they hired Meryl Streep or Tom Cruise for the movie adaptation. It's that each book had been marketed to readers. Each writer had some business sense behind their decisions. Either Lauren Weisberger or the acquisition editor at Broadway Books saw the enormous publicity value of a purported tell-all book set — a comfortable distance from libel suits — at the most influential fashion magazine in the world. The ambitious John Grisham read books about writing thrillers before using his legal training to write *The Firm.* Robert James Waller's slim romance novel was packaged as a literary romance novel (written by a man who tantalizingly might have drawn it from real-life) and possibly helped by a massive book-buy at selected bookstores to drive it up *The New York Times* best-sellers list.*

My point is that each best-seller was the product of artistic inspiration, backed by business decisions that drove their success. As an indie writer, you will need a similar set of tools to operate your own profitable business. Like Weisberger, you can identify "hot spots" in the *zeitgeist* that your story could cover. Like Grisham, you can educate yourself about how to write effective sentences, build suspense, and convey emotion. Like Waller, you can package your book for a target audience (although you shouldn't adopt the dodgy book-buying tactic).

Because here's a secret: successful artists know their business. They are willing to learn how to grow, how to hire people to do things they don't do, and give them the time they need where it's most important: creating works that sell.

But Weisberger, Grisham, and Waller started where you are, knowing nothing. They learned along the way. Many writers came from advertising such as James Patterson, Faye Weldon, Dorothy L. Sayers, and Frederic Dannay and Manfred B. Lee (Ellery Queen). They understood packaging, the power of a memorable phrase, and how to reach potential buyers. Nowadays, many in the indie world take courses like Mark Dawson's "Ads for Authors," and use that knowledge to get their books in front of buyers.

But building a business is not about just learning advertising. Whether you're just starting out, an author who's lost your traditional publishing contract, or somewhere in between, you need to lay the foundations of your business. You need to make some decisions.

This guide will help you work your way through them.

> For those who make a point of pride in saying they have never read anything by John Grisham, Tom Clancy, Mary Higgins Clark or any other popular writer, what do you think? You get social academic brownie points for deliberately staying out of touch with your own culture?
> **Stephen King**

---

* I was at bookstore in Charlotte, N.C., in 1991 when a well-dressed woman brought a stack of *Bridges* to the counter. As book page editor at a newspaper, I took note of the title and wondered why someone would buy so many copies of a then-unknown book.

Chapter 2

Evaluating Your Resources

Key Points to Remember
- Success depends on the ability to tell a story, keep writing in the face of obstacles, and luck.
- Develop the ability to receive feedback, persevere in the face of obstacles, and get the tools you need to be productive.

> Financial necessity can be extremely clarifying. When your goal is to make enough money to pay the rent, writing loses a lot of its artistic mystique and becomes something much more mundane: a job.
>
> **Malinda Lo**

To set up an author business that will survive, you need six things:

1. Financial Resources
2. Goals
3. Writing Talent
4. Business Knowledge
5. Computer Knowledge
6. Artistic (visual) Knowledge

Of these, 1, 2, and 3 are of critical importance to your success; 4 is important to acquire; and 5 and 6 can be outsourced to people who have that knowledge.

Let's look at them:

Financial Resources: The money you invest in your business. I'm assuming that you want to make money selling your works, so that means keeping an eye on how much you're investing, how much you're spending, and how much you're receiving from sales. This means, yes, keeping track of everything. Bookkeeping. It's not something you have to do every day, and if you set up a system — meaning a spreadsheet, paper ledger, or accounting software — you can easily keep track of income and expenses and warn you of trouble before it's too late. It's a little annoying, but it'll save you a lot of trouble, especially at tax time.

Goals: Understanding what you want to do and why. It means thinking about the future, even if it's only "I want to write one / two / three books a year." Setting your goal now — and you can change it as you go on — will help with your motivation, especially on the days when you have a huge to-do list and don't know why you got into this weird business.

Writing Talent: I have read and collected material about writers and creativity for a lot of years. I even published a collection of stories

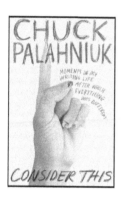

through Penguin (*Writers Gone Wild*). Over and over again, there are three things successful writers need:

- The ability to tell a story.
- The ability to keep writing.
- Luck.

Note what I didn't say. I didn't say "talent" or "genius." Those are exceptional traits and you either have them or you don't. The ability to tell a story is a bit trickier. You've listened to a six-year-old tell a story, and it's a chain of events on the order of "There's this knight, see? And he rides his horse to the castle. But there's this dog. A big dog! And it's growling at him. So he pulls out his plane and he fliiiiies over the dog's head. Oh, and he takes the horse with him …"

So I'm saying is, there are stories, and there are stories that touch readers emotionally. You can learn how to tell a story. You can even learn about the tools to employ, like three-act structure, scene and sequel, and character tags.

What you can't learn is imagination. That comes from within, fed by your life experiences, mother wit, and confidence in your judgment.

Chuck Palahniuk learned this lesson. In his great book on writing, *Consider This,* he tells a story about the day his writing instructor gave him a book to read. It was a short book, written by a well-known author. Chuck took it home and read it. Several times. And each time he finished it, he wondered why the hell he was asked to do this. The characters, as he put it, "were hard-pressed and put-upon cornpone hound-dog types just scraping by in the burnt-over backwoods hills of whatever." They did nothing exceptional, and nothing exceptional happened to them.

When he returned the book at the beginning of the next workshop, the instructor asked him if he loved it.

Palahniuk hedged. He didn't want to tell him the truth, that the book would benefit humanity only from the heat it provided if it was burned. How could he reveal his ignorance to his instructor, who handed him a book published by top people in New York City? So he said, "I really loved the language."

The instructor nodded, took the book, and left it on the table.

The session started. Students in turn read their work and everyone discussed it. And the book lay on the table, taunting Palahniuk with its presence.

Because, you see, he *hated* the book. He hated himself for not saying so, and that bugged him throughout the evening.

The class ended. Most of the students left. Someone opened a bottle of wine, and those who stayed chatted about movies. It was in the middle of a discussion about Robert Altman that Palahniuk broke.

"I hated it," he said.

They looked at him, puzzled and surprised. He hastily explained that he didn't hate Altman. It was the book his instructor had asked him to read, the one that was still on the table before them. "So I'm stupid," he concluded.

Silence. His instructor smiled. "I didn't give you the book to enjoy." He picked up the book and considered it. "It's awful …" and he grinned. "I wanted you to see how terrible a book could be and still get published." Only then did he shelve the book.

So here's my point: no matter how wretched you may think you write, there are books worse than yours out there. Besides, how do you know your book is terrible? You are not its reader.

Business Knowledge: When you start a business, you create a living thing that needs money to live. It takes in money, and it excretes money. So long as that happens, it will keep living. Cut off the supply of money, and it will wither and die.

So business knowledge is what you need to know and do to keep that creature alive outside of writing stories. It's what this book is about.

Computer Knowledge: A lot of work can be done on the computer. You write and edit your books on it. You'll go online and build your website, format your books, process art (for covers, blogposts, catalogs, swag), do social media, and answer and send emails,

That means you have to have a powerful computer, maybe more powerful than you think. Sure, you can write on any computer, even an old IBM-PC from the mid-1980s with the clickety-clack keyboard, running on an 8088 processor with WordStar 4.0.

But if you're laying out a 300-page book with art on every page, or filming a video for YouTube, you'll want a computer with more horsepower, and a larger monitor to boot. You want to make sure your software is up to date and protected against hackers.

The difference in your productivity can be astonishing. My last computer, bought in the mid-2000s, was a Compaq Presario bought off the shelf at Best Buy. It worked fine for word processing, but it slowed down when I edited a video. Year after year, as it absorbed new versions of Windows, it slowed down. I would turn the computer on, walk upstairs, get my coffee, chat with Teresa, and come back when it was finished.

When it came time to buy my new computer, I shopped the stores and online for a long time, until I met a computer geek who told me I needed a more powerful model than what he sold. Fortunately, I have two kids who knew computers. With their help, I bought the parts at PCPartPicker.com: 3.6 GHz 6-core processor, liquid CPU cooler, one-gigabyte motherboard, 16GB RAM, 3TB internal hard drive and 500GB solid state drive, a 24-inch

> Don't be a slug. Write it down, because you will not remember it in the morning. I get up at 3 a.m. to write. I force myself to write. The muse only comes to you when you're sitting . . . in front of the computer.
> **Richard Ford**

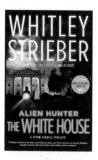

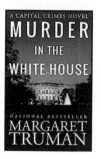

Papyrus font, the most mocked font after Comic Sans.

monitor, the latest version of Windows, and a cool keyboard with klicky keys that pulsates in color.

It's the type of computer gamers buy. It cost $1,800. Expensive, but turn it on, and about 10 seconds later it's ready to go. It's so powerful it can handle any big file I throw at it. It moves faster than I type, and I no longer have to fight my computer, or worry about it crashing. If I treat it like my last computer, I'll be rocking this baby for the next 10 years. Well worth the expense.

I'm not saying you need to buy a computer like mine, but if you can, buy a bigger model if it will remove a stress-causing problem. You have a lot of problems to deal with already; a slow computer shouldn't be one of them.

Artistic (visual) Knowledge: Acquiring an education in art is useful in dealing with artists, if only to provide feedback. But some people don't have any eye for art, just as there are people to whom music is a bunch of noise and gourmet food no different from what you can get in a frozen dinner.

This is not meant as an insult. It took me a long time to realize this. Not every person reacts to music the way I do. I listen to ELO's "Mr. Blue Sky," and feel the happiness of a new day, and the choir kicking in near the end has brought tears to my eyes. But to Teresa, ELO is only the answer to a crossword puzzle clue. And that's *all right.*

Learn what you are sensitive to and what you are not. Perhaps you have no idea what makes a good cover. That's fine. Educate your eye by looking at other covers in your genre, and pick out their common elements. Thrillers usually have a man, woman, or a couple running down a street. Political thrillers place them in front of the Capitol or the White House, following the rule in movies that all windows in Paris look over the Eiffel Tower. Romance covers provide clues to their sub-genre: woman in a beautiful ball gown (historical), a hunk's manchest (erotic), or in a kilt (Scottish laird). If the artist's cover approaches that, approve it and move on. If you're unsure, ask people whose advice you trust.

The same goes for any creative endeavor. There are people who can do it all, but there are also examples of groups who come together and inspire each other in ways they can't do by themselves.

As you publish more books, you may learn the nuances of typography, and why book designers shudder when you suggest Times Roman for the body text or Papyrus for the title font. If you're really observant, you'll learn why you shouldn't lay out your books in block paragraphs with no indent and a line space in between.*

---

* Libbie Hawker's plotting guide *Take Off Your Pants!* is laid out in that style.

Intangibles

There are also three mental skills which can help you succeed:

The ability to receive and process feedback. Your editor came back with suggestions for tightening your story. Your beta readers dislike your hero's choices. Sales have flatlined, and your book description needs tweaking. Amazon ads are not showing increased sales.

It's easy to blame the customers, or say the editor was not right for your work, or the readers just don't understand.

But what if they're right?

That's the question, and you won't find the answers in the back of the book. The hardest part about running a business, and life in general, is that it's nearly impossible to tell what is the right thing to do.

But the wrong thing to do is dismiss out of hand contrary advice or observations without examining them first.

That's what accepting and assessing feedback is about. You set up an action like sending a book to beta readers. You get their responses. Then, you sit down with a bracer, like a strong cup of tea, meditate for a moment to achieve inner peace, and read their suggestions as if they were made about someone else's book.

It's tough love I'm giving here, but if you can get through it, it'll give you so much in return.

If this will help, remind yourself they're doing it, not because they love criticizing, but because they see value in your words. They *want* to help make it better. They're on your side. The editor's on your side. The reviewers … well, maybe they're on your side. It depends.

But the point stands: the ability to receive and process feedback will help you in the long run. As you get more experienced, you'll stand a better chance of recognizing what is good advice for you and what is not. And that will only help you, too.

The ability to persevere in the face of obstacles. Suppose you were three novels deep in your series, when you realize, while you're writing the fourth, that sales have fallen off dramatically for #3. Readers hate your hero for what he did to that unfortunate dog.

Should you dump the series and start another? If so, should it be in the same genre? Or should you ride it out, change the ads, and see if they pick up? Maybe there's another option you missed.

Or suppose you hear that another author is trash-talking you at a bookstore. Do you confront him? Talk to the bookstore owner? Or do you decide to never return to the store?

What if you gave your spouse the manuscript of your first novel and they didn't like it?

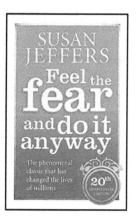

Over the course of your career, you will be faced with obstacles that will kill your momentum. You may even ask yourself if it's worth going on.

Only you can answer that question. When I have encountered an obstacle, my reaction varied from avoidance (sometimes for weeks, or even longer) to getting angry enough to confront it immediately. In the case of one passion — acting — I gave up completely.

Sometimes, my energy level played a role in my decisions. When I'm tired, distracted, or depressed, it was much harder to summon the energy needed to confront the problem. Keeping my life on an even keel — exercising regularly, getting enough sleep, and eating right — did a lot for my mental health and boosted my confidence.

In the case of your series, this is when you may want another person's opinion. Take a look at the reviews and see if there's a problem with the story. Maybe the best response is to carry on as usual.

A few decades ago, I came across a self-help book that contained a nugget of wisdom solely in its title, a piece of advice so powerful that I didn't need to read the book.

It was *Feel the Fear ... And Do It Anyway*.

I think a lot of us operate on that basis. On those days when we go to work knowing we're going to get fired. When we go on a date with someone we suspect is no longer into us. The last visit to our parent in the hospital. We're full of fear in those times, and we wish a fairy godmother would appear, wave her wand, and make it all better. Only we know that will never happen.

We feel the fear, but we go forward anyway.

The ability to acquire, design, and use the tools to get work done. Running your business is a job. It takes work. Every day.

You get the credit for success. You also get the blame for failure.

So this means putting routines in place that help guide you through your work day. Time for plotting, writing, and editing your books. Time to arrange covers and editing. Time to devote to marketing. Time to answer emails.

These require tools to keep your work flow under control, track important tasks, and keep you on an even keel.

Unfortunately, I can't give you a complete list of things to get, a sort of "business in a box" that you can open up and use. Your needs depend on the jobs you've taken on, the time you have available, and other factors.

You might be a retiree with a lot of time on your hands, but health problems that limit your energy. Or a mother with a couple small kids (bless you). Or you have a full-time job. You may be focusing on ebooks only, or you've decided to do print books and sell them at book festivals and craft shows.

Whatever you do, you'll need to think about how you're going to keep track of your business data, your paperwork (are you going to save your manuscripts for donation to a library?), your emails, your projects, your reading, and your schedule.

Fortunately, you won't have to do this all at once. It'll be a natural process, because you'll realize what you'll need to do when it happens. The moment you make your first business purchase, you'll need a way to record it. When you start selling books, you'll need to record that as well. The *Career Indie Author* will guide you through that process, offering ways to record expenses and sales, and keep track of your income and projects.

Chapter 3
Self-Test

Key Points to Remember
- Self-discovery is the process of learning who we are, not who we want to be.
- Determine what you can afford to lose; it will help guide your decision-making.
- Criticism is inevitable. You don't have to please everybody, just yourself and your readers

People do not spring forth out of the blue, fully formed — they become themselves slowly, day by day, starting from babyhood. They are the result of both environment and heredity, and your fictional characters, in order to be believable, must be also.

Lois Duncan

Let me tell you a story.

For most of my life, I wanted to be a reporter. Growing up in Warren, Ohio, I read my hometown newspaper, the *Tribune-Chronicle*, and the *Cleveland Plain Dealer* on Sunday. I loved seeing the reporters in *All the President's Men*. I fell in love with the drama of chasing the story, and the camaraderie in the newsroom. In high school, I took a journalism course taught by a reporter for *The Charlotte Observer* and got up at 5 a.m. to intern at the evening *Charlotte News*. At 15, I joined *The Charlotte Observer* as a copy boy.

Eventually, I entered the journalism school at the flagship University of North Carolina campus in Chapel Hill. I worked on the student newspaper as a reporter and copy editor, and even snagged an unpaid job as campus stringer for *The New York Times*.

The next summer, I landed an internship at the *Raleigh News & Observer*, and discovered what being a real-life reporter was like. Making phone calls. Asking questions. Being ignored or cursed over the phone. Making mistakes. Terrible mistakes.

Despite my dream, I discovered that I was not temperamentally suited to the job. I *hated* conflict. I *hated* criticism. I had a hard time getting to know people quickly, ingratiating myself with them, dealing with deadline pressure, and every day felt like going into battle.

I learned the hard way that it's difficult to assess our abilities, our needs, our faults, and our talents.

This insight applies also to a career as an author. You can write a story, but succeeding at writing is a different goal. Managing yourself forces you to be both boss and employee at the same time. Being the boss also means dealing with co-workers and freelancers who might not deliver what you want. Can you handle them?

That's what this self-test is about. It asks hard questions to help you see your core strengths and goals.

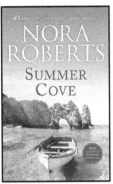

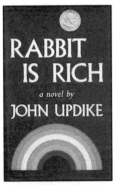

Remember: your goal is to understand if you want to build a business. There's no wrong answer! You want to align the structure of your business with your goals.

But if you want to make money at this — and please remember that, despite whatever the book evangelists say, it's not as easy as it looks — you want to build the systems and procedures that will support you on your journey.

Write your answer to each question below. This isn't a multiple-choice test, but I've added possible answers to encourage you to think deeper.

What is your goal as a writer?

- ► I want to write full-time
- ► I want to reach readers regardless of sales
- ► I want to create a profitable sideline
- ► I want to express myself and don't care about sales

What genre will you write in?

- ► Will they be written as part of a series or as one-offs?
- ► Can you write to your genre's expectations?
- ► Do you know what they are?
- ► Have you read many books in this genre?

What level of writer are you?

- ► Beginner
- ► I've written stories and taken a class / read *Writer's Digest* / read a book on writing
- ► Already published

How much money can you invest?

- ► Define this as the amount of money you're willing to lose.

Can you set up a website?

- ► Are you willing to learn?

Answers

Like I said, there's no wrong answer, so give yourself 100%. Congratulations! Let's review the questions and discuss your answers.

What is your goal as a writer?

What's motivating you to write? Some people were destined for the writing life: Stephen King, Nora Roberts, John Updike, Philip Roth, and J.K. Rowling. Before them, it was Charles Dickens and Arthur Conan Doyle, Virginia Woolf and Jane Austen. They wrote because they couldn't help it. Some overcame huge barriers to their success. Stephen King and his family lived in a single-wide trailer and he worked day jobs while typing his stories on a school desk. Think about Jane Austen, living in a time when few women were published writers. Think of the barriers she had to surmount, living in rural England, without support from fellow writers, magazines, the example of other women writers. And still she wrote.

At the other end, well, you can call them dreamers. They imagine the writing life like they see in the ads in *Writer's Digest*, spending their days on the beach, pen in hand, writing in a beautiful notebook. They see themselves, new book on the shelves, going on tour and meeting fans and doing media interviews.

In between might be someone who read her fourth dud romance in a row, tossed the book on the pile for the library book sale, and said those immortal words: "I can write better than that."

So the romance reader tries to write a book. She signs up for NaNoWriMo (National Novel Writing Month). She cranks out 50,000 words in a month, a novel about the size of a Harlequin category romance. At the end, her back aching, all she has to show for it is a mess of words that needs serious revision. Oh, it tells a story, and there's a happy ending, but some of the dialog sounds clunky, her heroine feels a little too drippy, and there are sections with notes like "[something exciting happens here]." And the sex scene! Can you even *do* that with kumquats?

She learned that writing a novel was harder than it looked.

She's faced with a decision. She could double down. She could read a book or two on plotting romances. She could take an online course. She could join a writers group and let them read five pages and see what they say.

Or she could tuck the manuscript in a drawer and stop, happy that she wrote it. She can pull it out later and reread it, amused at her characters and that one bit of great dialog — not to mention the kumquat — and leave it at that.

Nothing wrong with that at all. That's what self-discovery is about.

For you and me, the answer is somewhere in between. We have the desire, but not the full dose of confidence. We can't give up the itch, but it's difficult to scratch it. We may be afraid of people judging us by what we write. We may be afraid of rejection. We have these characters inside us, wanting to get out, but freeing them feels like unleashing King Kong on New York City. Is the world prepared for *that*?

Fortunately for us and our therapists, this little quiz is not concerned with *that.* We only want to know if you want to make money from your writing. If so, that means accepting a home truth I'm about to drop:

If you want to make money telling stories, you must consider your readers.

That means telling your stories in a way that entices them into listening.

Imagine trying to survive as a storyteller in the days before the printing press. You're in the marketplace. You have your blanket spread and you raise your hands and call out, "Oyez, oyez! Come and listen to the tale of the noble King Arthur, his beauteous Queen Genevieve, her noble lover Sir Lancelot, and the devilish Dragon of Derry!"

Pretty scary, right? What if no one listens? What if they *do* listen and hate you! This is why writers write and hate public speaking. But if you want to eat, you have to catch their attention. You have to humor them. You have to excite their curiosity, maybe their lust (this is a romance, you know). Maybe stick in some local gossip about the lord, to entertain the adults, while the kids squeal when you describe the Dragon of Derry stomping about the land and looking at them over the city wall (remember to point dramatically in that direction).

You know, I'm curious to know what happens next. I better get back to the point.

Consider your readers. Not the generic, faceless readers. *Your* readers. They haven't met you yet, but they'll read your words, see your story in their heads, feel the feels you create, and they'll want to know more. Some of them will even follow you to find out what happens next.

They're *your* readers, and if you want to make money at this, you must attract them, cultivate them, and work to satisfy them.

It's a big job, and yet not so big a job, because you're going to attract them doing what you're doing naturally: telling stories.

Let's go back to the marketplace. It's a busy day. The street is crowded. You're telling your story of Art, Gwennie, Lance, and the Dragon to the people.

Know this: *most of them will ignore you.*

That's all right. You've done it yourself. You've read a book by an author, and you don't seek them out for another book. There are authors you actively dislike, just as there are a few who you love without hesitation.

You're *their* fan, and now you'll be trying to find fans of your own.

Just don't overthink it. Know your audience. Tell your stories the way you want to, mindful of the tropes your genre readers expect, and, with luck and savvy marketing, you'll find them.

Consider your readers also applies to everything outside your story. Your book covers must send the correct genre signals. Your website should be easy to navigate. The book description should tantalize your readers. Even the title and author name (if you're using a pen name) should have a zing that makes

Readers, after all, are making the world with you. You give them the materials, but it's the readers who build that world in their own minds.
Ursula K. Le Guin

I don't really write for readers. I think that's the defining characteristic of being serious as a writer. … And if people like it, great, and if they don't like it, well, that's that — what can you do? You can't go round and hold a gun to their head.
Will Self, who later wrote "The literary novel as an art work and a narrative art form central to our culture is indeed dying before our eyes."

them memorable. All of that should be taken into account with *your* readers in mind.

I emphasize *your* readers to reinforce the point that you don't have to appeal to *all* readers. That never, ever happens, not even to best-selling authors. Not everyone likes Stephen King, just like not everyone liked Charles Dickens. Really! Look at his one-star reviews on Amazon.

What genre will you write in?

Genre is an artificial category created by bookstores and publishers to make it easier for customers to find a book. Back in the day when bookstores roamed the plains like dinosaurs, their shelves displayed books in broad categories: literary, poetry, general commercial fiction, science-fiction / fantasy, romance, and mystery / thriller. Children's books were segregated and ranged from baby's first book to the Hardy Boys / Nancy Drew series aimed at ten- to twelve-year-olds. Young Adult didn't exist.

Books that mixed genres existed, but one had to dominate. Isaac Asimov wrote mystery novels, but they had robots in them so they were science-fiction. Jude Deveraux wrote a time-travel novel, but it was a romance so it was shelved there.

Newbie writers with money on their minds frequently ask what's the most popular genre. It is romance, followed by mystery / thriller, followed far behind by science-fiction and fantasy. But you can make money with less-popular genres. Trad publishers will reject Westerns, medieval romances, and horror novels, because they can't make enough money on them to cover their costs. You don't have that problem. The key is to write really good books and find the readers who will appreciate them.

Examples abound. Wayne Stinnett loves novels set in South Florida, like those from Carl Hiassen, Dave Barry, and Paul Levine, so he set his Jesse McDermitt series there. He has published 18 books over the last seven years. Cecelia Mecca loves medieval historical romance, so she wrote one that was so good an agent said it was publishable, but she couldn't sell it. Traditional publishers weren't interested in the genre. So she published it herself, and she is still writing and selling books today.

If you are still unsure which genre to choose, here are two suggestions:

● **Look at your library.** What books do you read and reread? If you like that genre, you'll be more interested in writing in it than one that you think is successful but know nothing about. Plus, you already have a head-start on your reading.

● **Visit K-lytics** (*k-lytics.com*). Alex Newton's program scrapes Amazon's book rankings and charts the ups and downs of all the fiction and nonfiction categories. He offers free downloads of certain reports (like his most recent

> It's wise to plan early on where you'd like to go, do serious self-analysis to determine what you want from a writing career. … When I began, I thought I'd be comfortable as a straight genre writer. I just kept switching genres as my interests grew. I've since been fortunate that — with a great deal of effort — I've been able to break the chains of genre labeling, and do larger and more complex books. But it's difficult, and few people who develop straight genre reputations ever escape them.
>
> **Dean Koontz**

A lot of the humor (and possibly a lot of the power in the Discworld series) comes from thinking logically about those things which we don't normally think logically about, that we just accept. For example, in a horror story we just sort of accept the idea of werewolves and vampires without actually going a little deeper into it. It seemed to me that a thinking creature that spends part of its time as a wolf and part of its time as a human is going to be a very interesting creature, with a very interesting psychology.

Terry Pratchett

one on the Wuhan virus' impact on book sales), and sells special reports on certain genres. With his membership plans, you get access to the data (the 30 main categories and 420 subcategories at the premium level; and the 2,550 sub-sub categories at the elite level).

Series or one-offs? This decision will have a major impact on your earnings.

Simply put: readers love series. They fall in love with your characters and want more of their adventures.

Here a key fact to understand: the most successful authors, the ones who create a career writing fiction, write in a series. In every genre:

- Mystery? Arthur Conan Doyle and Sherlock Holmes. Rex Stout and Nero Wolfe. Erle Stanley Gardner and Perry Mason. Patricia Cornwell and Kay Scarpetta. Sara Paretsky and V.I. Warshawski. Sue Grafton and Kinsey Milhone. Lee Child and Jack Reacher.

- Romance? Many popular writers do not write in a series, but a significant percentage write series surrounding a family or location, like Nora Roberts, Marion Chesney, and Mary Balogh.

- Fantasy and science-fiction have series like Game of Thrones, Dune, and Wheel of Time.

Can *you* write in a series? Can you stick with the same characters or would you get bored with them, like guests who stay too long at your party? You can get around issue that by setting up a world and telling stories about different characters. Terry Pratchett built his phenomenal fantasy Discworld series by alternating books among several major characters: witch Granny Weatherwax; guardsman Samuel Vimes; the wizardry professors at Unseen University; and the reformed conman Moist von Lipwig.

Can you write to your genre's expectations?

The biggest mistake you can make at this stage of your career is to assume that you can write any story, so long as you think it's profitable. This suggests a degree of contempt for the reader ("they'll swallow anything"), and you'll find that spending a month writing a book in a genre you're not fond of is akin to self-torture.

You have to know the genre's expectations. Romances require — no, *demand* — a happy ending. Or at least a happy for now ending. That's even expressed in acronyms: HEA and HFN. Yes, Jude Deveraux got away with an ambiguous ending in *A Knight in Shining Armor*. But that was her 19th novel in nine years. If you get to that stage of the game, then you can try writing against expectations. For your first book, stick to the tropes.

Which is not to say you can't play around some. Remember, readers don't want the exact same thing. They want the same thing, only different. How to

IDEA

make it different? Combine your book with another subgenre, or change the setting, or flip the gender of the characters. A good rule of thumb is 80% familiar, 20% new. Don't go into counting words, however, just remember to inject something readers haven't seen before.

What level of writer are you?

The answer to this question determines where you should go next in your author journey.

If you're a beginner, then your apprenticeship has begun. You need to come to grips with the parts of a story and acquire the tools of your trade.

There are many ways to go about it, including — according to some people — nothing. Michael Anderle (founder of the 20Booksto50K Facebook group) is notorious for his writer journey, which consisted of writing a story, and pressing [Publish] when he was done. A computer programmer, he borrowed a term from that industry and called it a "minimum viable product."

Anderlee is a successful author and publisher, so it's easy to think that you can follow his example as well. You're welcome to try, but here's the rest of his story:

• His story was slammed by readers for its poor grammar, typographical errors, and indifferent prose style. However, they also loved the story and were willing to get his next book. They gave him a chance to get better, and he took it.

Good writing does not equal a good story. Nobody would accuse soap operas of emulating Proust, but they acquired an audience of rabid fans willing to settle down every day to watch "my stories." Why? Because they showed beautiful people in beautiful surroundings being emotionally engaged with each other.

In other words, they told a compelling story.

• Anderle learned from his mistake. He republished a reedited, corrected version of his first few books, and a fan of his organized beta readers to look over future books.

• Anderle is a fast writer. Taking advantage of Amazon's promotion of new books, he released books on a monthly schedule. Combined with placing his books (all in a series, naturally) in Kindle Unlimited — an all-you-can-read service that pays authors for every page that is read — and he fulfilled his 20 Books to 50K goal well before 20 books.

• Anderle is comfortable running a business. Over the years, he's dedicated himself to, as he calls it, "Pattersoning the shit" out of his business. Like James Patterson, he frequently writes and releases his novels and works with collaborators to increase his output. In short, Anderle has become the owner of a fiction factory, an indie publisher version of Harlequin, the Stratemeyer

Syndicate (the Hardy Boys and Nancy Drew series, among many others) and a descendant of the pulp magazines of the 1920s and '30s, churning out as much product as the market can bear.

That's his path; let's discover yours. In the back of the book, are resources which I've found useful, such as books, online courses, and areas that you want to concentrate on. These are the tools you can use to create memorable, emotional stories readers will give you money to read.

TIP

One suggestion: don't be like me and buy a lot of books. I have three shelves full of "how to write better" books. How many of them have I read? Not as many as I would have liked. I enjoyed reading them, but is your goal to enjoy reading these books or getting better as a writer? If the latter, you'll progress much faster if you get a few books and use them, or sign up for a course and stick with it, until you're sure there's nothing more to learn from them.

How to learn: Book are your tools, so use them and use them up! Write in them. Outline your thoughts on the opening blank pages. Create your own index of important concepts and other material you want to return to. The pages of my most useful books are covered in ink and highlighters, and I'll sometimes argue with the author or expand on what I've learned. Brain researchers say that it's easier to recall facts by writing them down rather than through reading alone.

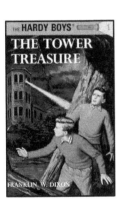

The process of transferring information from the page to the eye to the brain to the hand to pen on paper helps you better understand these concepts, and remember to use them when you turn to your stories.

An intermediate step can be you've written stories and **taken a class / read Writer's Digest / read a book on writing**. This is a wide, wide category, and means you're closer to the goal of writing stories you're proud of, and willing to learn more.

There's not much more to add here except check out the resources in the back of the book.

If you're **already published**, congratulations! You don't need my advice here, except that I hope you're still willing to learn more about stories, writing, grammar, and the business.

How much can you afford to invest?

How much does it cost to publish a book?

Nothing. As in zip, nada, free. There are articles out there that list figures for editing (developmental, line, and proofreading), cover design, formatting, printing, and distributing your book, with a bottom line that is breathtaking. But, my hand on my heart, it is also true that, if you do all the work, you can publish a book for nothing.

Knowing how to
lay out newspaper
pages and resize art
proved useful for
Peschel Press'
nonfiction books.

But there's a catch, as you'll see in the next question.

How much does it cost to publish a good *book?*

Aye, there's the rub.

The answer can be "the same." I published *The Casebook of Twain and Holmes,* a collection of Sherlock Holmes pastiches featuring Mark Twain, for free.

But, like the Michael Anderle example above, I had resources that enabled me to do this.

• I have my wife, Teresa, willing to edit my stories. Believe me, if you want to stress-test a marriage, either hang wallpaper together or have your spouse critique your work.

• I have mad copyediting and page layout skills from my years at a newspaper.

• I also learned there how to manipulate artwork using Photoshop.

• And I have an artistic daughter who colorized my cover.

Let me ask again: how much does it cost to print my *book?*

Now we're moving closer to the right answer, which is: it depends. We'll get deeper into this question later, with resources and dollar amounts, so if you go into this assuming that, to get someone else to do everything, it can cost you about $1,500, you're in the ballpark.

Before you head to your fainting couch, remember that this figure is not set in stone. You can pay a lot more. I've heard from people that they've paid someone else (who did everything) between $3,000 and $5,000 to produce a book.

Now, if you have the money and you find a reputable person, this might be a worthwhile investment. But remember that, if you want to run a business, you'll have to sell enough books to cover that cost.

Even $1,500 is a lot. If you're selling ebooks for $3.99 and realizing 70% of that, you're earning $3 per book. That means you'll have to sell 500 copies to get into the black. And that's before paying other expenses, such as buying a website name, buying ISBNs, and advertising.

(Like I said before, DON'T PANIC. Take deep breaths. Once you see the totality of this business and understand a concept called "cash flow," you'll feel, well, maybe not better, but not as panicked. Be patient and you'll see.)

Getting back to the point, before you start building your business, you must know your goal (money / fame / self-fulfillment), you must lay down a path to follow (what genre and series / no series); and how much you're willing to lose on this venture.

I'm not suggesting that you will lose this money. This is really the amount you're willing to *invest* in yourself. But like any bet, you should do it with the understanding that, if it doesn't work, the money's gone.

So think about it. Discuss it with your partner. Write down the figure.

Think of it as a starting point. You can always increase it later, but you have to start somewhere.

Can you set up a website?

What the heck? Are you going to ask next if I know how to change a tire?

No, but it's not a bad idea; at least learn the basics like checking your fluids and the amount of air in your tires.

But when it comes to your career, there are a few rules I consider absolute:

- Write at a comfortable frequency.
- Finish what you write.
- Publish what you write.
- Own a website.

It can be built any way you like, whether through sites that do the hosting and supply the software (such as Blogspot, WordPress.com, Wix, or Squarespace), or something a little more complicated like installing WordPress yourself on a hosting provider like SiteGround, HostGator, or Bluehost.

I've seen some advise starting a Facebook business page (using your personal page for commerce is against their rules), and they make a good argument for it. But the answer depends on how much effort you're willing to put into it.

- Do you like engaging with people socially? If you don't, you're better off avoiding social media.

Even if you do, you still need to be careful with your time. Posting on Facebook / Twitter / Instagram, etc., and monitoring comments might take up more time than you want to invest.

But with your website, all you need to do is post a page for each book, create a cool front page, set up your newsletter (if you're so inclined), and that's it. You don't need a blog (again, if you're not interested, don't). You only need to update the site with each new book.

Having a website establishes your credibility and gives people a way to contact you for whatever reason (book signings, fan mail, etc.). People who hear about you or your books can search for your name and find something.

Many authors don't do this. I've seen search results that begin and end with an Amazon listing. Or their name will be on a third-party website like Fantastic Fiction, which categorizes novelists and their series.

Or, you could dispense with a website entirely. I've seen ebook-only authors who do that. You could do that as well, if you're really concerned about your privacy and you don't want your family to know about your werewolf bondage erotica.

Are you willing to learn? In an early draft of *Career Indie Author,* I suggested that every author should start with a WordPress site.

For those who don't know, WordPress is a software program that you use to build a website. There are hundreds of millions of WordPress sites out there. The software has a learning curve, but it does not require programming knowledge to use.

To confuse matters, there are two flavors of WordPress. There is WordPress.com, a website that can host your WordPress-powered website. WordPress.org hosts the software (although many hosting providers also give you the option to install WordPress directly from them, which is a lot easier).

But over the last few years, I've changed my mind. I fell into the trap of thinking that anyone could buy a website name from a domain name registrar like GoDaddy or Namecheap, buy space on a server from a hosting provider, install the WordPress software, configure it, choose a theme and design their website.

I'm not saying you *can't.* I'm saying that it takes time to learn, and if you're a storyteller with little computer experience, you may not be interested in maneuvering through the various hoops to get your website up and running.

It's a lot easier to check out a site like Squarespace, buy your domain name there, and have them host your site. All you'll need to do is pick a design for your site (a design is called a theme) and tweak the colors and text to suit you. It'll be more expensive because they're doing the work for you, but they also act as your tech person. You're paying for convenience and to not be hassled. They keep the software updated and make sure the site's online 24/7.

But don't limit yourself to Squarespace. While it's cool to have a website that looks contemporary, it's not necessary. Most readers who visit you are not going to be aware if your site looks out of date. Most won't care, so long as they can find your books and learn where to buy them.

But if you want to DIY, WordPress is the way to go.

Chapter 4
The One-Page Business Plan

Key Points to Remember
- A business plan lays out your goals, your team, and how much you're willing to spend.
- It is not a law that has to be obeyed, but a map to a journey.
- Change the plan as you learn more about yourself as a writer and what you're willing to do.

It's the worst name in publishing. The worst mistake of my career was not taking my mother's name after my first couple of books. I'd be John Gregory and I'd be selling, no kidding, 10 times as many books. When people like my books they don't know how to tell anybody else. They say, "I just read this book by this guy, John somebody, Le-somebody." And the person goes, "Oh, John Le Carre?" and they say, "Oh yeah, probably."

John Lescroart

Now we're ready to build your business, and we'll do it on one page. This plan provides a way for you to think about your writing as a business.

The form is found on the next page. Here's how to fill it out:

Author or Pen Name / Genre / Estimated Word Count: Is your name easy to remember? Easy to spell? Does it fit with other popular names in your genre? Maybe you feel more comfortable if you created an author persona, or need to stay private. There's nothing wrong with modifying or even adopting a completely new name. Joanne Rowling adopted J.K. Rowling because it was gender neutral and reminded you of J.R.R. Tolkien. For her romance novels, Jude Gilliam changed her last name to the more evocative Deveraux. James Dover Grant probably would have been a best-selling thriller writer, but you have to admit Lee Child is much easier to remember and probably helped him get there faster. The author of the classic erotic novel *The Story of O* wrote under a pen name that was not revealed for four decades.

As for genre and word count, they were set by the trad publishers and vary widely. Romances and mysteries tended to be shorter, down to 50,000 words. Fantasy trends longer, especially epic fantasy, which can run 80,000-120,000 words. Science fiction has been as short as 50,000 and rising above 100,000 words.

Nowadays, any length is fine if the story is told well. Only epic fantasy fans seem to like shipping container-sized books, and contemporary romance readers prefer 50,000-60,000 words.

Company Name: A company name is not required unless you have to file official paperwork, such as incorporation papers. It's an optional box to fill out when you load your book onto Amazon. Check the best-selling indie books in your genre. I'll bet many of them don't list a publisher and note that it is sold by Amazon.com Services LLC.

Still, since Adam named the animals, we can be compelled to follow

Peschel Press Logos

Peschel Press

Odessa Moon

Career Indie Author

YOUR WRITER'S BUSINESS PLAN

AUTHOR or PEN NAME / GENRE / ESTIMATED WORD COUNT

COMPANY NAME / BRAND COLORS:

WHAT SETS YOUR BOOKS APART?	TEAM AND KEY ROLES
	•
	•
	•
	•

TARGET READERS	SIMILAR AUTHORS & TITLES
•	•
•	•
•	•
•	

SALES CHANNELS	MARKETING ACTIVITIES
•	•
•	•
•	•
•	•

VERSION / PRICE / ROYALTY	EXPENSES
•	•
•	•
•	•
•	•

INVESTMENT / SOURCE	EBOOK-TO-PROFITABILITY GOAL
•	
•	
•	
•	

DEADLINES FOR FIRST WORK

First Draft by	Revision Draft by	Editing Draft by	Beta Readers by	Publication by
Words per day	Words per day	Words per day		

Logos for Bass Ale, Knopf, the Great Seal of the United States, Ramones, and Terry Gilliam's Poopoo Pictures.

his lead and name our business. I chose Peschel Press because I didn't want to publish one kind of book. I wanted an imprint. I also felt that it would look more professional, even if I did name it after myself (just like Knopf, Ballantine, Baen and other publishers).

It was also out of habit that I created the company's logo, which I display as a colophon on the spine of our books. Logo is an abbreviation of *logotype*, a word derived from the Greek words *logos* (for "word") and *typos* ("imprint"). This unique symbol represents your company, much in the same way that a heraldic shield identified a knight on the battlefield.

Just about anything can be used as a logo. It can be a word, such as "Facebook" or "Coca-Cola" in a unique design or font. It can be a geometric symbol such as the red triangle for Bass Ale. It can be a drawing such as the running borzoi for Knopf books. It can incorporate all three styles. It can be modified from public domain sources; the Great Seal of the United States inspired the Ramones' logo. It can have a meaning obvious to the customer, or be a private joke, such as the half-naked medieval monk climbing a ladder drawn like a strip of film, the logo for director Terry Gilliam's Poopoo Pictures.

A good logo should be distinctive and easily recognizable whether used on a billboard or on the spine of a book. It's a difficult combination to pull off, but when it works — watch out!

A logo makes a powerful statement. Anyone (and everyone) can have a company name. Attaching a symbol to it makes it eye-catching and memorable, and makes it look like you have a real business, not a vanity press.

It should be used everywhere, such as your website, books (ebooks too!), printed catalog pages and flyers, swag, and press releases.

Brand Colors: Colors play an important role in branding. They can signify your genre, the type of books you write, and the type of pleasure readers can expect. A thriller writer with a website drenched in pink will probably not be taken as seriously as one with a black palette.

So think about what kind of books you're writing. Look at the popular covers in your genre. Can you identify the color palette? Consider using them as part of your website, swag, and personal brand.

Nail down the exact color, as well as the font for your company name and logo (if you have letters in your logo). Write them down. For colors, you can record the hexadecimal code, and the RGB and CMYK numbers. In addition, a company called Pantone assigns numbers to colors for use in the printing industry. Their Color Finder page (*pantone.com/color-finder*) makes it easy to identify a color by all of these numbers, so that the colors on your printed brochure (which uses Pantone), your website (RGB), and books (CMYK) are consistent. Save this information in a Word file, and you'll never have to guess again.

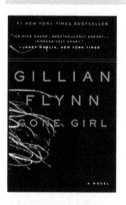

No writer is entitled to earn a living from his writing, or even to be paid for his writing; once you seek payment, you have to consider the market for what you're producing, especially during a time when supply outpaces demand.
Jane Friedman

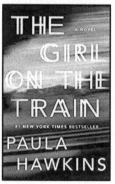

What Sets Your Book Apart? What makes your work unique? Crude humor? Oddball characters? An interesting world? Be wary of letting yourself be influenced by one writer. While people would love to see novels like Terry Pratchett's wonderful Discworld, imitators will only remind readers to turn to the original series. This is where wide reading will help you by providing plenty of inspirations to draw on. So give your world and characters something that sets your books apart.

Many writers begin their career knowing what they want to write. One popular alternative involves writing to market and writing to trend.

What's the difference? Write to market means deciding on a particular genre, and researching to learn the popular tropes, setups, emotional high points and other characteristics of that genre. For example, a cozy mystery is identified as a closed community (a small town, a bookshop, a bakery), an amateur detective, usually a woman, the possibility of romance (with the hunky homicide detective), and the story ending with a dramatic encounter between the detective and the villain.

Write to trend means looking at what's popular now. This means examining the best-seller list overall, possibly joining the K-lytics service (which identifies through the use of Amazon categories which niches are popular yet underserved).

Once you've identified a hot trend, you follow the same path as write to market.

For example, after *Gone Girl*, there was a spate of thrillers involving women who were worse or more than they seemed, like *Girl on a Train*. The Harry Potter series is another former hot trend that could have been exploited. In both cases, you're looking at BookWorld as a marketer, looking at what readers want and fulfilling their expectations.

Team and Key Roles: Do you have someone to edit your book, even if you're trading manuscripts with another author? Do you have a cover artist, website guru, or book formatter in mind? Note it here.

Target Readers: A book written for everyone is a book written for no one. No book is going to be read by everyone, even the Harry Potter series. The clearer the picture of your audience, the better chance you have of reaching them.

Similar Authors, Titles: These are called comps. They complete the statement "Fans of _____, _____, and _____ will love your book." This will prove useful not only in evaluating your novel idea — is your book appealing to those readers? — it'll help you when comes to advertising your book.

Sales Channels: The first choice is between going with Kindle Unlimited or wide, by which we mean Amazon, Kobo, Nook, Apple, Google Play, and an aggregate publisher like Smashwords or Draft2Digital to reach other markets. It's even possible to go direct to Kindle and use an aggregate for the rest, but in return for convenience you're giving up a share of the wealth. Draft2Digital, for example, takes 10 percent of your sales. That may not sting when you're making $10 a month, but once you hit $1,000 a month, losing $100 might make you reconsider.

Marketing Activities: While there are advertising options — Amazon, BookBub and Facebook ads, and newsletter deals on BookBub, BookGorilla, The Fussy Librarian, etc. — you may want to hold off on advertising your first book. It's better to learn how to use them effectively before opening your wallet. That still leaves social media posts, newsletters and newsletter swaps, press releases, blog tours … the list is nearly endless. Not all tactics are equally effective, so don't hold yourself to what you write here. You'll learn as you go.

Version / Price / Royalty: How will your book be published; the most common options are print, ebook, or audiobook (some authors issue a large print version, too). Price depends on your book's genre, size, and what your competition charges. Royalty payments are based on a percentage of the price, usually 70 percent, reduced if you go through an aggregator. Also, Amazon charges a delivery fee for your kindle ebook. So an ebook priced at $2.99 would return about $2 per sale. The price is based on what you think the market will bear. Checking competing authors — remember that list of similar titles? — will give you an idea of what readers consider a fair price.

Expenses: This is what you expect to spend to publish this book. Include indirect costs such as office supplies, computer equipment, and software.

Investment / Source: Write down how much you're willing to lose to publish this book, and where it'll come from.

EBooks to Profitability: Figure out how many ebook sales it'll take to cover your expenses. This'll depend on the price you'll charge and the sales channels you'll use. To make it simple, take the price, multiply by .7 (assuming a 70% royalty), and divide the total expenses by that figure. So, if you're going to spend $1,000 on a book you'll sell for 2.99 (2.09 per book royalty), you'll need to sell 1,000 divided by 2.09 equals 479 copies to begin making a profit. That gives you a ballpark figure of how much debt you need to pay off to make this work profitable.

Deadlines for First Work: One way to provide a motivation to finish your book is to set up a deadline for each stage. To set a first-draft deadline, take your estimated word count, and divide it by the number of writing days. This gets you the number of words you need to write each day to reach your goal. Do the same for the revision draft and then the editing draft.

Chapter 5
Deeper Into the Plan

Key Points to Remember

- A good pen name should be easy to remember, true to the genre and unique.
- Maintaining anonymity online is possible but it requires care and discipline.
- Beware author services that promise an introduction to Hollywood or best-seller "secrets,"

The first four chapters of *Career Indie Author* were given away as a reader magnet for my newsletter. But I found after writing it that there was more I wanted to say about the one-page business plan, so we're going to go through it again in greater detail.

Author or Pen Name

Give a thought for poor Elizabeth Taylor and Winston Churchill. They tried. They worked really hard, but fate conspired against them. They ran into the same problem each time they published a novel; their name got in the way.

I'm not talking about the actress and the statesman, but about the British novelist Elizabeth Taylor (1912-1975), and the American writer Winston Churchill (1871-1947).

I'm joking, of course. Taylor was a highly regarded literary novelist, and Churchill wrote several best-sellers. We don't know if they disliked sharing their name with someone else, but in their day, before internet search engines, they had time to establish their reputation before running into endless iterations of "do you know you share …?"

But bestselling thriller author John Lescroart believes his name cost him sales: "It's the worst name in publishing. The worst mistake of my career was not taking my mother's name after my first couple of books. I'd be John Gregory and I'd be selling, no kidding, 10 times as many books. When people like my books they don't know how to tell anybody else. They say, 'I just read this book by this guy, John somebody, Le-somebody.' And the person goes, 'Oh, John Le Carre?' and they say, 'Oh yeah, probably.'"

So before you publish your first book, take your time to decide on your pen name. The same goes for your publishing company (which is a separate issue we'll get to in a minute).

Names are important. They convey images and meanings. They signal

Too many writers think that all you need to do is write well — but that's only part of what a good book is. Above all, a good book tells a good story. Focus on the story first. Ask yourself, "Will other people find this story so interesting that they will tell others about it?" Remember: A bestselling book usually follows a simple rule, "It's a wonderful story, wonderfully told;" not, "It's a wonderfully told story."

Nicholas Sparks

to the reader your nationality, gender, intellectual level, and even the types of books you write. Would you expect "Brad Thor" (his real name, BTW) to write romances? Would you be disappointed if you picked up Agatha Christie's *A Daughter's A Daughter* and not find Hercule Poirot or a dead body in it? That's why she wrote it as Mary Westmacott.

If you use your name, which version of it? I write as Bill Peschel, but I could have chosen William Peschel. On a book cover it looks balanced (seven letters in each part) and conveys an intellectual tone. But what about W.E. Peschel? That disguises my gender. B.E. Peschel? Awkward sounding.

Billy Peschel? Forget it. Ditto for Willy Peschel.

What about my middle name? Then I would have been Ed Peschel (sounds like he fixes cars, not prose) or Edward Peschel.

Instead, I went with Bill. I'm used to it, and when I publish fiction, I'll use W.E. Peschel to differentiate myself from the nonfiction, annotating author, while still keeping it in the same family of last names.

Teresa avoided this trap when she chose Odessa Moon as a pen name for her Steppes of Mars series. It's easy to remember, easy to spell, and she liked the repetition of Os, which reminded her of the two moons circling Mars, Deimos and Phobos. The URL odessamoon.com was available, and there were no books written by that name at Amazon.

Here are some more factors that goes into choosing the right name:

Full names signal seriousness. "William F. Buckley" rolls stentorian off the tongue. "Billy Buckley" fixes your pickup truck. "Bill Buckley" sings country songs. "William F." is your professor.

Initials for fantasy fiction. Think J.R.R. Tolkien, M.A.R. Barker, and J.K. Rowling. George Raymond Martin added his confirmation name Richard when he was 13. When he started writing, he initialized Raymond Richard into George R.R. Martin, a memorable name that hints at the fantasy content in his work.

Pen names or initials to flip or hide your gender: This was formerly a woman's preserve, like George Eliot (Mary Anne Evans), James Tiptree Jr. (Alice B. Sheldon), and Robert Galbraith (J.K. Rowling). The few men who have written romance fiction have done the same, like Leigh Greenwood. But men writing psychological thrillers with strong women characters are doing it as well: Riley Sager (aka Todd Ritter), J.P. Delaney (Tony Strong), and S.J. Watson (Steve Watson).

Pen names for secrecy. This is particularly true for romance and erotica writers. Fordham University professor Mary Bly invented Eloisa James to write her historical romances to avoid potential problems. In the most notorious case, Anne Descios adopted Pauline Réage for *The Story of O* (1954), a pen name which was kept secret for four decades.

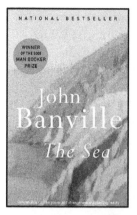

Booker Prize winner
John Banville also writes
crime novels as
Benjamin Black.

Different names for different genres. Irish novelist and Booker prize winner John Banville, described as "the heir to Proust, via Nabokov," also writes excellent crime novels as Benjamin Black. When he was starting out, mystery novelist Lawrence Block wrote soft-core porn under pen names such as Jill Emerson, Sheldon Lord, and Andrew Shaw.

New name, clean record. Traditionally published authors whose sales have flagged are frequently asked to start a new series under a different name. This became a popular tactic when Barnes & Noble would reduce orders for an author's new work if their sales show a decline. Releasing a new book under a name with no sales record was terrible for authors trying to build an audience for their work, but it got around the B&N penalty.

Too much fame. Worried that people were buying his books because of his name, Stephen King began publishing books as Richard Bachman (it helped that he was prolific, too). J.K. Rowling published her mystery novels as Robert Galbraith because she didn't want to disappoint fans looking for her fantasy work.

Extreme secrecy. No examples, because we don't know who they are. But there are writers who publish a lot of novels under what looks suspiciously like a pen name, and whose Amazon page and author website doesn't display their picture or personal information,

It could be someone running a fiction factory, who hires ghostwriters. Or, it could be someone who doesn't want the world to know their real name. (It could also be someone ripping off other authors or even fanfiction, but that's beyond the scope of this book. Just be aware that, if someone thinks they can make an easy buck scamming readers, they will try.)

Suppose you are a woman who wants to hide your identity online. Maybe you write stories that would embarrass your family. Maybe you've been through a traumatic relationship and you don't want your ex to harass you. Can you publish your stories and keep your identity secret?

You can, and here's how.

Keeping Your Name Offline

WARNING

To disguise your online identity so you can't be traced is possible, but only if you're careful and consistent, and even then, you might not succeed. Here's one possible situation: you write something in a novel that offends someone and they sue you for libel. They file a lawsuit against your pen name, and the judge orders the online vendor to serve you the legal papers. Depending on what happens next, the vendor may be forced to reveal your true identity.

Note: I AM NOT A LAWYER AND THIS IS NOT LEGAL ADVICE. I'm just spitballing a way your identity could be revealed.

This is not necessarily true for the wealthy, who have access to legal strategies to keep their identity separate from their business. Think incorporating in Delaware, setting up shell corporations and offshore bank accounts, and hiring lawyers who knows the ins and outs of high finance.

This is not to meant to scare you. It's perfectly possible to fly under the radar, but only if you tell no one. Friends can't know; they'll gossip. Your relatives especially can't be told, and maybe even your spouse. All you need to do is piss one of them off to find that your secret has become a weapon to bludgeon you with. Remember, two people can keep a secret, but only if one of them is dead.

Here are some issues to consider.

Your Online Bookseller Accounts

Your accounts with Amazon, PayPal, Facebook, and other ebook retailers will have to be in your real name. No pseudonyms allowed. Of course, to pay your bills you have to use your credit cards, which are in your real name, and if you want to get paid, you have to provide them with your bank information.

However, you can publish your books using a pen name. Amazon will let you use your pen name within your KDP account (you still have to log in with your real name).

Your Author Website

If you want a website, you'll have to buy a domain name, and you'll have to buy their privacy option to keep your name secret.

The domain name — the name of your website after typing in "https://www" — must have a contact name and address. That's the law, and there's no way around it. However, the law doesn't say it has to be the person who bought the website. The privacy option (for which you pay a yearly fee) will list the company as the contact name. It doesn't mean they own the site (you still do), but they act as a layer of protection.

While writing this section, I decided to check how my websites are listed. So I visited Whois.net (*whois.net*) and ICANN (*lookup.icann.org*), two major organizations in the domain registration world, and looked up Peschel Press (*peschelpress.com*). The only information that my searches turned up is the state the domain owner is from.

It turns out that GoDaddy, the company I bought my domain names through, added a free basic layer of protection. They offer higher levels of protection, such as protecting you from spam, keeping your state out of the directory, and protecting against domain hijackers. I don't know if they're worth purchasing — I haven't had a problem in these areas — but you might.

Part of Bill's books listed
in The Library of
Congress' database.

U.S. Copyright

Copyright can be filed with the Library of Congress in your pen name. Or, if you want to make it simpler, don't bother. Copyright is automatically granted the moment you finish your work. So you can publish your book with the copyright notice, and it is protected. If you file for the copyright, however, and your work is stolen, you can sue and receive damages from the thief.

We file our copyrights, but not in hopes of winning money from future lawsuits. Registering your work means you'll have to send The Library of Congress copies of your book, which they shelve. How cool is that?

Email

Creating a truly anonymous email account that can't be traced back to you can be far more technically complex, involving using a virtual private network (VPN) service and other techniques.

The easiest way would be to create a Google Gmail account to be used only by your author persona. Set up the account and use your pen name instead of your real name. Google will send a confirmation email to your phone, but instead of using your home phone, buy a burner phone such as the Motorola Tracfone, and give them that number. The idea is that you're not going to give Google any real information that someone can use to trace you. If Google finds out, they'll cancel the account, but that's a minor risk to take.

From then on, use that email account solely for your author business. Never send it to anyone you know. Never share this email address with anyone who knows you.

This is not a foolproof method, however. A determined pursuer with access to powerful tracing tools might be able to locate you. But this should protect you from the general public.

Here's one way how carelessness could make this scheme go wrong. I have a lot of emails associated with my websites. Because they get a lot of spam, I reroute them through my personal Google account. Yes, Google reads all my email, but they do a wonderful job filtering 99 percent of the spam. But there is one difficulty. If I reply to an email from peschel@peschelpress.com, they will see that it comes from my bpeschel@gmail.com account. Which is fine; I don't care. But if you route your pen name's email to your personal account and reply, you've blown your cover. So always go direct to your pen name's Gmail account to read mail, and reply from that account.

Chatting Online

If you use the Google Mail plan above to secure your email account, you can move on to set up social media accounts with it.

The only problem might be Facebook. That platform has a hard rule against setting up a personal page using an alias. Which means you also can't set up a business page using your pen name.

You can go ahead and try. Facebook won't know that you're using a fake name. Just be aware that they can delete your account if their algorithms catch you. Also, while you can accept people as Facebook friends, you shouldn't reach out to your real-life friends and family with invitations. Remember, they don't know you're using a pen name.

Also, no matter what the social platform, never say anything that can be traced back to you. Don't mention your birthplace. Don't mention people you know. Don't mention where you went to school. Nothing personal.

Public Appearances

Filming Bill's short segment for *Mysteries at the Museum* took two hours and felt like a gentle interrogation.

If you're trying to hide, why would you go out in public as your alter ego? All it takes is one photo online for someone to recognize you.

Think that's impossible? Here's my story.

A few years back, I appeared on the Travel Channel show *Mysteries at the Museum*. It was a short segment, about seven minutes, about the disappearance of Agatha Christie. In between "recreations" of her life, I popped up to say a few words about it. I probably appeared on screen about two minutes in all.

Within the next year, three people told us they had seen me on the show. One of them was a family member who knew about the appearance, but didn't remember which episode until she saw my face on the screen. What a shock to her system! Another was a local librarian who never met me, but assumed I was related to a woman with the same last name who came in frequently (Teresa, of course).

Teresa demonstrated how to make cloth grocery bags, as described in her book, below, on ABC27's *Good Day PA* show.

What were the odds that one brief appearance on a modestly rated show, rerun a couple times, would be seen by three people who knew me?

If you're dedicated to keeping your pen name a complete secret, you have to avoid publicity.

How to Pick a Pen Name

Now that we've considered why you may want a pen name, let's get into how to find the best one for you.

Not all pen names are created equal. If you want one that'll help your sales, here's what you should think about as you page through baby name books and look up your family tree.

1. It should be easy to remember, like Lee Child, J.K. Rowling, or Stephen King.

2. It should be easy to spell, even to people who only hear your name, as in

an interview. If they hear Kate, and you spell yours Cait, it'll be harder to find you.

3. It should be appropriate to your genre. Romance pen names tend toward the flowery, while thriller pen names sound tough on the ear, with hard consonants. That's why Frank Spillane adopted a nickname and became Mickey Spillane.

4. Plug the name into a search engine. Try it with quotation marks around it so the search engine will return results using the full name. Is anyone else using it, like a singing star, a serial killer, or adult film actress? Try again; you don't want your name to compete against someone more popular. Remember Winston Churchill and Elizabeth Taylor.

5. Search for it on Amazon. Any competition?

6. Go to a website that sells domain names like NameCheap (*namecheap.com*) or GoDaddy (*godaddy.com*) and type the name into their search box. You want your name to be the domain name of your website. If it has already been taken as a ".com" (pronounced "dot-com"), try again. You don't want to mess around with another domain type like ".org" or ".net." Most people who want to look you up will be most likely to type ".com." You don't want to do anything that puts an obstacle between the customer and a sale.

If you find a name that's available, and you're planning on buying a website, go ahead and buy the name! A year's right to the name can run you about ten bucks; if there's a sale it can drop to a buck. Even if you don't use it right away, you have it ready to use.

Genre

There are three possible answers to the question "what genre are you going to write in?":

1. You already know because, hey, you're a writer. Of course you know.

2. You know the general category — mystery, romance, young adult — but not the subcategory (cozy mystery or police procedural? Post-apocalyptic thriller or political thriller? Young adult romance or new adult chick lit?)

3. You have no idea, but you want a profitable niche to write in.

Let's turn to Alex Newton, whose K-lytics program (*k-lytics.com*) scrapes Amazon's data for his database reports. As of February 2020, here are the top-performing categories with, in parentheses, the estimated daily sales of the genre's top title (all of them with a rank of 100 or higher):

At the top is Literature & Fiction (653), followed by Romance (452), Mystery (436), Thriller & Suspense (436), Nonfiction (206), Science Fiction & Fantasy (206), Children's eBooks (185), and Teen & Young Adult (124).

The genres move up and down from month to month, but this is a good general representation of their potential. I have seen indie authors earn six-

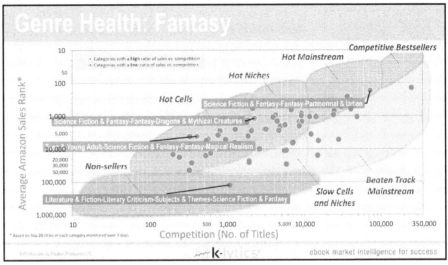

K-lytics maps the number of titles in a category against their average sales rank to identify niches where there are a lot of readers and relatively few books. Authors who write to trend look for these hot spots and write novels targeting them.

figure incomes in the romance, mystery, thriller and suspense, and science fiction and fantasy categories, so I believe that any story, told with imagination and energy, will do well in those genres.

But if you want to learn which subgenres are *currently* performing well, go to Amazon and check out the best-seller list. Or, visit Alex Newton's K-lytics website and sign up for his service. There's monthly membership plans available, or you can buy individual reports. He regularly puts out free reports and sometimes has a special offer if you share his website on your Facebook page.

But chasing trends does not guarantee success. If you're not excited about that genre and your story, readers will sense it. They may not know what a dangling participle is, or care that you don't know the difference between affect and effect, but they can tell when you're phoning it in; when you're condescending to them.

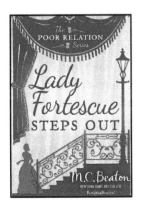

What Sets Your Books Apart?

The answer to this varies, according to your interests, talents, and inspiration. The question could be also phrased as "what's one major aspect that you're bringing to your stories that will excite readers?"

It could be an emphasis on humorous observations of humanity (Douglas Adams). Or writing about older characters doing unexpected things (Marion Chesney's Poor Relations romances). Or what about a heroine who brings her city-bred attitudes and prejudices to the country, which makes her unpleasant and sympathetic at the same time (M.C. Beaton's Agatha Raisin)?

Marion Gibbons (1936-2019) wrote historical romances like *Lady Fortescue Steps Out* (p. 43) as Marion Chesney and mystery novels as M.C. Beaton. After her death in 2019, her publisher rereleased her romances under her more popular mystery pseudonym.

To find your answer, you must read. Read the popular books in your genre. Read the classics of your genre. Read good books in other genres. Read them with a pen in hand, noting what struck you about their plot, pacing, how the characters talk, how they appear on the page; in short, anything that's worth remembering.

If a quality does not come to mind, be patient. Perhaps it will come out in the writing. But it's worth thinking about, because recognizing your unique voice and infusing your fiction with the qualities that define you will help you elsewhere in your business. You'll have a better handle on branding and publicity. Writing book descriptions and plotting future works will be easier because you'll have a path to follow.

Note that this is different from "writing to market" and "writing to trend" — two phrases you hear frequently when indie authors gather to talk shop.

"Writing to market" means recognizing what readers expect from a certain genre and giving it to them. "Writing to trend" is similar, except that you're focusing on what's hot now.

It used to be that agents and editors warned writers against hopping on the latest hot book. In traditional publishing, plotting, writing, revising and editing a novel could take one or two years, or even longer. By the time your magic academy book was ready to be published, readers were done with the Harry Potter books and were looking for something new.

Not so in indie publishing. If you think of an idea for a psychological thriller in the vein of *The Silent Patient, Gone Girl,* or *Sharp Objects,* you can push your book into the marketplace within months, not years, and not have to convince an agent / editor / publisher to support it.

Team and Key Players

Here's where you set your lineup of support players. Who will edit your book? Will you have more than one? What about beta readers or a proofreader. Do you have a cover artist in mind?

Target Readers

College-educated married women in their 40s? Girls aged 15 to 19? Ex-military who have seen combat or wish they had? There's a book for each of them, and one genre will probably not satisfy them. The college-educated married woman might fancy books by Liane Moriarty, while the teens will grab the new *Twilight* sequel or Young Adult novel. Ex-military readers might grab the Bad Company series of space opera adventures by Craig Martelle and Michael Anderle. You can expect some crossover readers, but there's bound to be a core group for your genre. Write for them.

Similar Authors, Titles

This is a test of how well you know your genre. Write down the authors and books that are similar to yours. Consider the amount of violence (none to a lot), the level of romantic heat (kisses to explicit), the mix of genres, and setting. When you're deciding on your target audience, they'll be particular about the amount or lack of sex and violence in it.

This list will keep your book on track as you write it, and is especially useful later for your book description and ad campaigns.

Sales Channels

There are two paths: exclusive ebook distribution through Amazon's Kindle Unlimited (and print books everywhere else; you're allowed to under their rules), or "going wide" putting your ebooks / print on the major channels (Amazon, Nook, Kobo, Google Play, Apple's iBooks) and using an aggregator like Draft2Digital or Smashwords to hit the rest of the bookstores. Some authors prefer going direct with Kindle and an aggregator for the rest, saying it saves them time placing their books and updating the accounts. It's up to you; I prefer keeping as much money from sales as I can.

Marketing Activities

With public appearances, book festivals, advertising, blogging, newsletters, social media, you could spend 100% of your time promoting your book. You won't get anything else done, such as writing, eating, sleeping, or learning the names of your spouse, children, and friends. So pick a few things and do them as best as you can.

I would not recommend spending money advertising your books until you have a couple of them out. For books in a series, I've heard from authors that sales pick up after the third book is out. Three books in a series shows whale readers — the ones who read several books a week and love series — that you're going to stick around and feed their story hunger. It also allows you to spread the cost of an ad over the sales of several books rather than just one.

Version / Price / Royalty

By version, I mean ebook, trade paperback, audiobook, large-print edition, radio-play version (like an audiobook only with actors), translations, and a graphic novel. In the beginning, focus on ebook and trade paperback; those you can format yourself or hire someone at a reasonable cost to do it for you. Keep the other versions in mind, because having multiple streams of income will make it easier to build your income and weather downturns.

> "
>
> If you look at most of the great artists of the twentieth century, they were also amazing marketers. Andy Warhol was a marketing genius. ... Paul McCartney is a self-promotion whiz; he knows what he's doing. So to color all previous artists as not having anything to do with self-promotion is really a disservice that people pay to themselves.
>
> **Austin Kleon**

The price you charge for each version depends upon your reputation (if you have any), and what competing books are charging.

Economists call your decision "price signals." Simply put, the price of an object conveys a message to the buyer. A low, low price suggests that the item might not be good quality, or that you're desperate to sell it. But too high a price will scare off budget-minded readers, as well as readers who can afford a slightly lower price. You're looking for that sweet spot in between.

What price range? I've seen an 80,000-word novel go for as low as 99 cents (even free), while some authors have priced theirs at $5.99 and even $6.99. These are authors who have had best-selling books and are also in KU.

Calculating the ebook royalty at 70% of the retail price is a good starting point. Amazon charges a "shipping fee" based on the book's file size, so it'll end up being less. Print royalties are based upon the price of the book and the company doing the shipping. Look up "Amazon paperback royalty" to find their formula. With IngramSpark, the payment per book could be even less, depending on the price, the bookstore discount, and IngramSpark's 15% share for itself.

Expenses

List the price of the services and products you'll need to get this book off the ground. It may be more expensive than you think, because you'll need to include indirect expenses such as buying a URL, webhosting, design software, and subscriptions such as Vellum, Office 365, and Photoshop (you may have access to cheaper or even free services, so don't take my list as a shopping list).

What about hiring people like editors and cover designers? You know your needs better than I do. If you're confident about your storytelling skills, you may want a copy editor. If not, then a developmental editor to go over your

Type of work	Price per word
Editorial Assessment	$0.014
Content / Developmental Editing	$0.024
Copy Editing	$0.017
Proofreading	$0.01
Copy Editing +Proofreading	$0.019

plot, a copy editor to check your spelling and grammar, and maybe even one more pass to finish up.

Where to find these people? Check with your fellow authors, or the Facebook groups 20Booksto50K and Mark Dawson's Self-Publishing Show. Their archives are full of recommendations. You may find people who are willing to work for less than the average. Cover designers who are just starting out, for example, may give you a break on price until demand for their work picks up.

One good source for price information can be found at the Reedsy website (*reedsy.com*). Reedsy offers many services, and one of them is a marketplace where authors can find editors, marketers, and cover designers. Reedsy only admits people who meet their standards. This means that their prices are higher, but there's a greater chance that they'll do good work (remember, in this business, anyone can hang out a shingle and claim they're a cover designer, agent, or editor).

As of 2020, here is their suggested fees for editorial services (from *blog.reedsy.com/freelancer/how-to-set-your-freelance-editing-rates/*):

These fees are not set in stone. They rise and fall from editor to editor according to their needs, the genre they work in (higher rates for business and self-help, for example, and lower for romance and thrillers) and how much time it takes to do the job.

How to Hire an Editor: Many will do a sample edit for free or a very low price. Send them the requested manuscript pages from the middle of the book, which is more representative of your qualities as a writer. Treat this like the ideal dating situation. You want someone you're comfortable working with. Someone who can talk to you about the reasons behind their decisions.

NEVER accept their edits without going through each one of them. Keep a pad beside you and write down what they found so you can learn from it. Also, it's possible an edit may have changed the meaning of your story. Always, always, double-check their work., no matter how simple. One author asked an ebook formatter to fix a spacing issue. She didn't realize the fix screwed up the rest of the ebook until a 1-star review told her. Oops!

WARNING

Investment / Source

This is potentially the toughest question to answer. We're funny about money, where we get it from and how we spend it. If you doubt me, ask a traditional author how much was their advance for their last book. They won't tell you unless they really know you — and even then they may fudge the number.

Ask an indie author at a convention like 20Booksto50K, and chances are they'll tell you how much they made last month, how much advertising they used and where, and even how close they are to this year's goal.

That's because indie authors recognize that their success does not mean that anyone else failed. The trad-pub world is intensely competitive. There are only so many slots available, and plenty of authors who want to fill them. This creates a zero-sum game. Add to that publishers' insistence that writers don't reveal their advances — because that could make other writers demand more from them — and that creates a climate of silence and secrecy.

Indie writers don't face those pressures and believe in paying it forward. They're willing to share what they've learned, because the more writers publishing good books, the more readers are willing to try indie authors.

However, the climate of sharing does not mean writers *must* open their books to anyone who asks. They have no obligation to do so. Some are uncomfortable doing so. The indie writing community also recognizes the right to silence. If someone you ask says no, accept it.

Getting back to your investment, write down how much you're starting with and where it's coming from (savings, spouse's salary, or cashing in your *Magic: The Gathering* cards). This amount is not fixed, of course. You may need to add more as your career progresses. But I lay down a marker, a visible amount that says, in essence, *this is how much I'm willing to lose.*

"Whoa!" I imagine you saying, "what's this about losing? I want to earn money."

True, but if you know, to the penny, how much you have, this will guide your spending. The temptation is great to spend money like it's water from a stream.

Learn from others' failures. During the dot-com boom of the 1990s, Silicon Valley was awash in cash from venture capitalists. The internet was new, and its potential seemed limitless. Anyone with an idea could find someone willing to give them bags of money to realize it.

Some of their ideas paid off, and you know them today as Amazon, eBay, PayPal, and Facebook. A lot of them also crashed and burned. There was even a website called Fucked Company that posted anonymous accounts from employees detailing unethical behavior, spending sprees by management, and other reasons why these dot-coms went out of business.

Fucked Company demonstrated the seduction of spending money without a visible limit. Lottery winners have experienced the same temptation. Don't let this happen to you.

Ebook-to-Profitability Goal

> "Annual income twenty pounds, annual expenditure nineteen [pounds] nineteen [shillings] and six [pence], result happiness. Annual income twenty pounds, annual expenditure twenty pounds ought and six, result misery."
>
> Mr. Micawber's recipe for happiness,
> from Charles Dickens' *David Copperfield*

The purpose behind all this planning is to make enough money to support yourself in the style you want to become accustomed to. That means making more than you spend, and the time to begin calculating how to do that is as soon as you get your idea but before you devote months to writing it.

Given your skill set, the book's editorial needs, your marketing plan and the time you have available, you should come up with an estimate of how much it will cost to produce the book.

This means making a list of the estimated cost to fulfill these steps. Here's a suggested list. Note that some of them are optional:

1. Create the cover art
2. Lay out the trade paperback
3. Write the book's ad copy (the text that goes on the back cover, and on your online book pages)
4. Hire a developmental editor
5. Hire a copy editor
6. Create the ebook version
7. Marketing costs (including advertising and arranging appearances at bookstores, conventions, and libraries)
8. Copyright fees
9. Fees to license copyrighted material (articles, art, music for marketing)

Figure out the sales price for the trade paperback and ebook. You set the book's price based on the manufacturing cost and the seller's cut, with a couple bucks added for your profit. This means that your book could pay you anywhere from $2-5 per book. Depending on the site, you would get between 50% (Google Play) and 70% (Amazon) for each ebook sale. It can be less. Amazon pays you 35% for ebooks sold in markets such as India and Japan. Ebooks sold through Amazon pay you 70% of the retail price of $2.99-$9.99 and 35% otherwise. This means a $2.99 ebook will earn you about $2.

With both sides of the equation decided — cost of production versus royalty per TPB/ebook — calculate how many ebooks you need to sell to recover your investment. We use ebook-only sales because that will make up the majority of your income. As the years pass, you'll learn what percentage of your income comes from areas other than ebooks and adjust your thinking accordingly. For now, assume 100% of your income comes from ebook sales.

Look at the number of sales. How do you feel about it? Remember, it's not an accurate assessment. We wrapped your indirect expenses into your first book. If you publish 12 books over the year, those expenses would be spread out over 12 books. However, this is not an exam, but a way of educating you about the way a business owner thinks.

As the owner, you have to juggle competing demands. You don't want to run out of money, but you want a good-quality product. You want to make a profit, so you want to keep expenses down. But if you lower your expenses too

> I love deadlines. I love the whooshing noise they make as they go by.
> **Douglas Adams**

> A journalist is stimulated by a deadline. He writes worse when he has time.
> **Karl Kraus**

much, you might cut the quality of your book so much people won't buy it.

This is why a lot of people prefer working for someone else who has to think about these things.

Fortunately, the key to your success, your ability to tell a compelling story, costs only your time.

Deadlines For First Work

Some writers find it difficult to finish a book. Some are motivated by spite ("I'll show them! I'll show them ALL!"); some by ego ("I have nothing to declare but my genius"); some by a driving desire to write.

The rest of us — and I include myself — need deadlines.

I've had a near-finished draft of *Career Indie Author* hanging around for several years. I spent years on it, and I sputtered out before the finish line, when it reached 133,000 words.

With some tightening, and finishing the marketing section, I could have published it. But in the interim, I've published more than a dozen books, read books and taken courses on self-publishing, and I saw a way to make this better. More concise, so you didn't have to wade through my meandering thoughts. Like what I'm doing now, but with even less focus. I also learned more about the business, and realized that some of my advice, while still correct, did not represent what beginning writers needed to hear.

At this moment, I am rewriting this book to meet a deadline. It's July 8, 2020, and I have to be finished by Aug. 14. Then I have to produce the book and have it printed and delivered by the time Teresa and I teach a class on business at Cupboard Maker Books on Sept. 20.

This is the best kind of deadline, because there are consequences if I fail. Teresa will be disappointed in me. I'll be disappointed in me. We won't have books to sell at the class, and the authors will wonder, rightly, how I can lecture about running a business when I demonstrated that I can't run a business.

No pressure here. Nope, none at all.

So, back to the math. When I started this rewrite, I had 36 working days. I don't know how many words this version will be, but if I do 2,000 words a day — a combination of repurposing the first draft and adding new words — I'll reach 72,000 words. I'll be editing and laying out the book during this time, and the cover and back copy are already done. If I stay the course, I can hit my goal.

So this is why I want you to do the same, at least for this first book. If you haven't completed a book yet, here's your chance to do so.

The key to making this work is to *set a consequence for failure that has teeth in it.* Announce your goal to your spouse. Post it on your Facebook page. Deny yourself a favorite treat and vow not to indulge until you succeed.

But give yourself permission to fail as well. If this is your first time, you'll also be learning about what works for you. While compiling the *Career Indie Author Quote Book,* I learned that what works for one writer will not work for another. A deadline that spurs one writer on shuts down another writer. Some create detailed plots of 30,000 to 40,000 words, while others start on page 1.

Then there's Chuck Palahniuk. In his writing book *Consider This,* he talked about compiling his book in scenes as they occur to him. He'll print a draft and carry it with him. He'll show it to friends and ask for suggestions and ideas. He'll rework the draft and print a new version and repeat the process.

This is the most detailed, convoluted process I've ever seen, but who am I to argue with the author of *Fight Club* and other great books?

10 Services To Avoid Or Be Wary Of

The self-publishing gold rush is over, and there are plenty of people who've decided that they can make more money selling you the tools to go prospecting than do the job themselves. Some are worth the money, but many of them are ineffective, expensive, distracting, not worth the cost. How can you tell the difference?

One easy scam to spot is when you receive an email or a phone call from someone offering a service. Reputable companies and agents never, never, *ever* approach you this way. Hard no.

Another red flag appears when someone charges for an introduction. It could be a "literary agent" who asks $500 to show your book to publishers. This is a hard rule: agents never charge for something they do on commission.* Same thing with introductions to TV and movie producers (see #1 below). There was one service that claimed a connection to a reputable Hollywood agency. No matter what, avoid them.

Based on my decade inside book publishing and two decades on the outside looking in — buying plenty of how-to books, writing books I couldn't sell, and attending conferences — I've come across many dubious products and services. Either they're ineffective, ethically dubious, or work only under the right circumstances. In all cases, they distract you from your primary job, which is to write books and reach readers.

So here's my top 10 services to avoid, listed in order from "absolutely never" to "maybe under the right conditions."

---

* "But what about agents who charge a reading fee?" It appears some reputable agents are doing this, and you should avoid them. They're not interested in acquiring clients, and rather than simply say "no submissions," they're making money off you. Remember, the money is supposed to flow *from the agent to you,* not the other way around.

Part One: Never Use

1. Anything Hollywood Related

> "
>
> If I wrote about the stories of nice people who lived in Hollywood, everyone would be bored to tears by page 2.
>
> **Jackie Collins**

Anyone who promises you an introduction to a Hollywood producer, talent agent, or agency in return for a fee, is selling you a promise that is never, never fulfilled.

Yes, authors have sold their books to the movies or television. Yes, producers and agencies are looking for material that they can make into the next *Artimus Fowl, The Expanse, Harry Potter,* and the Jason Bourne movies.

What they aren't doing is looking at the books being mailed to them (legally risky), scanning the shelves at book shows (where you paid a premium to display your work), or reading a treatment created by a vanity press who charged you four grand for the privilege.

(For chutzpah, one company offered to turn your book into an 8-10 page treatment, then a full screenplay that would be sent to its "Hollywood partner." All you had to do was send them the book and $20,000, and they would do the rest.)

So how *do* works get optioned for television or the movies? Two popular ways are a) a producer reads a story or book and decides to buy the rights; or b) the author has a Hollywood agent who markets the property. Sometimes, a writer meets a producer who is starting out — and they form a relationship that leads to film work.

If you want to learn more about authors' sometimes fraught and litigatious relationships with the studios, check out *Hollywood vs. the Author,* an anthology edited by Stephen Jay Schwartz. For a funny book about the insanity of movie making and writing scripts for Hollywood, read Thomas Lennon and Robert Ben Garant's, *Writing Movies for Fun and Profit: How We Made a Billion Dollars at the Box Office and You Can, Too!*

2. Buying Social Media Followers and Reviews

No, no, no, oh hell no!

Have I made myself clear?

Yes, celebrities have done it. They've also been caught doing it. And you know? Nobody cares.

As for you, early in your career, suddenly coming up with hundreds of reviews for your first book is going to look suspicious. Having thousands of followers for your social media that consists of your book cover is going to look *really* suspicious. If the social platform's algorithms catch on, they go away and you've lost money.

Plus, if Amazon thinks that you've bought your reviews, they're going to go away.

Finally, the reviews from these services suck. Their reviews are not convincing. And who reads five-star reviews anyway? If I want to know about a book, I'll read the ones that are three-stars and below. They're going to tell me what they didn't like about the book, and I decide if that will bother me. And then I'll still read the first few pages using the "Look Inside" feature.

3. Contests and Permafree Giveaways

> Always deliver more in perceived value than you take in cash value.
> **Jeff Blackman,** business consultant

Permafree means you write your novel, set the price to zero, and give it away. Again, and again, and again.

The hard truth is that price matters. People respond to price signals. There is the right price for everything, even books. If the price is too low, people wonder if there's something wrong with it. If it's too high, they won't buy it.

What's the sweet spot for books? It starts with how much effort you put into it. Is it well-written? Does the cover look like what you'd see in a book-store? Is the description taut, vivid, and exciting? You could sell it for $4.99 or $5.99. Some best-selling authors try $6.99. That's the beauty of indie publishing, you can lower the price, proclaim a half-off sale, and still make a profit.

If you give it away, you'll get takers. There are plenty of people who will grab it. But will they read it? Many will put it on their Kindle and never look at it again. They're hoarders, collectors. Or they're new to reading ebooks and decided to load up, not realizing that the quality might vary wildly.

Same thing with running contests, where people sign up for your newsletter for a chance at a prize, such as an Amazon gift card or books in your genre. These people are not here for you; they're here for the free. Many of them will go away, but some will stay behind but not open your newsletter, making you pay for dead leads.

So should you never give away your books? Of course not. But use price signals rationally. Give away a sample of your work, or in conjunction with a special offer, such as a BookBub promotion or a special advertising campaign. Kindle Unlimited lets you give away your book for up to five days. When done in conjunction with a promotion on a newsletter site like Book Gorilla or Bargain Booksy, you'll expose your work to fans who might come back for more.

Be smart. Your work has value. Protect it.

4. Book Trailers

If people love watching movie trailers, they'll love watching book trailers just as much.

But check out book trailers on YouTube. Look at how many views they get. Is it worth the investment? I think not. No matter how good the trailers look, viewers know that it tells them little about what's in the book. That can only come from reading a sample, either at the author's website or at an online store.

Consider investing in book trailers a sop to your ego and nothing more.

5. Online Blog Tours

Appropriating the idea from book tours, blog tours are supposed to put your name and book before potential readers. Instead of visiting bookstores, you "visit" a series of websites that specialize in posting book reviews and hosting author visits.

You could arrange the tour yourself, emailing sites and coming up with a schedule. There are services that arrange blog tours. All you do is write them a check, supply them with a variety of blog posts, and they do the rest.

The reality is disappointing. If you check these sites, they're visited by people who are looking for free books. They're run by people with little or no name recognition, and who can be guaranteed to pump your book as if it was the next big thing. What they end up doing to wasting your money and your time. Time and again, authors who have taken this path found that blog tours are a lot of work, and they can't see the results to make it worth your time and money.

6. "Write a Best Seller" Courses

I'm not talking about writing courses. I'm not even objecting to courses on what makes a book popular.

I'm talking about instructors promising that you, too, can write a best-selling book. They'll say things like "publishers don't know what makes a book work, but we do!" They promise to show you the twelve things all best-selling books have in common. They promise to reveal their "secrets" of best-selling authors, as if agents and editors knew them all along but didn't want to tell you.

There are books out there that go up to the line, like Al Zuckerman's *Writing the Blockbuster Novel*, and Donald Maas' *Writing the Breakout Novel*. There's even *The Bestseller Code: Anatomy of the Blockbuster Novel*, in which its two authors used data-mining to find commonalities among best-selling works.

When you see courses and books that promise you a gold mine, ask yourself: where are their customers' gold mines? If they give testimonials, look them up on Amazon. Do they have multiple books out like best-selling authors, or just one or two? Are their ranks high? Do they have a lot of reviews?

While you can use software like K-Lytics to assess the market for books, success comes from creating vivid, memorable characters who touch the readers' hearts. That's something that can't be taught.

Part Two: Use Sometime

7. Services You Can Do Yourself

This is tricky, because what you consider a valuable service I may not.

For example, I file a copyright notice with the Library of Congress (*eco.copyright.gov/*). I've been doing it for years, and while I've had my run-ins with them — sometimes because I filled out the form wrong — they've been good about correcting my mistakes. It just takes awhile because they're real humans working in Washington, D.C., and they can only do so much in a day.

You can pay someone to do this for you, but it'll cost a lot more, and as with anything you buy, the quality might vary. Chances are they'll do fine with novels, but if it's that simple, why not do it yourself?

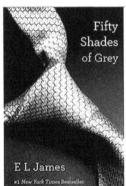

Editing services are useful, but again, the quality of the editor varies. Look at their credits. If they give references, check them out. How long have they been editing? Are they from the trad-pub world? Do they specialize in a particular genre? Do they offer to edit a few pages or a chapter to demonstrate their skill? Some will offer do a few pages for free; they'll say on their website.

Ebook or trade paperback formatting? It's possible to do both yourself. There are free ebook services at sites like Draft2Digital, and Amazon offers its Kindle Create software, too. Authors love Vellum (Mac) for its ease to make ebooks and paperbacks.

So before you hire someone to do it for you, try it yourself first. Only then can you decide if it's worth spending the money to let someone do it for you.

8. Swag

Giving away free stuff at book signings is cool. We do it, too, and through trial and error, we've learned that there's good swag and ineffective swag.

Good swag is something that will hang around the reader's house and remind them of you and your books.

For example, I've seen authors give away bite-sized candy bars with their book cover printed on them. It looks neat, but after the reader unwraps the candy and eats it, what do they do with the wrapper? Throw it away.

Authors also give away pens with the book's name on them. Those work, until they run out of ink, and vanish into the trash. A writer who specialized in books similar to *50 Shades of Grey* handed out small hairbrushes with her brand on them. Saucy and memorable, although I'd be reluctant to explain to my kids why it's in our bathroom!

One good method of evaluating the effectiveness of swag is to check the trash cans after an event. Any swag there represents wasted money.

After trying a variety of swag, we settled on four items: printed bookmarks, cloth bookmarks, cloth grocery bags, and catalogs.

Bookmarks are always useful. The catalogs are cheap to produce and can be used again and again. The cloth bookmarks and bags also bear our Peschel Press label to remind our readers where they got them from. As for production, the printed bookmarks are outsourced to a printer; Teresa, who sews, makes the cloth grocery bags and bookmarks; and I design and print our catalogs using Microsoft Publisher and my laser printer.

This demonstrates that there isn't a one-size-fits-all strategy for your business. If Teresa didn't sew, we wouldn't offer cloth bookmarks and bags.

In addition to being given away at events, swag can also be used strategically when you're launching a book. If you think your book and your story can attract media attention, think about sending swag impressive enough to draw their attention. Like the author who sent fresh French macarons to New York media outlets to promote her New Adult novel. For the thriller writer's book about a photographer caught in a web of deceit, his publisher sent disposable cameras (back when cameras contained film, not microchips). Even if the reviewers don't promote the book, they could write a story about the swag.

If you decide to go that route, two words of advice: go big. This is your one chance to impress the media; make your swag count.

9. Design Your Covers

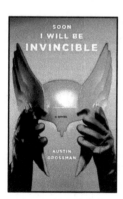

Kidd's design for Austin Grossman's superhero novel is one of our favorites.

If you're a graphic designer like Chip Kidd, you might be competent enough to do your own covers. If your covers look like they could be featured at Lousy Book Covers (*lousybookcovers.com*), please reconsider.

If you need to invest money in your book, a professionally designed cover and good quality editing will give you the highest return. If you can't afford a bespoke cover, there are book designers at sites like Go On Write (*goonwrite.com/*), Rocking Book Covers (*rockingbookcovers.com*), Affordable Book Covers (*stunningbookcovers.com/*), Mariah Sinclair (*mariahsinclair.com/*) and Cozy Cover Design (*cozycoverdesigns.com*) who offer pre-made covers for a lower price. All they need is your book's page count (it's a trade paperback), trim size, and text (title, author name, and tag line), and they'll do the rest.

When shopping for covers, make sure they're genre specific. Check Amazon's bestseller list in your category and look for common elements. If you're using a designer, listen to them. If you're not sure about a cover design, ask your friends or a group online. Show them the cover and ask: "what genre is this?" The responses may surprise you.

10. Book Awards

I'm going to step on the electrified third rail with this one. While plastering your cover with gold medallions is not unethical, it's not a wholly pure act either.

It boils down to the award's reputation. There are the big literary prizes — Pulitzer, Booker, National Book Award, Los Angeles Times Book Festival — and the genre awards such as the Edgar, Anthony, RITA, and Dragon awards. Lesser-known competitions such as the Tony Hillerman Prize and the Writer's Digest awards can still signal a book's quality.

(And while I'm mentioning awards, this has nothing to do with contests held by organizations, such as the Romance Writers of America's Golden Heart or Rita Awards, nor writers' groups, such as Pennwriters, which hold writing contests at their annual conventions.)

Then there are the skeevy awards; contests that are more interested in collecting fees from authors than judging talent. Some have tons of categories, making it possible to give awards to dozens of "winners." Some "book festival" prizes are named for big cities, enabling you to proclaim that your book won at the London Book Fair, when neither you nor your book were anywhere near the city.

True, some book buyers are swayed by the sight of a gold medal on your cover, even from a dubious contest. It comes down to how you feel about it.

Two sites that sell pre-made covers – Cozy Cover, and GoOnWrite – are among many supplying indie authors with covers that look as good as those from traditional publishers.

PART II
Execution

I already know
the ending;
that's where I
start.

Toni Morrison

Chapter 6

Writing Your First Book

Key Points to Remember
- Successful commercial fiction is 90% tropes and 10% original.
- Learn narrative tools such as scene-and-sequel, transitions, and use all the senses.
- To write consistantly, develop habits that signal to your subconscious that it's time to write.

You know what's fucking scary? The fact that I could literally change my life at any moment. I could stop talking to everyone that makes me unhappy. I could kiss whoever I want. I could shave my head or get on a plane or take my own life. Nothing is stopping me. The world is in my hands, and I have no idea what to do with it.

Sarah Coghlan

While I want *Career Indie Author* to focus on the business of being a writer, I also want to share some advice on writing your first novel.

I've read dozens of advice books over the years that go into detail about creating characters, developing plots, and marketing your book to agents and editors. What I haven't seen is a metaphorical writer's toolbox so you can get an idea of what goes into a book.

This list is not intended to be comprehensive. It's a list of tools to explore with the help of the Resources chapter in the appendix. It's the kind of crib sheet I wish someone had given me, a 50,000-feet-high map of the landscape.

These guidelines are meant for writers of commercial fiction. Writers who express themselves via their work wouldn't necessarily pay attention to who their audience is or what they expect. Literary writers probably pay far more attention to status and image than is good for them or their books. Gertrude Stein probably did not care who read her books, while Jonathan Franzen expressed reservations in interviews after Oprah Winfrey selected his book *The Corrections* for her book club.

Readers

- Know your audience. This means not only knowing the tropes for your genre, but the amount of sex and violence it contains.

Paradoxically, your books should leave room for your self-expression. A book that follows 100% of the tropes that doesn't contain anything that sets you apart as a writer could result in a bland and boring product. Self-censorship is as bad as unrestrained self-expression.

As a general rule — and this is a personal belief only, based on decades of reading — an effective commercial novel is 90 percent tropes and 10 percent unexpected material. It is in that 10% that can be found whatever it is that makes your books unique, memorable, and exciting.

Let me use as an example Terry Pratchett's Discworld series. The first book, *The Color of Magic,* was a parody of Fritz Leiber's Fafhrd and the Gray Mouser sword-and-sorcery series. It was set in a familiar fantasy world with wizards, magic, fantastic creatures and races and familiar character types, written with a light touch seen in other fantasy stories.

The opening of *Magic* was familiar to any reader of fantasy fiction: a swordsman and a thief are sitting outside the large city of Ankh-Morpork, watching it burn down (a common occurrence in a world where most buildings are wooden). They meet a young man in a shabby robe fleeing the city. They learn that he's Rincewind, a wizard so incompetent that he can't remember spells. They ask how the city came to be afire, he tells them, and away we go.

The novel's worldbuilding is familiar to anyone who read fantasy novels or played *Dungeons & Dragons.* Rincewind, his backstory, and the magical trunk following him on dozens of legs, is the 10 percent Pratchett contributed.

Over the next three decades, that germ of an idea expanded into a multifaceted world, vividly populated with fascinating characters and compelling ideas about society, technology, and humanity. His series stands as a major fantasy achievement.

So know your audience, but know yourself as well, and find a way to bring them together in your work.

- **Readers read for a reason.** Some want to experience strong emotions, such as horror, eroticism, or adventure. There are also readers who see the dark side in their daily lives (think morticians, ER workers, police, and firefighters) who crave calming reads that take them away for awhile. Some like stories that teach them something, and others love a puzzle to think about, like in *The DaVinci Code.* Know who your book is for and what they expect from it and write to it.

- **Poorly written books have their fans,** if they move readers. A vivid imagination excuses a lot of sins. Think of Edgar Rice Burroughs's Mars series. The hero, on Earth, looks at the red planet, falls into a reverie, and suddenly he's there on the surface of the red planet, in the thick of the green six-limbed warlike Tharks. The action is so overwhelming that we don't care how he got there. Burroughs made it work.

Plotting

- **Strong characters drive stories.** Do your characters want something? What are they willing to do to get it? Characters who are acted upon and who don't act in return are dull and passive. In Kevin Kwan's fourth novel *Sex and Vanity,* the heroine Lucie Churchill struggles throughout the book not to fall in love with George Zao. It's a negative motive, and not very exciting.

Compare her to Rachel Chu, the heroine of Kwan's first novel *Crazy Rich Asians.* She is dropped into her fiancée Nick's wealthy life and eccentric family and is pressured to break off the engagement. Sounds like a negative motive, too, right? Except that she wants to marry Nick. She puts up with the pressure, but along the way she learns how to overcome the machinations of Nick's mother. By the end of the book, you're rooting for her.

What is it about a character that makes him or her memorable? Is it Philip Marlowe's determination to protect the weak, even if it impoverishes him? Is it when Wren Hayden — from Mary Balogh's *Someone to Wed* — wills herself to face the ton despite the port-wine stain disfiguring her face? Is it Rico's struggles to survive boot camp and his moral education in Robert Heinlein's *Starship Troopers?* What important struggles do your characters face?

Give us a reason to care about your characters.

• **Stories transfer emotions.** We want to feel passion, rage, jealousy, righteous anger, striving and accomplishment. Not all emotions are energetic; there's also deep nostalgia for family and community, pleasure in a beautiful landscape, laughter in characters wittily crosstalking.

• **Stories need a unity.** The first chapter in a novel and the first paragraphs in a short story can contain the seed that blooms at the end. But each chapter can have its own unity as well, as do scenes within the chapter. Look at the memorable stories you've read and see how they do it.

• **Gun and clock.** If your story drags, install a gun and/or clock. A gun is a device — a weapon, a badly maintained furnace that will explode, a nemesis pursuing the hero — that will go off and drive the characters toward the climax. A clock is any kind of tick-tock — a literal clock, a pregnancy, a year at Hogwarts — that defines the end of the book. Install one (or both) and your story has an endpoint.

• **Mix up the pacing.** Indiana Jones can infiltrate a Nazi archaeological dig, find the Well of Lost Souls, discover the Ark of the Covenant, get captured and imprisoned, escape, destroy a transport plane, chase the truck carrying the ark on horseback, climb aboard, beat up the bad guys, steal the truck, drive to Cairo, and arrange for its transport aboard a tramp steamer. Now *that's* a full day. But he still needs downtime to patch his wounds, rest, and romance his ex-girlfriend before conking out.

It's the same in writing. Short chapters, long chapters; scenes with lots of dialogue, scenes with less. Vary them so readers don't get bored or fatigued.

Writing Techniques

In no particular order, because all of them are equally important.

• **Use all the senses.** Characters experience their world through sight and touch, but tastes, sounds and smells can also trigger nostalgic associations

IDEA

worth exploring.

- **Scene and sequel.** A story is a collection of them. Scene is where something happens, and sequel is your main character reflecting on the scene and plotting a new course. In a mystery, a scene is the detective questioning a witness; the sequel discussing the witnesses' statements with another officer and deciding their next move.

Scenes spark the actions in the sequels, and the reverse is true. In the sequel lies the seed for the following scene. But this can also happen at the beginning of a book. Recently, I sampled a story which opens with a man discovering himself in a new body. He's trying to sneak into a castle, wondering about his new body, and suddenly thinks of his girlfriend and wonders what she would think of him now. This seems to come out of nowhere (it *is* the opening pages), but wouldn't it have been more effective if he caught a whiff of something that reminded him of her? That's the invisible sequel (his past) creating a scene.

- **Character tags.** Dashiell Hammet's detective brushed at his moustache when he was thinking; Terry Pratchett's cop Sam Vimes smoked cheap cigars; Christopher Moore's Fool waved a puppet head on a stick that talked; Douglas Adams' Arthur Dent wore a bathrobe and hungered for tea. These characters had depth, but also carried markers that when repeated helped the readers remember them.

- **Avoid similar names.** Names that look and sound alike confuse readers. Was Brian the scientist or was it Bryce? Don't name one woman Anne and another Anna.

Make up a style sheet as you write. Put on it character names, details, and anything else that needs to be checked, particularly if they have complicated spellings. Send the style sheet along with the story to your editor / beta reader so they can check your work.

Names also carry emotional or cultural signals that can color your character. What would you think of a strong man named Percy, or a beautiful woman named Gladys?

- **See the world through your character's eyes.** This means no objective measurements. The man isn't 300 pounds; he fills the doorway, and the floorboards creak when he walks. The clothesline pole may be T-shaped, but a man in a spiritual crisis sees a modified cross.

- **Establish your character's authority.** There's two types of authority: knowledge and emotional. If your protagonist is a cop, show him doing cop things and talking like a cop. If he's a butterfly collector, he dreams of flying to Wales to hunt the High Brown Frittilary. In *My Cousin Vinny*, Vincent Gambini's girlfriend, Mona Lisa, is a gum-chewing, high-haired unemployed hairdresser from Queens. But she's an expert on cars, and her testimony about the suspension system on a 1964 Buick Skylark is convincing and funny.

Then there's emotional authority. If your heroine was dumped at the altar, and she flies off on her honeymoon alone, she can be attracted to the hunky wedding photographer, but she also needs to mourn for her shattered dream. If she's not hurt, why should we care about her?

● **Details establish your authority.** You could write a book-length description of the Oval Office at the White House. You can describe each stick of furniture, the color of the walls and ceilings, the make, origin, history, and feel of the carpet. You can identify the objects on the bookcases, the flags on the stands, the telephones and buttons on the president's desk, the number of doors and whether it's drafty or humid depending on the weather.

When you're describing the Oval Office in fiction, you'll have to choose which of those details to use, depending on your novel's point of view. The omniscient view would be described according to what the author thinks is important to reveal, while that of a character would depend on what that person sees. A Secret Service agent responding to an alarm would see the room very differently from a 10-year-old visitor brought in by her parents.

Now, multiply that quest for accuracy by all the locations in your book, and you have an idea of the task ahead of you. Make the reader see what your characters see.

● **Mind your transitions.** Describing this requires a chapter to explain. Read up on how the pros do this. Transitional sentences guide the reader from paragraph to paragraph so they don't get lost. It can be as simple as a single word (also, furthermore, remember), or as long as a sentence. Not every paragraph needs one, but when it's needed, the reader can subconsciously sense its absence.

● **Voice is natural.** Boy, I wish this hit me years ago. You don't think about how you talk, nor should you think about how you write. I don't think authors care about their voice; they're too busy paying attention to their characters.

● **Revise to clarify meaning.** This defines your voice. It means knowing the definition of words. It means replacing static verbs like "is" with verbs that convey action. Someone doesn't walk across the room, they stride, amble, or sidle. And if the walk isn't interesting, why are you describing it? Cut it. Let the character get there on their own.

Personal Habits

● **We are creatures of habit.** When I walk down to the TV room first thing in the morning, I turn on the WiiFit and prepare to exercise. It's a habit so ingrained that if I go downstairs at that time of day for any other reason, I feel the urge to exercise. Bizarre, I know.

> "
>
> One of the hard things, and this relates certainly to commercial fiction as well as writing for television and movies, is just getting the voice down. Once the voice is there, it's easier.
>
> **James Patterson**

> "
>
> Your writing voice is the deepest possible reflection of who you are. The job of your voice is not to seduce or flatter or make well-shaped sentences. In your voice, your readers should be able to hear the contents of your mind, your heart, your soul.
>
> **Meg Rosoff**

When you sit at your desk, do you turn on the computer and load up solitaire? Or do you write? Chances are, you taught yourself to play cards and surf, and it's now a habit. So learn to build positive habits (and delete the game). To make it easy on yourself, start with a small goal, and build it up over time.

● **Keep writing.** Once you're in a book, drive through until the end. If you're pressed for time each day, set a goal of 50 words. That'll keep your head in the game, and it can inspire you to write more. If you never write "The End," you train yourself to never finish a book. This is a fatal bad habit if you want to succeed (see, above, "We are creatures of habit").

● **Recognize the dead zone.** That's when you're so deep into the book that the initial creative rush from a new story is gone, but you can't see the end. Your energy can flag. Professionals work even when they don't want to; that's what makes them pros. Try the 50-word minimum goal to get you through the rough patches. Set a deadline with teeth. Promise yourself a bottle of (cheap) champagne when you type "the end." Whatever works for you.

● **There is no one right way to tell a story.** There are good ways and poor ways, fashionable ways and unfashionable ways. Look at *Crazy Rich Asians*. Kevin Kwan's book breaks several rules that should have made it unpublishable. He describes in detail fashions, jewelry, customs, and institutions like he's a descendant of Charles Dickens. He breaks the fourth wall by talking directly to the reader! In footnotes! He pulls it off because *Crazy* is a wonderful book, and he found an acquisition editor willing to go to the mat for him with the publisher.

When You Finish Your Book

Celebrate. You've completed a draft of your book, revised it (you did remember to spell-check it, right?), and sent it off to an editor or beta reader for feedback. Congratulations! You're ready to move on to the next step, building your business.

Chapter 7

Your Basic Business Set-Up

Key Points to Remember

- Set up your tickler file system to remind you of important time-sensitive tasks.
- A simple filing system makes sorting notes and papers easy and quick.
- Begin recording income, sales, and expenses so you won't have to catch up at tax time.

The complete novelist ... would own the concentration of a Trappist monk, the organizational ability of a Prussian Field Marshal, the insight into human relations of a Viennese psychiatrist, the discipline of a man who prints the Lord's Prayer on the head of a pin, the exquisite sense of timing of an Olympic gymnast, and, by the way, a natural instinct and flair for exceptional use of language.

Leon Uris

This part is not as much fun as writing your book, but it's vitally important to do. It'll save you a lot of time and trouble later, I promise. I'd like for you to make space in your office to store business papers, buy office supplies, and set up procedures for recording sales and expenses.

With a few exceptions, how you fulfill these tasks depends on your preferences. I'm not going to demand you buy a four-drawer file cabinet if you feel a two-drawer model will work, or a cardboard box. While you should store all your files in one cabinet in your office, you may choose to have one cabinet in another room, and a cabinet nearby for critical files. Your work flow will be interrupted while you decide where to file that invoice, but you may decide that's an acceptable price to pay.

So let's get to work. The goal behind setting up your office and office supplies is fourfold:

1. You want your files close at hand to make it easier to retrieve information and to store it when it's no longer needed.

2. Keep your office supplies in one place and easily accessible. You want to lay your hands on fresh paper or a toner cartridge when the printer runs out without having to stop your work and run to the store.

3. You want a simple organization of your papers so you can file them easily and find them easily. The same goes for the files on your computer. If you can't find it, you don't have it.

4. You want to schedule weekly maintenance of your office, with specific tasks such as filing or disposing of papers on your desk, and backing up your files before problems arise.

Here's three tools I use that help:

1. A file cabinet and plenty of file folders

It should be near your desk, so you can reach it easily. A two-drawer cabinet should be good to start with.

Hint: When filing story ideas, think about using the label "Fiction [Story Name]." That will shorten the number of files you'll need to go through if you can't remember the name.

2. A rack holding 43 file folders on your desk

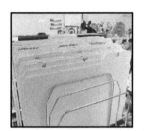

The tickler file on my desk. Seeing it every day reminds me to check it.

This will be your tickler file, a movable calendar that will remember tasks that have to be done on certain dates.

To create it, write the numbers 1 to 31 on the folders, and the 12 months on the rest. Arrange them so the numbers are first, followed by the months, starting with the next month after the current one. If it's January 1, the February folder should be in front.

Each day, open that day's folder. If it's empty, rotate it to the back of the date folders.

On the last day of the month, look in next month's folder. Move any date-sensitive notes into the proper date folder.

This allows you to keep track of anything for the next 31 days (using the numbers). For anything beyond that, tuck the note into the proper month. So if you've decided to apply to speak at a book conference, but they won't accept submissions until Sept. 15, put the note in the September folder. On Aug. 31, you'll see the note and move it to the proper date folder. I like putting it in four days before the deadline, to remind me to get on it.

This system makes it possible to remember those small tasks that are vital, such as paying my state's sale tax on the books I sell (in Pennsylvania I have to file in January and July).

3. A paper notebook, with a pen

> [N]ovelists who take the bitterest view of our modern condition make the most of the art of the novel. ... The writer's art appears to seek a compensation for the hopelessness or meanness of existence.
>
> **Saul Bellow**

I keep my notebook with me. It's a cheap, small notebook that I can put in my pocket, or a slightly larger model that I can carry easily. I devote a page to each day and keep track of my exercises, my current writing project, and any other tasks that need to be done. I also use it throughout the day to write notes, ideas, story ideas, useful quotes, and keep track of the number of words I write. Because it's a cheap notebook, if I lose it I don't feel like the world will end, and it can take all kinds of abuse.

I add checkboxes to my notes. They draw my attention to tasks or ideas I want to go back and process or save. When I can, I go through the pages, day by day, and mark with an X or a checkbox at the top of the page to remind me of work I haven't done.

Your Filing System

At first, the idea of having a file system seems ludicrous, maybe even pretentious. You're writing short stories, maybe sketches. A couple of printed pages. Maybe keeping a notebook. Not much of a threat to your sanity, right?

After a year of steady writing, however, and the situation has changed. You have a file cabinet, notebooks, and binders containing your working papers. A computer with an external hard drive. A desk with a printer, scanner, Wi-Fi box, monitor, a cup for hot drinks and a cup with pens.

And books. Lots and lots of books.

How do you organize it? What do you keep and what do you throw away?

Organizing your work does not need to cause trauma. You need to have a system in place and a procedure to sort and file your papers quickly and effortlessly.

I recommend buying a copy of David Allen's *Getting Things Done: The Art of Stress-Free Productivity*. Allen contends that we use our brain inefficiently. We use it to store our to-do lists, track our projects, remember small tasks from our non-work life, and retain deadlines and other vital information. This overloads our brain, causes us to forget important events and tasks, and frustrates us when we're trying to decide what to do next.

Allen devised a system that lets you capture all your material, thoughts, notes, and emails, either on paper or on software, and store them in logical places. With the help of a tickler file, we can track tasks that have to be done by a certain date, or future tasks we can only do at a certain time, like applying to give a workshop at a convention. By letting the tickler file remember for us, we free up our brain space for other tasks. At the end of the week, we sort through our inbox, process, file, and trash each item, and review our work for the coming week. The more we do this, the more we trust our process and happily get on with the creative, productive work.

Allen also helps us break down projects into manageable tasks that can be done in a workday, and sort reading material into slots that can be accessed during our down time, such as waiting for an appointment or during the afternoon, when we can't do creative work.

Creating an index in the front of books helps me remember important points and find them again.

There's much more to the system, so get the book. I have read my copy several times; it is one of the few books that I have annotated and indexed so I can refresh my memory and get back on track.

Writing by File Folder

The backbone of Allen's *Getting Things Done* system is the A-Z folder system. Typically, we file our paperwork in folders arranged by subject, arranged in alphabetical order. Obvious, right? But it means that from the start you have a bunch of subject folders that are difficult to root through. It's easy to lose track of where important material went.

He recommends starting with 26 folders, with the option to break out material if they all belong to a single project. Only when you have a thick sheaf of papers do you break out another folder to store them.

I use this system on my computer, and created a technique I call "Writing by File Folder." I have a lot of ideas for stories and books. More than I can use in a single lifetime. They can be great nuisances at times. I can be in the middle of a novel, and realize that a character can be broken off into a series. In my spare time, I may come up with several story ideas about that character, each of them demanding that they be written *right now*.

Instead of haring off and writing that story and losing track of my current project, I capture the idea, write it down, stick it in a folder and forget about it. Once it's out of your head, you know that you can come back to it later and see if it's worth pursuing.

Writing by file folder helps me store material for future books, especially nonfiction works. I start with 26 folders, lettered A to Z, and when I come across a newspaper clipping, magazine article, speech transcript, book review, printout from a website — anything that pertains to my book idea — I throw it into the proper folder and forget about it.

That's how I wrote *Writers Gone Wild*. For years, I came across fascinating stories about writers from book reviews and feature articles, and I would print them out, label them on the side with the author's name (or subject, such as sex, feuds, frauds, reviews, etc.) and file them in the proper folder.

For material on websites, I cut and pasted them into a Word file and saved them in the A-Z folders, plus folders on subjects such as feuds, bad reviews, fraud, and love affairs, in my *Writers Gone Wild* main folder. I also have a folder reserved for interesting art such as author photos, advertisements, and movie clips.

I have a similar system set up for other books in the series, including Hollywood, comic artists and writers, and sex. I still throw material into the WGW folders for a possible sequel.

To handle future book projects, a set of 26 folders has already been set up. By selecting them all and copying them, I can move to a folder with the new book's title, open that, and select paste. That saves me time setting up a new book idea.

So whenever you come across a story, online or in a book, copy it to your folder. For computer files, consider using a system that renames it to something you can use to find it again. For my *Gone Wild* books, the files are organized by the last name of the person involved, with a few keywords identifying its contents. For a story about Alfred Hitchcock's treatment of his actresses, it might be called "HITCHCOCK Blonde Obsession.docx." If a date is needed, I use a six-number code consisting of the year / month / day (e.g., April 1, 2021 would be 210401).

A
Art_Holly
B
C
Calendar
Crime
D
E
F
Feuds
G
H
I
J
K
L
M
N
O
P
PDFs
Q
R
S
Sex
T
U
V
Videos
W
Wallpaper
X
Y
Z

The file tree for *Hollywood Gone Wild*.

Scrivener's Binder function lets me see my chapters and research files and click easily among them.

I am a fiction writer only to the extent that my characters are invented. In every other sense, I'm still a reporter.
Patricia Cornwell

Other Filing Systems

Writer have found plenty of ways to keep track of their material. Here are a few of them:

● MS OneNote. OneNote also has optical-character recognition software built in that will scan articles that can be pasted into a file. Its accuracy depends upon the quality of the scan. I have found it able to "read" a high-quality file with nearly 100% accuracy. Even if it delivers 75% accuracy, it is still faster than keying in the document manually.

● Firefox's Scrapbook plug-in

● Firefox's Zotero plug-in (*zotero.org*)

● Scrivener, useful for large single projects. I used it to write *Career Indie Author* and the *CIA* and *Writers Gone Wild* quotebooks.

● Evernote

● DevonThink and Ulysses: For projects involving lots of documents, such as biographies or detailed historical fiction.

Tracking Your Work

The more books you publish, the more you'll need to keep track of your work. You'll schedule meetings with cover designers, editors, and other subcontractors like book formatters. You'll want a place to record your public appearances, podcast interviews, and book conferences. You'll have to write down your income and expenses for the IRS. When you launch Amazon and Facebook ad campaigns, you'll have to record what keywords you're using and how they're doing.

In short, you'll need to use calendars, notebooks, and lists.

Calendars

When you're in the middle of a big project, you're not just thinking about the day's work. There will be times when you have to think several months ahead, and even into next year.

For example, as I'm writing this, Teresa is writing an email to her cover designer about book 3 in her Steppes of Mars series. Because the designer is booked seven months into the future, she has to reserve a place on his calendar for book 4 (which she started writing last month).

No one can keep this kind of schedule in their head. It's too easy to lose track of the days. You may not have a problem with solving a crisis at the last minute. But if a little foresight can help avoid those traps, that means you'll have more energy to finish your books.

That's where calendars come in handy. They range from wall-sized models that display a year to individual months that you can create with Microsoft Publisher in MS Office (see the sidebar on page 72).

Use MS Publisher to create a calendar

Microsoft Office, has a nifty program called MS Publisher that you can use for your business. I've used Publisher to create half-page brochures, three-panel flyers, and single-sheet flyers, but I love its calendar option. It lets you create calendars with a month per page, or the entire year. I use Publisher to create a calendar to track the course of a book project or when I need to sort out my schedule. I like the year-at-a-glance calendar on the wall, and my daily *Dilbert* desk calendar, but the MS Publisher calendar is my utility substitute, called up at a moment's notice to fill any role I need.

Calendars can be used to keep track of any important task, including public appearances, book deadlines, monthly writer's club meetings, tasks that have to be performed at a certain time, such as applying to festivals, launching ad campaigns, and tax deadlines. A 12-month wall calendar can let you plot your publishing schedule, starting with the manuscript deadline and including dates to have the manuscript edited, cover art created, and marketing efforts in place. You can even add tasks that you want to perform at the beginning of the month that are not tied to a particular date, such as checking your book inventory well ahead of public events so you can order new copies in plenty of time.

Plotting your life on a 12-month calendar lets you coordinate your activities so there are no conflicts. It lets you determine your productivity and estimate how much money you could earn. You can adjust your deadlines well ahead of time so you can stay on top of your work.

Thinking Outside the Box: Consider adding a multi-year calendar to your arsenal. Create a timeline, consisting of a single line, marked off by years and subdivided into months. Use it to keep track of notable events: book publications, public appearances, and any major signposts that you want to recall.

Notebooks

I've been carrying a notebook for more than a decade. I started small, a little 10-pager from a supply my dad saved from his job at the steel mill. That wasn't enough, so I moved up to a 25-page spiral-bound job you can fit in a shirt pocket. But my need grew. I'm up to a 200-page spiral-bound with plasticized covers that could fit in a pants pocket if they're big enough.

Oh, I resisted. Dorothy Parker sneered at writers who carried a notebook around. It seemed so pretentious. Can't you just write? It's like Olivier telling Dustin Hoffman, who was immersed in the Method technique, "why don't you try acting, dear boy?"

Parker was wrong. I can't work without my notebook. It's attached to my hand like an appendage. I love notebooks, and I think you should use one as well. I'm a notebook pusher.

Here's why.

1. Portable. You can carry one everywhere. If the spiral holding the pages together is big enough, you can clip a pen to it so you're never without one.

2. Requires no power, no software, no learning. Just grab and go.

3. Flexible. Start on page one (I start on page two, in case the first page gets damaged) and go straight through. Or keep a daily task list in the front section and use the back for recording speech, images, and ideas.

4. You can tear out notes for any purpose.

5. You can record anything and everything: to-do lists, story ideas, article drafts, bon mots and quotations from books and magazines. It's a commonplace book, diary, self-help assistant, partner, and friend.

6. Nearly unlimited storage.

7. If you lose it, well, you lost a notebook. It's not like you lost your smartphone.

Many authors use their notebooks to record their impressions during the day. Some of them have been published, so you can look over their shoulder and see their working habits. Other notebook-using authors include Agatha Christie (where she worked out her plots); Mark Twain (who drafted sketches and recorded ideas); Alexis de Tocqueville (he recorded by subject information used in *Democracy in America*; talk about writing by file folder!); Charles Darwin (scientific observations mixed with conversations and lists of books to read); Ernest Hemingway (experiences he would use in his stories, plus expenses, gifts and — for his first wife — her menstrual cycles); Jane Austen (dramatic sketches, verse, and moral observations); and Katherine Mansfield (everything including shopping lists and story drafts).

My notebook captures my scattershot thoughts for later resorting.

A page from Mark Twain's notebook.

Lists: I Hate Them / I Love Them

I love lists like I love diets. I've been on dozens of weight-loss plans, and I've written hundreds of to-do lists, yet I never reach my goals with either.

That bummed me out. I'd feel terrible when I go to the trouble to write down everything I have to do, only to get bored and irritated seeing that hectoring, nagging list, and throw it away. A few weeks later, there I am at the computer writing up another one.

I'm avoiding two lists right now. There's a printed sheet of paper on my desk with these items:

- Seven ideas for posts
- Next actions for two books (one of them crossed off as finished)
- Six items for Peschel Press business, including the January newsletter was done in February; the January sale report finished a week late; and I've added the rest of the year's books to my spreadsheet but I haven't crossed that off yet.
- Two handwritten tasks, unfinished.
- Two major projects born of recent ideas, also unfinished.

Does that make me a hate-lister? Probably. I'm not the very model of a Type A author. I'm as disciplined as Beetle Bailey, I am the despair of the writer I want to be.

Then I realized I was more productive with a list than without one. True, I never finished a single list I wrote out, but I still got things done. I didn't lose track of my tasks, and some of the things on there it turned out I didn't need to do now.

The Power of the Check Box

I have a powerful tool that helps me keep track of my work. Here it is:

☐

A checkbox. Simple. Elegant. Begging to be filled in.

I use it in my notebook to identify tasks that I need to accomplish. It could be a question that needs answering, a book that needs ordering, or a plot idea that needs to be filed away. When I review the previous week's work, I can spot instantly those tasks that I can check off.

I use checkboxes elsewhere. When proofing a paper manuscript, I place a check at the top of pages that don't need fixing, and a checkbox on those that do. When I'm reviewing those pages, I pull out the pages that need work quickly. In a 500-page manuscript (double-spaced), those seconds saved can add up!

The checkbox is useful if I'm taking notes, and I need to add a to-do item. I draw a checkbox and point to the item. The check box helps me on another notebook task. During downtime, such as sitting in the dentist's office, I'll page backwards through my notebook. A page with no unfinished tasks gets a big X at the top. All others get a big box instead. This makes it easy to go back, locate unfinished tasks, and decide if they need to be finished after all.

Nor am I alone in the pleasures of a checkbox. In her collection, *My Nest Isn't Empty, It Just Has More Closet Space*, thriller author Lisa Scottoline writes about her affection for checking off items from her to-do list. She draws a big circle next to each of them, then checks it off, "like a schoolteacher at the top of your homework." She even adds finished tasks to her list so she could add the checked checkbox.

Recording Book Sales

In the game of business, money is how you keep score. But there is a moral debate about the role money should play in our lives. When Swedish programmer Marcus Persson sold Minecraft to Microsoft for $2.5 billion (and pocketed $1.3 billion of it), he sent a series of messages via Twitter revealing his despair over getting everything he wanted.

He's right. There's research that shows a person's happiness rises with his income, but once it reaches $50,000 to $90,000 a year, the amount of happiness one feels levels off depending on where you live — (Possibly because people at that level are in high-stress occupations such as CEOs, A-list movie stars, and billionaires). At higher incomes, you think you're happier, but your emotional health doesn't reflect that. In other words, getting rich gives you more space to unleash your craziness.

Markus Persson @notch

The problem with getting everything is you run out of reasons to keep trying, and human interaction becomes impossible due to imbalance.

5:48 AM - 29 Aug 2015

↰ ⇄ 1,478 ★ 2,332

Markus Persson @notch

Hanging out in ibiza with a bunch of friends and partying with famous people, able to do whatever I want, and I've never felt more isolated.

5:50 AM - 29 Aug 2015

↰ ⇄ 995 ★ 1,794

Markus Persson @notch

In sweden, I will sit around and wait for my friends with jobs and families to have time to do shit, watching my reflection in the monitor.

5:51 AM - 29 Aug 2015

↰ ⇄ 466 ★ 1,104

Existential misery? You're soaking in it!

Yes, you can't take it with you, and the best things in life are free, but there's a big difference between the questions "How can we afford to eat?" and "Where shall we have lunch?"

Until we get to that level, we have to watch our nickels and dimes, and here's two popular alternatives recommended by several writers that have the bonus of not requiring you to learn Excel.

Software Solutions

If the prospect of using Excel makes your toes curl and your fingers cramp, there are alternatives worth looking into:

Trackerbox (StoryBox Software, *storyboxsoftware.com*): Written by author Mark Fassett, Trackerbox ($60) runs only on Windows computers. It imports

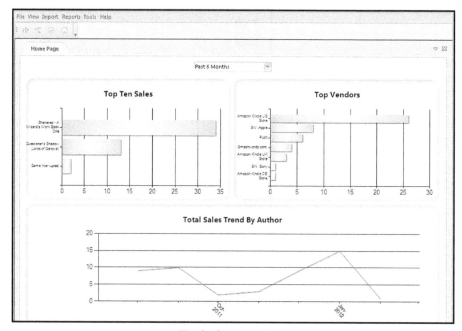

Trackerbox in action.

sales reports from 20 sites (including Amazon's Kindle, KDP and Amazon Vendor Central, but not IngramSpark), lets you run simple to complex reports (e.g., multiple titles, authors, and vendors), export reports in a variety of formats and sort the information just about any way you like. It comes with a 45-day free trial. At the end of the period, a purchase gives you a key that unlocks the software. Fassett has released minor updates and a major revision to the software since 2015.

BookTrakr (*booktrakr.com/*): This service offers a two-week free trial. It logs into your accounts at Amazon KDP, B&N NOOK Press, iTunes Connect, Google Play, Kobo Writing Life, Draft2Digital, and Smashwords, gathers your sales and new reviews, and you a daily report.

Book Report (*getbookreport.com/*): This plug-in for your Chrome or Firefox browser works only for Amazon's KDP, but it does so very nicely. The service is free until your income rises above $1,000 a month, after which you'll be prompted to pay.

The Excel Solution

To keep track of book sales on Excel, Eric Lorenzen offers an Excel spreadsheet on his website (*ericlorenzen.com/2015/01/20/tracking-book-sales/*). Anyone can download it for free.

It's a beautiful piece of work.

Eric Lorenzen's book sales spreadsheet.

Lorenzen's spreadsheet breaks down sales by book and market. Each page is devoted to a single book. On that page you record your monthly sales, royalties, and number of free books given away. The last page automatically totals the sales of all your books, so you can tell how well each book is doing, as well as your overall sales. He even put in a section that totals your sales for each month, both for each book and overall.

This is not the place for a tutorial on using Excel. If you don't know how to use it, don't download Eric's spreadsheet and learn along the way, unless you have plenty of time, are very patient, and have *Excel for Dummies* on hand or your Google-Fu is powerful.

But at some point in your career, assuming your sales rise, you or someone you know should learn Excel or one of its clones. Spreadsheet software is a necessary part of probably every business out there, and once you get into the habit of using one, you'll see why.

So whether your solution involves a spreadsheet, software, or an abacus, a record-keeping system must be in place to track your book sales.

Recording Income/Expenses

Keeping records is an important part of your business. There are two reasons why: one that's important for the business and another that's important for you.

It's important for you to do this because it's another tangible way to reinforce that you are operating a business. That there is an entity outside yourself that you are building and bringing to life, much like Dr. Frankenstein did with his patient.

To think about it another way, ask "What is a business? Is there a physical, tangible thing that I can point to and say, "this is the business?"

You have objects associated with your business, such as your books and your marketing materials. You might even have an office dedicated to running your business. But the business is a fiction. It is a story that you are telling your readers, your suppliers, your booksellers, the IRS, and even yourself. If everyone buys into the story, then you have a business.

Take the Hogarth Press. That was the business started by Virginia and Leonard Woolf in 1917 to hand-print books by themselves and their Bloomsbury friends. In the first year, they published a book containing a story by each of them, and earned £14 in profit. They published two books the next year, and five the year after that. It grew from a hobby that gave Virginia a way to relieve stress to a for-profit venture. Virginia relinquished her interest in the business, and Leonard continued running it with a partner until 1946, when it was acquired by Chatoo & Windus.

So what is the Hogarth Press? It was controlled by the Woolfs, but it was not integral to the Woolfs. They were able to pass it along to other interests, until now it's an imprint owned by Random House.

Will your business last as long as Hogarth Press? That's up to you. What's more important is that you treat it as a living thing, and living things need sustenance and maintenance in order to live. Keeping track of your business expenses can help bring your business to life, both in your mind and in the eyes of equally important entities, such as the state and the IRS.

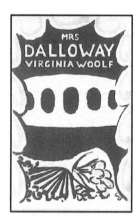

Hogarth Press first editions, designed by painter Vanessa Bell, Woolf's sister.

Managing Your Business

Teresa and I needed some way to evaluate what we're doing, and holding ourselves responsible for what we do and don't do.

This means, uncomfortable and fraught with peril as it may seem, it boils down to having someone look over your shoulder to see what's going on, what needs to be done, and what you're going to do next.

It could be your spouse. It could be a friend. It could be the internet. It could be yourself.

Here's how we do it at Peschel Press: on most Sunday nights, Teresa and I grab our favorite beverage and meet in the office with our unwilling slaves (a.k.a., our adult children). We go over the previous week's minutes. We cross off the finished tasks and go over what needs to be done. Do they still need to be there? Does it need to be modified? We add new tasks to the list, focusing on what the next action should be, that specific task that could be done in a day that would push that project forward. The list is prioritized so that the most important items are at the top.

Then we check the 12-month calendar, see what's coming in the next week,

> The novelist says in words what cannot be said in words.
> **Ursula K. Le Guin**

and decide if there's anything that needs to be done in advance.

That's it. There's no recriminations over the tasks left undone. Even a Type A author would have a problem finishing the dozen items we usually have on the board.

Sunday is also the day I look through the previous week's entries in my notebook and make sure nothing was missed.

That's it. The Sunday business meeting is also a time for us to consider new ideas, reconsider the value of old ones, and make mid-course corrections.

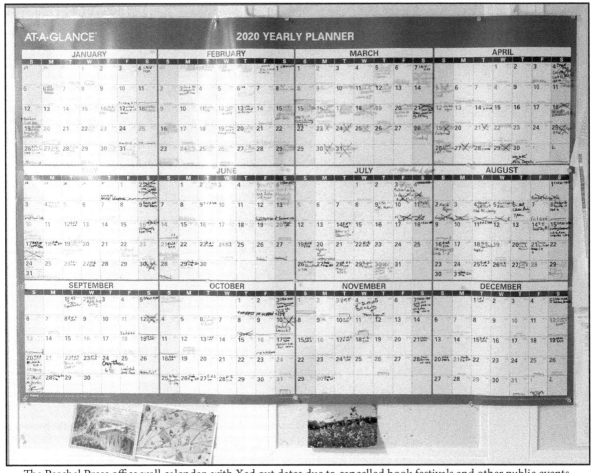

The Peschel Press office wall calendar, with Xed out dates due to cancelled book festivals and other public events.

Chapter 8
Building Your Website

- -

Key Points to Remember
- You must have a website to display your books and help fans and businesses to find you.
- If you're not comfortable with running a website, choose a service that does the job for you.
- A social media presence is useful, but they control what you can say and do, not you.

- -

Websites promote you 24/7. No employee will do that.

Paul Cookson,
marketing consultant

Career Indie Author is intended to be a map, showing you the terrain of indie publishing and inviting you to explore. Some paths are well-marked and represent the best practices many authors have used to their profit. Others have been tried and found wanting, while somewhere in between are techniques that worked for some but not others.

One thing for sure, doing everything suggested in these pages is not recommended. Some techniques may not work with the kind of books you write. You may not have the enthusiasm to produce videos or podcasts. You may not have the money to hire a great cover artist or design a cool website. Then there's time. There's only so much you can do in a day.

And you know what? *That's all right.* Pick and choose what you think will work and make incremental improvements. Unlike traditional publishing, your book is not dead if it doesn't sell quickly. You can rebrand, change covers, write better descriptions, run ads, and even rewrite the book. Nothing is required, except to keep writing and publishing books.

Except, second to having books to sell *you must have an online presence.* That means a website. It doesn't have to be a flashy website boasting a cutting-edge design. It doesn't even have to have a lot of bells and whistles content, such as a forum, video, or a blog.

But if you want to be taken seriously as an author, if you want readers to find you and your books, and where to buy them, you have to show them online. And that means a website.

So let's break down the process by deciding what your options are and their plusses and minuses. I'll tell you the cost, the amount of time you need to put in, and the expertise you need to master.

If you intend to make a career out of selling your books, if you're in it for the long haul, you must have a website that you own and control. When your site is hosted by someone else — Google's Blogspot,

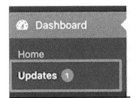

WordPress Updates

WordPress is very popular software. It is used by more than a quarter of all websites *in the world*. This makes it a rich target for hackers, so follow this rule:

Update your software!

WordPress regularly updates its software to add features, fix bugs, and plug security gaps. Minor updates are done automatically. Big changes ask you to click the update button. The same goes for plug-ins. Hackers can exploit flaws in plug-ins. Just look for a number to appears next to Update on the dashboard and follow the instructions!

Facebook, WordPress.com, Wix, Squarespace — your fortunes are tied to their algorithms and policies. If the company vanishes, so does your website, like the musicians who set up shop at MySpace, or the bloggers who hung out at Geocities. Worse, if they decide you violated their policies, they could kick you off the platform. Game over.

How to Begin

I prefer to run a website built on WordPress, but I have a lot of experience dealing with websites. You may not feel that way. Fortunately, there is a way for you to have a cheap, good-looking website and still retain some control over it.

First, a few basic definitions:

Domain name: This is the address of your website that has to be typed into the search bar. It begins with "www" — I know, I know, officially it's http://www.yourwebsite.com, or even https: — bear with me for a moment. Sites that let you build a website for free give you some leeway in creating a domain, but they'll stick their name in it as well like "www.blogspot.billpeschel.com.". You can also pay a yearly fee for your own domain name (they say buy but, really, you don't own it for life, unless you cough up the dough), but if you want to use it at Wix, you have to upgrade from their free plan. We'll get into that shortly.

Web host: The company who sells you space on their servers (a box with a lot of memory) where your website is stored.

If you're starting out, it's fine to start at Blogspot, WordPress.com, or Wix. They're great places to make you familiar with websites and what they can do. Eventually you'll want a domain name that you own where people can find you. A home that you can decorate exactly as you want it.

There are three kinds of websites: those free to set up, those you have to pay a monthly fee, and those you own. The boundary lines between the first two options are blurred because a service such as Wix or Weebly offer both free and paid plans. Keep that in mind as we discuss the options below.

Free Plans

If you know nothing about websites or computer programming, these are ideal places to start. They have free plans that allow you to build your website using a template, which is a bare-bones skeleton of a webpage. To do things like change the color, fonts, and add stuff, you drop icons onto a page to make it look the way you want it to. This is called "drag and drop programming," although no code-writing takes place.

Squarespace is the premium example of this type of website.
WordPress.com — not to be confused with WordPress.org — lets you use the

Squarespace

WordPress.com

Wix

Weebly

Blogger / Blogspot

WordPress software while they handle the hosting. **Wix** and **Weebly** are older services that have changed and improved their offerings over the years. Wix doesn't offer a free plan, only a 14-day free trial, but it's included here because it operates like the other free-plan services.

The advantage of these plans is that they're inexpensive, you can get a website up and running quickly, and you don't have to deal with technical issues such as buying a domain name, finding a company to host your website, telling its servers where to find your domain, and running the website.

The disadvantages are that, as we said earlier, your fortunes are tied to the fortunes of the company. If the company goes down, your site goes dark. You'll have to find another hosting service to get your website back online, but you've lost any search engine optimization juice you have built up by being in the same place over a long period of time. Until the search engines catch up to your new location, you can expect to see a drop in visitors to your website.

Another disadvantage of these plans are that unless you pay more, they make you use a domain name that identifies you as a cheap author. Instead of having a domain name such as www.billpeschel.com, you will have www.wix.billpeschel.com. I don't think you'll be penalized too much for having this type of name, but it's not going to help you either. Eventually you're going to want to live at www.YourName.com. So why not start now?

The company also has the right to run ads on your pages. If you don't want to see colon-cleansing ads next to your author photo, you'll have to pay to get them removed.

Another free option is **Blogger**, run by Google (*blogger.com*). It's a free blogging service, easy to set up, and because it's run by Google, the company already knows where you are. Because Google hosts these sites on the blogspot.com domain, you'll sometimes hear them referred to as Blogspot sites. Blogger sites are very limited in design options. I've seen some that look very nice, but plain. If you don't mind that, this could be an ideal solution.

Paid Hosting

The next step up from free hosting is paid hosting. At some point, you may get tired of seeing your name connected with the hosting company in the domain name, you may want more bells and whistles, and you may wish to remove the company's ads for miracle medical cures from your blog (this is why you're paying nothing).

These companies offer paid plans from five dollars a month on up. You'll be able to buy a domain name. The ads will vanish.

Buying a paid plan from these hosting providers could strike a very good

HTML Made Simple

Hypertext Markup Language (HTML) is the language used to design webpages. You won't need it to design your website (unless you love coding!) but bits of it are used in writing blog posts, particularly if you want to **bold,** *italicize,* and underline your words. The command is turned on by typing the left caret key (found above the comma key; it looks like this: <), a first letter of the style you want, then the right caret key (found above the period: >). To turn off the command, you add a backslash (found above the question mark key) like this: </b>, </i>, or </u>. Now you're programming!

balance between your need to have a good-looking site without having the computer knowledge to handle the problems behind it. I come from an amateur computing background. I've been working with computers since the 1980s. I'm comfortable with them. I used to build webpages using HTML code. I've worked on a number of blogging software platforms. So that's why I use WordPress with a hosting provider to run my company.

But you may not have that computing knowledge. You may not be interested in learning how to code a webpage. (Which by the way I'm talking about a very simple coding such as to bold (<b> to turn on and </b> to turn off) or <u>underline</u> or <i>italicize</i> words.)

As for cost, they are comparable to Squarespace and the other plans. Depending on the plan you choose, a paid hosting provider may cost anywhere from five dollars a month on up. I pay roughly $10 a month to use WordPress at HostGator. So I think that washes out.

Design Your Own Website

The third option is to hire a hosting service to host your website, install blogging software such as WordPress, and design your site from the ground up. This can be a complex undertaking but will result in a professional-looking website that will make you look as big online as any best-selling author. It allows you the freedom to put up whatever material you want to support your books.

The disadvantage, of course, is you're responsible for anything that goes wrong on the website. The hosting provider is responsible for keeping your website up, but if you don't keep WordPress and its plug-ins updated, you may visit your webpage one day to find it's been hacked.

Then there's the problem of setting up your website and designing the pages. WordPress has canned themes that give you a good start. Most of them are pretty bland, so if you want one with more flair and flash, you either have to learn how to do it yourself, or hire someone to do it for you.

When you hire a person to design your website, they'll work with you on the design. When it's done, all you'll have to do is post blog posts and keep the site updated. It will cost you money, but a polished author website will leave a better impression on potential readers than a free webpage at Wix or Blogspot.

Again, there is no one correct answer. You will have to decide for yourself how much time, money, and energy you want to devote to this, and the only way to find out is to jump in and see for yourself.

Website vs. Social Media

There are people who decide to ditch the website in favor of Facebook,

Twitter, Instagram, and Pinterest. This is not a good idea.

Social media can help market your books, but it does not replace the power and effectiveness of your website. You can invest a lot of time and effort in social media, and have fun doing it, but social media has significant shortcomings.

Note we're talking only about using social media to promote yourself and your books. We are not talking here about advertising on social media platforms, which will be discussed later in the book.

Social Media Sites Are Not Permanent

Remember MySpace? That was the place to be in the early days of the internet. Then it fell out of favor when Facebook came along. How long will Facebook be here? No one knows. What about Twitter? In 2019, it's overall usage has dropped, and it has been criticized for the way it censors and bans tweets and users.

But as long as you keep paying your hosting company, your website will always be there.

You Are Not In Control

Any account can be suspended by Twitter for any reason, even Auburn's football team.

Social media sites are moderated by bots and your enemies. Say a photo-scanning bot decides the cover of your vampire novel is too bloody. *Zip!* Down it comes, and your account is suspended. Doesn't matter if you're about to release the new book in that series, it stays down until you can convince FaceTwitTumbInsta to put it back up.

You may think I'm exaggerating, but Amazon has specific no-nos about covers, such as no guns pointed at the reader, and no blood showing. Sometimes, it'll refuse to publish a cover without explaining why. Facebook's bots search for nudity and have pulled pictures that it thought contained nudes, but didn't.

Then there are the problems with censorship. If you irritate someone off with your opinions, you can be reported for making harassing statements. They can harass you with an anonymous complaint. Twitter formed a group of advisers that has been used to suppress free speech it doesn't like. Even Scott Adams, the creator of *Dilbert* reported that he had been "shadow banned." This meant that he could look on his timeline and see the tweets he made, but Twitter made sure no one else sees them.

On your website, you can talk as you please. You cannot be censored.

Social Media Posts Are Ephemeral

Good: Social media is awesome because there are millions of people on them.

Bad: Social media is awful because there are millions of people on them, and they're all talking *at the same time.*

Actually, it only seems that way. A 2014 *Wall Street Journal* story found that just 13% of Twitter users have tweeted more than 100 times. But that still means you're among more than 125 million people.

And once that funny tweet or brilliant observation is posted, it sinks out of sight.

Search Engine Optimization

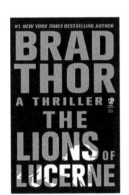

Search engine optimization (SEO) is the practice of writing and editing material that is published online in a way that allows search engines to rank your page high in searches for certain keywords.

Every day, Google, Bing, Yahoo, and other search engines scan millions of webpages. They use various methods to determine what is on each webpage and how valuable it would be to people looking for that kind of information. This process is done automatically using algorithms, without the use of human judgment.

When you are posting a webpage about your new book, there are certain things you can do that will help place your book high in the search rankings. If someone is searching for your book by title or author, your book page should appear on the first page of a search.

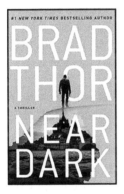

This is fine if all you want is an audience composed of people who know your name and the title of your book. But you can also use good SEO practices to place your page before people who don't know you or your book, but who are looking for books like yours.

Let's say you've written a political thriller set in Washington, D.C., and you think it would appeal to Brad Thor's fans. Add a paragraph to your book page's description that "fans of Brad Thor will love this book," and you will have increased your chances that your book will appear before fans searching for his books. It's a small chance, to be honest, but that's how search engine optimization works.

To increase the odds, and increase your exposure to Brad Thor's fans, you can act like one as well. Review his books and add a link to your book at the bottom of each page.

Once you understand search engine optimization, you'll begin to get an idea of what to add to your webpage to attract readers. Let's say that you're a quilter, and you've written guidebooks on how to design and sew quilts.

On your website, you have a page devoted to each of your books, with excerpts, and links to bookstores and websites carrying them. But you can also add pages that are not about your books, but about sewing quilts. You could have pages displaying your quilts. You can write blog posts that discuss the problems quilter's face along with your solutions. You can recommend books and classes that you found useful.

The more good, useful material you add, the more confidence search engines will put in your website. They'll conclude that you are an expert on the subject and respond by placing those pages higher in search engine results. Quilters who have never heard of you before will see your website placed before them more often. This increases the chances that they'll visit your site and buy your books.

Is there a secret sauce that will guarantee that Google will always place your website on the front page of its searches? No. There are best practices for search engine optimization but they change. Blame scammers for this problem. As soon as they figure out how Google ranks its pages, they throw up bogus pages in response. Google and other search engines change their algorithms, and the dance begins anew.

You'll need to educate yourself on what the correct current practices are. In general, if you don't try to game the system, if you put up good, high-quality material, you'll stand a better chance of winning in the long run than the people who take shortcuts to success in search engine optimization.

But here's one practice that will be useful no matter how the algorithms are designed: use good keywords.

A WordPress plug-in like Yoast SEO can guide you through the SEO process.

What is your page about? The answer, in anything from a single word to a phrase, is the keyword (as you can guess, keyword despite the singular "word" can also mean a phrase or a series of words).

For example, if you wrote a novel called *The Trouble with Angels*, the title could act as that page's keywords. In order to designate that as the page's keywords, you would need a WordPress plug-in such as Yoast SEO, which has a keyword box that you would fill in with that information. There are other keyword practices to follow. The keyword should be used several times on the page. You would refer to *The Trouble with Angels*, not "the book" or even "Angels." The keyword should appear in the page's title (the headline of a blog post, for example). And the keyword should be in the page's URL, such as "www.peschelpress.com/the-trouble-with-angels." If you have a photo of the book cover, it would be useful if the file name was "the-trouble-with-angels-cover.jpg" and not "43590821303.jpg," and its alternative name (called, in HTML-speak, ALT) should have the keyword there as well.

All of this can be done easily in WordPress with the Yoast SEO plug-in (there are others out there; this is the one I use). If done correctly, anyone who types in *The Trouble with Angels* stands a better chance of finding your page at or near the top of the front page.

Minimal needs

Your author website need only a few things:
1. A domain name you own.
2. A website built at that domain.
3. Information about each book, including the cover.
4. Links to where you can buy your books.
5. An author bio.
6. A way to contact the author.
7. Links to your social media accounts.

Everything else — blogs, essays, links to social media, podcasts, book trailers; the bells and whistles of marketing and promotion — is optional. Nice to have, but 100% of potential book buyers will visit your site to
     a. See your books
     b. Look at their covers and read descriptions and excerpts
     c. And maybe learn something about the author.

Your Own Domain Name

Building a website is done in two steps: buying the domain name, then buying a web hosting plan.

A domain name is the site's name that you see in the address box at the top of the browser. The domain name for Google is "google.com." The browser adds the stuff to the left of the name ("http://"). As you add pages to your website, where to find them will be to the right of your domain name separated by a slash ("/"). This web address is called the URL (universal resource locator). So when you visit Google News, its URL is "https://www.google.com/nws", where "google" is the domain name, ".com" is the top-level domain (discussed below) and "nws" the webpage the news feed is on.

You buy your domain name online. There are many companies that sell domain names, usually with web hosting, such as NameCheap, BlueHost, GoDaddy, iPage, 1and1, and HostGator. Searching for "best domain name registrars for [year]" can get you the latest opinions. Go to a site, type in a name to see if it's available and how much they charge.

The price of a name varies with the seller, so shop around. Generally,

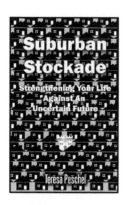

Teresa maintains two authorial brands. She writes nonfiction books under her name, and science-fiction romances as Odessa Moon.

expect to pay about $10 to register a name, and maybe $15 to renew it each year. Multi-year discounts are available.

What name should you use? Your author name or pen name. It should also be a .com, such as "BillPeschel.com". Don't worry about the capitalization, by the way. It doesn't matter. If you type in Google.com, gOOgle.Com or GOOGLE.com, you're taken to the same site.

What if my name is taken? You have two options: a) change your name; b) see if your name is available in another top-level domain.

What is a top-level domain (TLD)? That's the ".com" at the end of your domain. That designates sites that are "commercial" (for profit). Two of the best-known TLDs had specific functions — .net (for computer network-related organizations), and .org (for non-profits). This proved unworkable, unenforceable and has been abandoned.

There are other TLDs available that are geographically based (.us for United States, .eu for European Union), oriented for devices (.mobi), information (.info), or businesses (.biz). The best practice is to buy a .com name. Your readers are familiar with them, and if they type in your name, chances are they'll add the .com suffix.

If you have your heart set on your name, but it's taken, add a word at either end, such "BillPeschelBooks.com," "AuthorBillPeschel.com," or "BillPeschelWriter.com." Don't make the name itself different from your author name (like choosing BillPeschel.com if you couldn't get WilliamPeschel.com). Keep it simple for your readers!

Should I also get one for my book title? I wouldn't. If you're going to publish 20 books, buying a domain name for each will set you back hundreds of dollars a year, and they'll all point to the same website anyway. Stick to your name.

Do I need more than one domain? Only if you need to separate your audiences. Perhaps you write fiction and nonfiction books, or sweet Amish romance under one name and werewolf bondage erotica under another. Otherwise, stick to one name.

A Website At That Domain

Recently, I was listening to a podcast in which a book marketer was talking about websites, and how silly new authors can be about creating them. "They're easy to do," he said. "I can lead a class through them, and at the end they shake their heads over how scared they were!"

At the time, I was looking at the results of WordFence's evaluation of my website. My security certificate was out of date, my site had been placed on SpamCannibal's list of banned IPs, and I had a dozen broken links that needed to be fixed.

I had some choice words for that marketer, none of which I'll repeat except to say they began and ended with "you."

He is right in one sense. There's a lot you can do that's easy. Buying your domain name is easy. Setting up a WordPress site can be a one-click process. Learning to create pages, upload artwork, style for headlines and captions ... is tricky, but learnable.

Working through this process is a lot like making your way through a dark room. You're feeling your way around worrying about barking a shin on the ottoman or tripping over an end table. It's only when you reach a light switch, flip it on, and see the room lit up that you realize that you could have walked through without a problem.

But after your site is set up, there is still more to learn and do:

● **Design the website.** A canned theme will see you through fine. If you want a more personal look, in your company colors and a logo, you either will need to learn a bit of website design, or find someone to design it for you.

● **Protect your site against hackers.** Keep WordPress, your site's theme, and its plug-ins up to date. Your WP dashboard will signal when a plug-in needs to be updated. Installing the Wordfence plug-in provides added protection.

● **Learn about search engine optimization (SEO).**

Again, these skills can be learned, but you have to set aside time to do so. There are plenty of free and low-cost ways to learn, including books in your public library, YouTube videos, websites, even getting advice from your writer friends. Try those resources first before dropping money on courses.

Information About Each Book

Devote a web page to each book. If you're writing a series, create a page for the series with links to the individual titles.

This page should contain:

● Art of the cover

● Great reviews or blurbs.

● A description of the book. Use the same book description on your Amazon book page or on the book's back cover (if there is one).

● An excerpt from the first chapter. This can be put on its own page, but be sure to add bookstore links at the bottom of that page as well. You want to make the book-buying process as easy as possible.

● Links to the bookstores, both online and brick-and-mortar. This is covered in the next section.

Links to Where You Can Buy Your Books

The book page should have a link to every bookstore your book is at and every version as well: ebook, print, and audiobook.

Your Amazon links should also contain your Amazon Associate code.

What is Amazon Associates? It is a program in which you're acting as a salesperson for Amazon. You provide links on your website that contain your account ID. Anyone who clicks on that link and buys something from Amazon will earn you a commission based on a percentage of the price. This applies to anything, so if a visitor goes to Amazon to check out your 99-cent ebook and buys a $50 set of headphones instead, you get a couple bucks.

Not a bad deal, right? There's a right and wrong way to use these links. They're for your website. Not your newsletter, or any email you send. You also need to tell your website visitors that you're a member of the program.

Something About You

There should be a page describing you. What this consists of is up to you and how much you want to reveal. The best way to answer this question is to visit other authors' websites, see how they present themselves, and decide what's right for you.

While this is a place where you can be formal, there's no rule that says you have to be. If it's consistent with the image you want to project, feel free to be humorous, maybe even startling. Revealing things most people would not know about you makes you stand out from other authors.

If you display an author photo, make it as professional and on-brand as possible. Well-lighted or moody, it should show you off to good advantage. Look at the best-selling authors in your genre. They look polished.

Your bio should be on-brand. It should not be a list of your life, unless it pertains to your book.

A Way to Contact You

This can be a part of your author's page, or on a page of its own. WordPress provides a form that allows someone to type a message and email it to you. Or, you can provide a link to your email and your social media platforms.

Disguising your email address: Putting your email on a web page risks opening the door to getting your inbox flooded with spam. Using a contact form keeps that from happening. Using a Google Gmail account lets them skim nearly all the spam out. That's what I do.

Mailing List

Author photos for Odessa Moon, Bill Peschel, and Skye Kingsbury.

The most effective way of staying in touch with your dedicated readers is through a newsletter. It's the perfect match: you have something you want to sell, and they are there to hear your message. They *want* to hear from you.

Best of all, the process is so easy and nearly stress-free that if you can't send

Instead of asking people to sign up for your newsletter, call it your readers' group! This contributes to the illusion of intimacy, makes them feel more like they're joining you in your publishing journey, and less like customers to be exploited.

your fans an email saying "here's my new book," you might want to consider another line of work.

There are many services that help you add a signup box to your website, collect the emails, remove people who want to leave the list, and send your messages.

There are plenty of companies to choose from. The most popular ones today are MailChimp, Constant Contact, Mailerlite, and AWeber. Their services and fees vary, but most of them have a free level, then start charging a monthly fee once your list has grown beyond a set number of emails. They also provide additional services for a fee.

At this point, you can put a signup box on your website and leave it at that. But there are best practices that involve writing a reader magnet, building a funnel, and "warming up" your subscribers to encourage them to become superfans. Those details can be found in Chapter 11: Mailing List.

Website Security

One of the hazards of running your own website is the risk of hackers taking it over, or finding it infested with malware, ransomware, or adware. It's a terrible feeling akin to seeing your store vandalized and occupied by squatters.

This is not helped by stories spread by the media and self-styled security experts, that make it sound like hordes of hackers are swarming your site, attacking your door with a battering ram. It's enough to make you swear off owning a website, or sticking a toe online ever again.

Don't give in to that fear. Arm yourself with these facts about website hacking.

Websites get hacked because of a weakness in its defenses: To extend the store metaphor, if you have bars on the windows and locks on the doors, burglars cannot break in.

To break into your site, a hacker has to find a way in through a portal such as your login page or through a WordPress plug-in that has malware written into its code. If you follow the best practices for securing these portals, you'll take care of the majority of the attacks.

To be honest, I can't say 100% of them. I can't predict the future. A clever hacker might discover a flaw in WordPress' code and exploit it. Or your website host might leave a critical backdoor open. Like much of our lives, we can't predict when something unexpected happens. But securing your website will go a long way to deter the vast majority of attacks.

If your website is on a site like WordPress.com, Wix, or Squarespace, they'll be responsible for a lot of the security. All you'll have to do is choose a long password. Don't make it a consecutive string of numbers ("1234567").

IDEA

Don't use ("password"). Don't use this password on another site; hackers who steal your password from one site will try them against other sites.

When creating a password, group letters and numbers, such as "ABCD1234abcd!@#$." You get the complexity of this type of password, but it's easier to type in than "A#!$@Cb!caDdAaf."

If you're using WordPress and paying for web hosting, get a plug-in like Wordfence that specializes in keeping your website secure. One option it has — which WordPress should include — sets the number of chances you have to login with the correct password. After a preset number of failures, that person can't log in again anywhere from a few minutes to several months. Hackers use a program that scans the internet for the tell-tale sign of a WordPress login page, then attack it repeatedly with a combination of logins and passwords. This limits the number of times they can try. There are other options available as well.

TIP

If you think your website's been hacked but not sure, test it at *www.sitecheck.sucuri.net.*

What happens if your site's hacked? If malware is discovered on your site, your web host will most likely shut it down and isolate it. They will offer to clean your site for a price. The cost may be high. Services like Wordfence do the job better because they're expert in dealing with website security. Your web host know how to host websites, but that doesn't make them security experts.

Optional Website Add-Ons

Blog

The question is not why you should blog. As I've said before, there are very few things you must do. You must write books, produce them, and make them available for sale. You must have a website with information about your books and links to where visitors can buy them.

After that, everything is optional, based on the types of books you write, your business goals, your talents, and your desire. If you don't like to blog but you feel obliged to, chances are you're not going to be good at it. You'll write in bursts, posting daily when you're enthusiastic about it, less when you don't feel like it, or feel discouraged.

I know the feeling; I've experienced it, and it's bothered me for years. There are bloggers out there who have been writing daily for years. They've built large audiences of appreciative readers. Their comment sections are full of people discussing the post, many of them around long enough to create in-jokes appreciated only by the regulars.

Meantime, at my blog at *planetpeschel.com,* I've flailed wildly from week to

I've been suggesting to people is that almost every publication now has a big online presence. I think that there's a lot more openness to new writers on websites. I mean, I can see this with *The New Yorker* — the chance of getting something on the website is infinitely greater than getting in the print magazine.

Susan Orlean

week. I post irregularly about a lot of different subjects. I'm not consistent. In short, I'm a terrible host.

Weirdly, I'm a good commenter. On the sites I regularly visit, I contribute information, tell jokes, encourage and praise those I agree with, disagree politely when I'm not (with the occasional misstep). I've spent more time on other people's websites than on my own.

My problem is that I'm interested in too many things. My curiosity is wide-ranging: politics, comics, history, sex, culture, literature, writing, science, space, crime. At one time, I was regularly reading posts from more than 200 websites. I was a read-aholic, and while I was learning a lot, I wasn't contributing. I wasn't creating.

Something had to give. I cut back on my reading diet drastically. Now I'm down to about 20 sites, many of which post infrequently.

I use the free Feedly service to subscribe to blogs. It's a great way to keep up with writers and book marketers.

Blogging is not for everyone. If you don't feel you can do it well, it's best not to start.

If you are going to blog, think about what you want to share. It can be anything, but you can be most effective if each post aligns with your books. It can be to reveal something about yourself; some readers believe authors live a more interesting life. Here's where you can prove them right or wrong. It can be about writing, although unless you're selling how-to books, you don't want to write about this too often. If your books are about a certain subject, posting about this subject will demonstrate your competence in writing about it, and attract potential readers.

For example, say that you write a mystery series in which horses play a major role. It might be set on a ranch; it might involve a horse trainer or jockey; your characters participate in fox hunting. You're around horses, or you do a lot of research on riding, training, dressage, and history. Your blog will have posts on all of these subjects. If they are optimized for search engines, they are given a better chance of appearing high up in searches. You may be recognized as an expert. If you write about other authors who also specialize in horses, chances are you'll appear in their searches as well (it'll help your chances if you offer useful information on those subjects).

The Six Purposes of a Blog

There are six major purposes behind a blog. Some overlap — every blog is a form of self-advertising, after all — but if you're thinking about starting one, picking one purpose will clarify decisions such as how often to post and what to write about.

Self-Promotion

Types of posts: Book-focused: announcements, behind-the-scenes looks, interesting research, announcements of author appearances and signings.

Frequency: Irregular, increasing around the time of a book's publication and decreasing in between.

Goal: Draw potential readers to the website through search engine optimization. For example, a writer of books on space exploration can post articles about NASA's history, astronauts, space vehicles, and similar subjects. Frequent posts on these subjects will raise the site's profile in search engines, raising the chance that people seeking information on those subjects will find his site. Fiction writers can do the same thing by not only writing about their books, but about other writers and books in their genre. Associating their blog with other writers increases the chance that other writer's fans will discover these books.

Romance writer Marie Force's website is full of news about her new and upcoming releases: *marieforce.com*

Example: To spread the work of keeping a blog going, many writers form group blogs, such as Writers in the Storm (*writersinthestormblog.com/*) and Mad Genius Club (*madgeniusclub.com*). Many popular romance writers such as Meljean Brook (*meljeanbrook.com*) and Marie Force (*marieforce.com*) use their blog to feed fans and potential readers information about their books, with the occasional personal glimpses.

Community Building

Types of posts: All kinds, but designed to solicit comments and discussions from readers. Most effective posts express an opinion, the more strongly held the better. Also, posts involving memories that encourage readers to contribute memories of their own.

Josh Fruhlinger has built a community of fans around The Comic Curmudgeon, with his humorous commentary about newspaper comic strips: *joshreads.com*

Frequency: Daily, usually Monday through Friday. Unless trained to expect a post only on certain days, readers seem to prefer a daily routine. Since many of them surf the internet at work, a Monday-Friday schedule conforms to many workers' schedules.

Goal: Socializing and feedback. A community of like-minded individuals with varying experiences can be a useful source of information, a focus group for ideas, and the pleasure of people's company. To the writer, it can also be used to attract fans of your work, and an effective tool at book launches.

Examples: The Comics Curmudgeon (comic strips; *joshreads.com*), The Passive Voice (writing and self-publishing; *thepassivevoice.com*), Ann Althouse (politics, Madison, life; *althouse.blogspot.com*), The Archdruid Report (spiritualism, magic, occultism; *ecosophia.net*).

Advocate

Types of posts: Revolving around the cause you're promoting.

Balloon Juice comments on political news and causes from the liberal perspective: *balloon-juice.com*.

Frequency: Varies depending upon the flow of information and the writer's desire to promote his views. Blogs focused on politics at the state and national level can post every day, creating a community of like-minded readers.

Goal: To support opinions on an issue.

Examples: Ace of Spades (conservative politics, *ace.mu.nu*), Balloon Juice (liberal politics, *balloon-juice.com*).

Warning: Venturing into controversial subjects may drive away readers.

Self-Expression

Types of posts: Any and all kinds. Opinions, observations, memories, humor.

Frequency: Varying according to the mood and productivity of the writer.

Goal: Varies. It could be simply the fun of putting down on paper what you're thinking about that day. It could even be a variation on the journal.

Examples: The Bloggess (*TheBloggess.com*). Sadly, it seems that the blogs I used to follow are no longer around. What passes for personal blogs are now lifestyle blogs with corporate sponsorship.

Jenny Lawson's website charts the ups and downs of her life with her unique sense of humor: *thebloggess.com*.

Future Books

Types of posts: Drafts from an upcoming book.

Frequency: Varies according to the writer's productivity. One benefit of using a blog in this way is that the pressure of meeting a regular deadline forces you to work (or, as film director Robert Rodriguez put it: "Action comes before inspiration").

Goal: To come up with a finished book. *Writers Gone Wild* began online as a way to use up years of material I had gathered about authors. Teresa used this technique to write *Suburban Stockade,* and I wrote *The Career Indie Author.* Collections of posts can be sold as anthologies. Andy Weir published *The Martian* on his website and turned it into a Kindle ebook at his fans' request.

Wattpad lets you post fanfiction and original fiction before readers: *wattpad.com*.

Examples: The popular fiction site Wattpad (*wattpad.com*) is a collection of writers publishing future book material. Teresa's science-fiction persona,

Odessa Moon, serializes chapters from her Steppes of Mars series.

Expertise Display

Types of posts: Information about a particular field to demonstrate a

David Gaughran uses his blog posts to demonstrate his knowledge of Amazon and book marketing in general: *davidgaughran.com.*

depth of knowledge and expertise that leads to offers of work. It could be examples of book marketing, cultural reviews (books, movies, art), op-ed pieces, humor: Anything that can be used as a portfolio to approach magazines, editors, or other websites to seek work.

Frequency: Varies depending upon the writer's productivity.

Goal: To promote the writer as an authority on a particular subject.

Examples: The Hacker Factor Blog (internet security; *hackerfactor.com/blog/*), David Gaughran (book marketing; *davidgaughran.com/*).

The Illusion of Intimacy

The internet connects people, especially those with whom we have no direct contact. In my many years online, there are people who I know a lot about who I have never met in person. In fact, I know them better than I know my siblings! I know how they think, their sense of humor (or lack thereof), their beliefs, and their attitudes on everything from current events or whether they prefer Kirk or Picard.

What the internet does best is deliver the illusion of intimacy. Through your words, your fans will "read" you in the same way they're reading a book. They'll base their image of who they think you are on what they read, a prospect some writers find unnerving.

If you're one of those writers and don't want to jump into the social media pool, that's all right! There is no value in making yourself do something that you won't enjoy. Every time you write a post, you'll have to nerve yourself to press [publish]. Moreover, your fans will recognize that you don't want to be there, either.

But being on social media doesn't mean having to share everything about your life. Think about the celebrities and other public figures you follow. Do they share everything? Some seem to, but even they have their limits.

If you want an idea of how different authors share their lives, check these out:

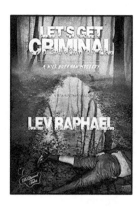

• Thriller author Lisa Scottoline publishes a weekly personal column in the *Philadelphia Inquirer* (*inquirer.com/author/scottoline_lisa/*). She has talked about her hatred of air conditioning, her Italian family, aging, her relationship with her daughter and her adventures in New York City, and her relationship with her fans. These columns have been collected into books exposing her thrillers to fans of her columns.

• Lev Raphael (*levraphael.com/*)is a former academic who has written books about the Holocaust (which his parents survived), Edith Wharton (who he specialized in at the University of Michigan), and his life as a Jewish gay man. He uses this material to write books in several genres, including mystery, memoir, and history. His blog posts at the *Huffington Post* (*huffpost.com/author/lev-raphael*), however, are varied: from books and plays he's experienced to family stories.

• S.J. Pangonas writes cozy mysteries set in Japan. Until she cut back on her book publishing, she blogged regularly about her writing life, her trips to Japan, and what she did during the week. She set monthly goals, then returned to them at the beginning of a new month to show whether she has met them.

• Kristine Kathryn Rusch and her husband, Dean Wesley Smith, use different strategies. Rusch publishes weekly her "Business Musings" column (*kriswrites.com/category/business-musings*) discussing publishing, marketing, licensing and other subjects. Smith blogs a daily diary (*deanwesleysmith.com*) telling us when he gets up, who he meets with, the progress of his pop culture store, the times of his writing sessions, and the number of words he types in. As you can imagine, this gets repetitive, but it's an excellent example of the daily life of a productive writer.

• James Lileks is a newspaper columnist in Minneapolis. For more than two decades, he has published a five-days-a-week column called The Bleat (*bleat.com*), where he mixes scenes from his life as a newspaperman and homeowner with some takedowns of particularly stupid articles, and snippets of pop culture from the 1920s to the 1970s. He keeps strict limits on appearances by his wife (who works for the state government), but has talked about his relationship with his daughter and his father.

Essays

Are essays different from blog posts? They can be, but not necessarily.

Essays are better-written blog posts that occupy a permanent, easily accessible place on your website. They are evergreen and contain useful information or emotions that promote your persona and your books.

On my website Planet Peschel, the Wimsey Annotations (*planetpeschel.com/the-wimsey-annotations*) can be considered essays on steroids. These pages explaining the cultural and historical references in the mysteries of Dorothy L. Sayers draw a lot of traffic to my website. Some visitors turn around and buy *The Complete, Annotated Whose Body?*

You can do the same with your website. If you're a historical writer, you could write essays that build your reputation as a writer of that period. If you're a genre writer, anything that draws on your knowledge of the genre, optimized for search engines, could draw that genre's readers. You want however many pages you can generate on your topic so that people searching for "Victorian medicine," "NASA space shuttle," or "Raymond Chandler" will find you.

Affiliate Programs

A potential source of revenue can be found by joining an affiliate program offered by a company or service. The most common one is Amazon's. After signing up, you create affiliate links to products (such as your books) and place them on your website or in your ebook (but not in your emails, including newsletters; that's a no-no). Anyone who clicks on an affiliate link is taken to Amazon, and anything they buy — whether it's your products or not — earns you a fee.

If you join the program, you must put a notice on your website alerting people to what you're doing. For example, here's the text at the bottom of my Peschel Press website. Feel free to copy it:

> **Amazon Associates Disclaimer**
>
> I am a participant in the Amazon Services LLC Associates Program, an affiliate advertising program designed to provide a means for me to earn fees by linking to Amazon.com and affiliated sites at no cost to you.

TIP

Because people from around the world visit my website, I try to accommodate their needs. I joined BKLINK, a free service that directs buyers of my Kindle books to the store in their country. The service lets me add my Amazon Associates code so that I could earn a little cash as well. For other stores, I use a similar service offered by Draft2Digital.

Chapter 9

Producing Your EBook

Key Points to Remember

- Metadata is all the information associated with your book: title, description, categories, etc.
- Formatting an ebook can be outsourced, but you can do it yourself with online tools.
- Amazon allows for multiple keywords to describe your book, so use as many as you can.

Ebooks have many advantages – publishers don't have to make guesses about how many books to print, books need never go "out of print," and hard-to-find books can be easily available. So far, the only limitation seems to be finding a way for the writer to be paid.

Kate Grenville

By now, you have your business set up. Your manuscript came back from the editor. You've checked the suggested changes, accepted some, rejected others, and got another pair of eyes to look over it one more time. You're ready to publish.

You'll need two versions of your ebook: one for Amazon's KDP and one for every other site called an EPUB file, because the file extension is EPUB, as in YourNovelTitle.epub.

Even if you're putting your book in Kindle Unlimited, you might want to have the EPUB handy, so if you go wide with it, you're ready to go. Because it's so easy to make, a formatter usually doesn't charge extra for it.

If you're doing it yourself, here's what you need:

- **The manuscript file,** preferably saved as a Word file (.doc, or .docx).
- **The cover** in either .jpeg (or .jpg) or .tif (or .tiff) format. Amazon wants it to be 2,560 pixels by 1,600 pixels (other retailers are fine with less). Its resolution should be 300 pixels per inch and less than 50MB in size. It should be saved in the RGB color format. If the cover's background is largely white, add a black border, 3-4 pixels wide, around the edge.
- **A book description** for the top of the book page. For added oomph, add a large headline, and use bold, and/or italics using Dave Chesson's book description formatter (*kindlepreneur.com/amazon-book-description-generator/*). Do this in advance, save it as a file, and call it up when you need it.
- **Keywords** for the seven slots allocated. Thanks to research by Dave Chesson of Kindlepreneur, we know the optimal way to use keywords. Each slot accepts any number of words up to 80 characters total, including spaces. The words can be put in any order and you don't need to repeat words. "Historical romance novel" works just as well as "historical novel" and "romance novel" and saves you six spaces for another word. These keywords can be used on all the ebook sites.
- **An author bio.** A short version of 50-100 words is recommended.

Writers do not choose their subjects at random — it is often the subconscious that makes that choice for them. So if you want to know about a writer, and about what really makes him or her tick, then simply look at the books. There's a lot to be found out there.
Alexander McCall Smith

You'll need four versions: long (200-300 words) for your website, short (50-100 words) for ebook sites that use this such as your Amazon author page; a few sentences for social media sites like Facebook and Twitter; and professional (500 words and up) for your media kit about your accomplishments so journalists can use it for profiles, reviews, and other articles.

• **Optional:** An author photo to go with your bio inside the book. This can also be used on your Amazon Author Page. If you don't want to use your image here, create a piece of art that reflects your brand. But put *something* there.

Going Meta With Metadata

Metadata may sound intimidating, but it is simply a collection of words that describe your book. Your title is a piece of metadata. So is the subtitle, author, genre, categories, keywords, and book description. That's all it is.

There's so much metadata that I designed a form to keep track of it. Having this information easily accessible lets me review prices, revise keywords, and grab a book description when I need it quickly for publicity purposes. I also use the form to chart the book's publication history.

I reproduced it below, and a copyable version is in the appendix and A Word file can be downloaded at *www.careerindieauthor.com/Resources*. Feel free to modify it to suit your needs.

Metadata for [BOOK TITLE]

About the Book

Title:
Subtitle:
Series / Number:
Imprint:
ISBN:
ASIN:
Number of Pages:
Illustrations, Number of:
Trim Size:
Interior: (white or cream)
Cover: (matte or glossy)
Short description: Distributors like IngramSpark limit you to 350 characters.
Full description:
Author(s), illustrators and other contributors / Bio:
Prior work for each contributor:

Location (for each contributor):
Affiliations (for each contributor):

Prices

Price: (print and/or ebook)

INGRAMSPARK (price / discount / returns?)
US:
UK:
EU:
CA:
AUS:
Global Connect:

Publication History and Notable Upgrades

Record what happened to this book during and after publication, including price changes, new editions, problems with uploading it, and any unusual situations worth recording. Repeat these headers for each bookstore (Kindle, Nook, Google Play, etc.).

First Published:
Latest Edition:

Discoverability

Amazon keywords should be completed before publishing your book, but the rest can be done during the process. Don't forget to write down your choices! For more information on finding keywords, see Chapter 12: Amazon.

For example, here's the keyword section for my book *The Complete, Annotated Mysterious Affair at Styles.* The order these words are entered does not matter. The algorithm will display this book whether a customer types in "Golden age detectives," "Edwardian female authors," or "poison country home Land Girls."

Amazon Keywords (limit 50 characters per line):
1. Golden age private detectives murder by poison
2. Traditional classic Edwardian period mysteries
3. British English country homes medical doctors
4. Female mystery authors novelists best selling
5. annotated history Britain England post-world war I
6. debut novels Belgium strychnine families
7. Land Girls William Palmer essays annotations

Categories (Amazon): (You're allowed to choose two, but later, you can ask them to add up to eight more.)

BISAC codes: (Used in Google Play and some other sites; *bisg.org/page/BISACSubjectCodes*)

Thema subjects: (Used in Google Play and some other sites; *ns.editeur.org/thema/en*)

Geographic region: (used at IngramSpark but not required)

Audience: (Academic, general trade, children, YA, etc.)

Table of contents:

Review quotes:

Adding Front and Back Matter

Material placed around the book's content is called matter. Front matter goes in front of the book, and back matter, of course, goes in the back.

The Chicago Manual of Style — a reference book used in the publishing industry, particularly by university presses — defines what matter goes where, but in Indie World the format is more flexible. Online bookstores ask only that the book's title and author name be placed at the beginning, and that the table of contents is accessible through the device's drop-down menu.

Here is what you can also have as part of your front and back matter.

• **Copyright notice:** This can range from the simple "Copyright 20xx by Your Name," to the more elaborate list of credits seen in many books. It can be formatted any way you like. In printed books, the copyright notice goes at the front, but many ebooks have them in the back. This lets the online seller's "look inside the book" show more of the story, rather than waste a page the customer doesn't need to see.

Here is a typical example:

> Copyright [YEAR] by [COPYRIGHT HOLDER]. All rights reserved. Published by [COMPANY NAME AND MAILING ADDRESS]. Cover art by [ARTIST, with link to their website]. Edited by [EDITOR, with link to their website]. Formatted by [FORMATTER, with link to their website].*
>
> ISBN: [ISBN Number].
> Library of Congress Control Number: [NUMBER].**
> Version: 1.0, [Month] [Year]

* You don't have to link to their websites, but remember commandment 8: "Thou shall pay it forward."

** The Library of Congress' Preassigned Control Number Program (*loc.gov/publish/pcn*) is a free service that helps them catalog the print edition of your book. Ebooks are not eligible. You fill out a form before the book is published. They give you a number to be printed on the copyright page. You must also send them a printed copy of the book. Join this program (like we do) only if you like imagining your book on their shelves.

- **List of publications:** A list of your other books. Traditional publishers place it before the title page. Because you're an indie author, you can place your list in both places and link your titles to the Amazon store. For the EPUB version, which will go up on many store sites, link your books to your website, where you have a page for each book, right?

- **Newsletter signup:** Asking readers to join your newsletter or readers' group is a standard marketing tactic. This *call to action* is usually accompanied by the offer of a *reader magnet*, a freebie given as part of the *onboarding sequence* (these terms are explained in the section on newsletters). Authors usually give away one or more of their novels, but I've seen some give away part of a novel, a prequel novella introducing a series, short stories, or something related to the book, such as character profiles, a map, or a dossier. This can be put in the front and the back matter.

- **Author's note, acknowledgements:** Writers like to include a personal note to the reader that acts like a "behind the scenes" feature on movie DVDs. Authors can also thank everyone who helped with the book, such as editors, beta readers, family, friends, and supportive spouse. This usually goes in the back of the book.

- **Author bio and photo:** Placed in the back of the book. Because it conveys the author's image and brand, it's a bad idea to toss off in haste the photo/bio. But overshooting the mark can be just as bad; a black-and-white photo of a mystery author in a leather jacket against a brick wall sets the proper mood, but posing in a trench coat and fedora, holding a gun, with a slinky blonde at your side is too "on the nose" unless you're writing a parody. If you're unsure, show the photos to people you trust, especially a bookstore owner.

- **Dedication:** Usually in the front. I've seen it on its own page, as part of the copyright, and tucked in after the table of contents.

GET THE NEWSLETTER

New releases, behind-the-scenes info, and general nonsense. I'll Never Sell Your Information. Promise.

Subscribe

A newsletter signup box could be as simple as this.

Formatting the Manuscript

You have two choices: hire someone, or do it yourself.

If you're comfortable working with software, it's worth a try. Amazon's Kindle Create makes it easy to format your novel and see how it looks on their devices. They even have a tutorial with sample files to experiment with (*kdp.amazon.com/en_US/help/topic/GYVL2CASGU9ACFVU*).

In the end, you'll have a file in the .kpf format (where you would see .docx on a Word document). You can't load this onto your Kindle. It's uploaded to KDP, which converts it into a Kindle-readable file.

Making the EPUB Version

For all the other sites, Draft2Digital can help. They offer a free tool that converts a Word file into an EPUB file. You might be able to use the same

*Book Sites
with Direct
Author Access*

BARNES&**NOBLE**

Google Play

front cover, but if it doesn't work, resize it to 1600x2400 pixels and you're good to go.

Press [Publish]

If you filled out the metadata form, and gathered all the material you need to publish your book, there is one last decision to make.

KU or wide?

KU is Kindle Unlimited, Amazon's all-you-can-read subscription service. You can put any or all of your ebooks into KU, and they can't be published anywhere else. However, you can publish your print edition anywhere.

Your book is in the program for 90 days, and is automatically renewed at the end of the period. You can pull your book from the program easily by going into the book's KDP Select page and unchecking a box. It's as simple as that.

Amazon calculates how many pages your book consists of, called the Kindle Edition Normalized Page Count (KENPC). The KENPC varies from book to book. KU subscribers check the book out, and Amazon keeps track of how many KENPC pages were read.

At the end of every month, Amazon sets the page-read rate. The amount varies, but averages a little less than half a cent per page. They multiply the number of pages read by the page-read rate, and that's how much you'll get paid. Authors with a high number of page reads earn a bonus between two and five figures on top of that.

To publish your book, here are the sites that allow direct access to their stores:

Kindle: *kdp.amazon.com/*
Kobo: *authorize.kobo.com/signin*
Barnes & Noble: *press.barnesandnoble.com/sign-in*
Apple: *authors.apple.com/*
Google Play: *play.google.com/books/publish/*

To reach the remaining storefronts, choose an aggregate distributor such as Smashwords (*smashwords.com/dashboard*) or Draft2Digital (*draft2digital.com/*). Or, you could give up some of your royalty share and use them to get to the major sites as well.

Making a Print Edition

Laying out a print version of your novel is more complicated than formatting the ebook. To do it well, you need to understand these tools in Word: headers and footers, page numbers, inserting art, page breaks, and decompressing art.

There are two services which make this process much easier. The Mac

Ebook, Print Converters

software Vellum (*vellum.pub*) has an excellent reputation for easily converting print and ebooks. It can be pricy ($200 for unlimited ebooks, $250 for ebooks and paperbacks) and you need either an Apple computer or an online Apple emulator to use it.

Draft2Digital also offers a free ebook/print converter. It has few options but seems serviceable for novels.

Otherwise, designers use InDesign or Affinity Publisher to design their books.

If you're interested in doing it yourself on Word, here is a brief, truncated procedure to demonstrate what you'll face:

1. Download an interior template Word file from KDP (*kdp.amazon.com/ en_US/help/topic/G201834230*). The template comes in a folder with many files, each one for a particular size book. The two most popular sizes are 6" x 9" and 5.5" x 8.5".

2. Paste the text into the template. Apply bold and/or italics where you want it. Modify the chapter heads using the Heading styles. Add the front and back matter.

3. Download a cover template for the same size book from KDP (and from IngramSpark if you're going there as well). If you bought art for only the cover, go to the cover designer and order a wraparound cover (art that covers the front, spine and back cover). Otherwise, use an art program like Photoshop to add color to the spine and back and add text: the title, author, and imprint on the spine and a book description on the back. Make sure it looks like a real book.

4. Proof everything one more time.

5. Create a PDF of the interior and cover templates. If you use art, before you do so, turn off Word's compression option. Click on a piece of art to bring up the Format tab, look at the Adjust panel, and click on Compress Pictures. Click on Options, then uncheck "perform basic compression on save." Make the PDF.

6. When you have PDFs of both the interior and cover, it's time to upload the book to KDP. After the files are uploaded, it will check for errors and let you know what's wrong. When they're fixed, you'll be able to download a PDF or review it on screen. You'll also be able to order a print proof so you can hold the result of your work in your hand. I strongly recommend doing so, until you're comfortable with the process and your skill at creating a book.

7. If everything looks good, tell KDP and your book will be for sale.

After that, consider putting your book up on IngramSpark. Ingram is a major distributor to the bookstore and library trade, and they're moving into selling books direct. If you have a trade edition, all you'll need to do is download from IngramSpark the cover template for your size book and readjust the art. I've successfully used the interior PDF created for the KDP edition.

The downside is that they charge a $50 setup fee, and after your book is publish, another $50 each time you upload a file (such as if you're making corrections to the book). But there are coupon codes out there that will waive both fees. They'll occasionally put the code in their newsletter, so sign up for it. The 20Booksto50K Facebook group was given a code, but that expires 12/31/2020. Also, ALLI (Alliance of Independent Authors) offers a code with membership.

If you decide to publish through IngramSpark, *do not put your book up on Barnes & Noble Press.* IngramSpark will supply the book to B&N.

PART III

Finding Fans

Wanting to meet an author
because you like his work
is like wanting
to meet a duck
because you like
pâté.

Margaret Atwood

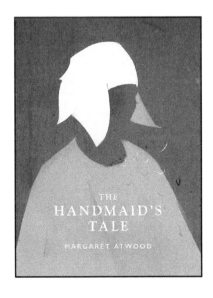

Chapter 10

What's Next

Key Points to Remember

- Think about your book as a product that can create multiple revenue streams.
- Revenue streams can include print, ebook, audiobook, and podcast.
- Demonstrating expertise in a subject can let you move into videos and public speaking gigs.

> When you have your revenue streams set up the right way, you can be confident the dollars are rolling in no matter what.
>
> **Desmond Ong**

A t this point, you're wondering where's the stuff about advertising and marketing. When do I start making money at this?

Not yet.

Very few first novels take off. Very, very few. Those that do have some kind of special oomph behind them due to high-level planning, throwing a lot of money at it, having great connections, or simply luck, propelling a book into the public consciousness and onto the best seller list.

- It's President Reagan spotted carrying Tom Clancy's first novel *The Hunt for Red October*.
- It's a publisher's eight-year-old daughter who read the first chapter in the Harry Potter series and wanted more.
- It's Andy Weir coming up with a compelling twist on the man vs. nature story, stranding an astronaut on Mars, publishing it on his website, then for the Kindle (where it hit the top of the best-seller list) before trad publishing took a chance on *The Martian*.

There have also been more moderate successes. Jami Albright's debut novel *Running From a Rock Star* was launched with the help of her many, many friends and her sassy Texas-flavored personality. T. Ellery Hodges' superhero novels *The Never Hero* and *The Never Paradox* are still enjoying good sales despite the long delay (more than three years now) in producing the third book.

So it's not impossible to create a best seller from one book, but unless you can come up with specific reasons how your book can make the lists, you're better off building your career slowly rather than spending a lot of money and effort on a longshot.

In other words, what should you do next?

Write more books.

How many? The conventional wisdom says that if you're writing a KU-only series, three books is the minimum to have out before revving up your marketing plans.

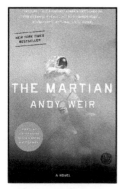

Why three? Because whale readers, the easiest ones to reach in your genre, like seeing at least three. It shows that you're not a one-and-done author, and if your reviews are good, that your books are worth trying.

Even if you're not in KU, having three books will help you spread the cost of advertising over more books. Spending a dollar that returns $2 in royalties is good. Spending a dollar to earn $6 is better.

Again, don't accept this as anything more than an educated guess. If your books are decently written, if you've nailed your genre's tropes, if your characters burst off the page, if your cover is on-genre, and your book description sings, you might do better. But wait for it to happen before you commit more resources.

Creating Revenue Streams

Now that you have one book under your belt, it's time to think about what to do next. I don't mean about the next book; I mean creating multiple revenue streams for each book.

That means not just having an ebook, but having it in Kindle Unlimited. Or if not in KU, then on all the platforms. If you're going wide, that's several revenue streams coming in (one each from Kindle, Kobo, Nook, etc.). If you're using the KU-only strategy, that's two streams: one from ebook sales, the other from KU payments.

Other revenue streams include:

• Print sales from KDP and IngramSpark.

• Direct sales to the public at book festivals, craft shows, street fairs, and conventions.

• Direct sales to bookstores.

• Audiobooks through Audible, Findaway Voices, and Kobo Writing Life.

Then there are other possible revenue streams:

• Through teaching, consulting and public speaking.

• Through YouTube videos and podcasting

• Through Patreon and Kickstarter

Most of you will probably stick with a combination of ebook and print sales, with some local appearances at bookstores and libraries. And that's fine. There are plenty of indie authors who are making five- and six-figure incomes publishing only ebooks and print books.

But it's nice to see Brandon Sanderson offer a leatherbound edition of his Stormlight Archive novel and raise more than $5 million on Kickstarter, and realize you could do the same down the road.

But first, write the books.

In the meantime, let's talk about marketing (at last!).

Chapter 11

Mailing Lists

Key Points to Remember

- A regular newsletter is the most cost-effective way to reach your readers.
- Providing the illusion of intimacy offers a safe, controlled view into your private life.
- Newsletter content is most effective when it aligns with the type of books you write.

Permission marketing turns strangers into friends and friends into loyal customers. It's not just about entertainment – it's about education. Permission marketing is curriculum marketing.

Seth Godin

Writing, revising, and publishing your first book is the first step toward building a business that will support you. At some point, you'll have to learn the tools of marketing, advertising, and publicity.

Marketing is anything that's doesn't involve writing the novel. Your cover art, book description, website, newsletter, even your author photo. All of these elements determine how readers think of you and your books, and affect whether they'll hit the [Buy Now] button or move on.

Truth be told, marketing can even play a role in your writing. You can *write to market* or even *write to trend,* paying attention to what's in the best-selling books in your genre and using them with your own unique spin in your stories.

This doesn't imply that you should be 100% about the marketing. If you do, chances are you'll write derivative stores that proclaim your cynical attitude clearly to the reader. They'll also lack your unique worldview, sense of humor, and life experience that make up your voice and set your books apart from all the others.

Your mailing list can be an important component of your business plan. An email list of readers who like your books and want more can give you a significant boost every time you release a book. Your list demonstrates the size of your audience to potential partners, such as traditional publishers, movie producers, and fellow authors.

Handled wrong, it can also be a waste of time and money. Indiscriminately handing out free books to attract signups will draw an audience of freeloaders who have no intention of paying for your work; worse, they'll make you pay the mailing list provider for their presence.

Terms

Before we begin, let's go over a few words you might be unfamiliar with:

• *Funnel:* The path the reader takes starting with your request to sign up for your mailing list, whether a clipboard on your table at a book festival, or a pop-up box on your website;

• *Landing page:* A page on your website where the reader can sign up for your newsletter; typically, the page is isolated from the rest of your site;

• *Reader magnet:* A freebie you're offering for signing up, such as a short story or a novella;

• W*arming up:* The process of converting a person who signed up for your list into a fan; usually consisting of sending a series of emails with special offers, a survey, or sharing personal information, creating an illusion of intimacy.

Planning Your Newsletter

There are five elements to consider in setting up your newsletter:
- **Content:** What you write
- **Graphic Design:** What it looks like
- **Provider:** Who handles your list
- **Frequency:** How often you'll send it
- **Reader magnet:** What you give subscribers to sign up

1. Content

What should you write in your newsletter?

Anything you want.

The best answer depends on the kind of relationship you want with your readers. Is it purely promotional? Then it's about your books and the promotions. Is it to convey a personal tone? That's when you write about your future projects, your trips, and your cat or dog.

To learn what works for you, join other authors' mailing lists and see how they market themselves.

Let's take a look at two of them, picked at random from the many I receive:

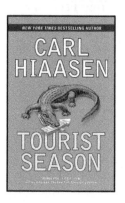

• Wayne Stinnett writes thrillers set in South Florida, the land of Carl Hiassen, Elmore Leonard, Dave Barry, and John D. Macdonald. His newsletter is short and friendly. One consisted of 373 words about his trip to Key West for Mystery Fest, describing his visit to Mallory Square and Ernest Hemingway's home. This is an ideal alignment of his interests with his books.

He also does a bit of networking. He mentions meeting John H. Cunningham, another author with South Florida connections, and provides links to his books. Stinnett also wrote another 124 words on "What I am Reading," promoting the latest book in the Road series by his friend Michael Reisig.

Apart from the banner ad promoting his latest book, the tone of Stinnett's

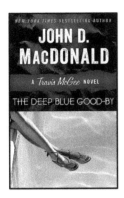

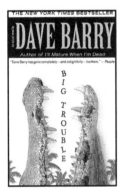

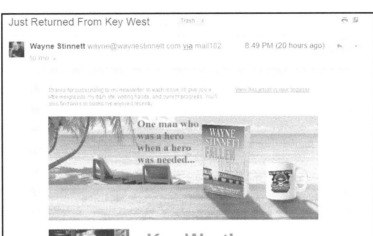

Just Returned From Key West

Wayne Stinnett wayne@waynestinnett.com via mail182   8.49 PM (20 hours ago)
to me

Thanks for subscribing to my newsletter. In each issue, I'll give you a little insight into my daily life, writing habits, and current progress. You'll also find links to books I've enjoyed recently.   View this email in your browser

One man who was a hero when a hero was needed...

What I'm Reading

This past week was perfect timing. My good friend Michael Reisig, has just finished his latest in the Road Series Road to Key West. He sent me an advance copy the day before I left to go to Key West for the annual Mystery Fest. Reading about Kansas and Will's latest exploits, while there in the place it all begins, made it really easy to fall right into the island cadence of Michael's work. If you haven't read any of these great stories, you're really missing out. Just click on his name, up above, and you can start at the beginning. Michael helped me out immensely when I first started writing. This new book is without a doubt his best one yet.

Semper Fi
Wayne

Key West!
Welcome aboard all you new Subscribers!

About four hours ago, I pulled back into the driveway of our home on Lady's Island, South Carolina, after nine days in the Florida Keys and Key West. It rained nearly the whole 700-mile drive down there and a good bit on the way back. But, while we were in Key West, it was sunny, hot, and brutally humid. I loved it! We were anxious to get home, but it's always hard to leave the Keys in my wake.

Monday through Wednesday, we played tourist. Yes, we went to Mallory Square. And yes, we laughed at the cat juggler, Southernmost tight rope walker and other street performers. We watched the sun slip into the Gulf of Mexico and we wished on green flashes that never occurred. We tried to go up to Marathon to see Dan Sullivan playing at Faro Blanco, but a truck fire on the Seven Mile Bridge thwarted our plans. Nobody was hurt, but the truck burned completely and blocked both directions for an hour and a half.

On Thursday, the day before the annual Mystery Fest kicked off, I attended a cocktail party with my wife and daughter at the Old Town home of John Cunningham, the author of the Buck Reilly Series. We had a wonderful time, the highlight of the conference. Look for Buck Reilly to make a cameo appearance in the upcoming Rising Storm. We also talked about doing a collaboration, where Buck and Jesse work together. This might have to wait a little while though. John's books are set in the present and mine are set in past, currently 2008. Here, John and I are hanging out by his pool, enjoying rum punches.

Wayne Stinnett's newsletter meshes perfectly with his thrillers set in South Florida. It makes you want to get a refreshing beverage and join him on the beach (and in his books).

If you choose a service to manage your mailing list, schedule times during the year to make a copy of your email addresses. This makes sure that if your service suddenly goes under, or (horrors!) erases your list, you're not totally up the creek.

newsletter is informal and friendly. The email's subject line, "Just Returned from Key West," makes it seem less like a newsletter and more like a personal note. It certainly looks better than my last newsletter that used "Newsletter July 2017."

● On the other hand, romance/thriller writer Marie Force's newsletter is slick, polished, and professional. It opens with a big banner ad announcing the publication of her latest book, *Can't Buy Me Love*. Below it is a group of icons linking to her website's blog, online store, reader groups and social media (Facebook, Twitter, Instagram, and YouTube).

Under the headline "Thank You for a Great Release Week!" she praises the readers who reviewed her book, quoting some of them by name (first name only to protect their privacy). At the bottom is a list of links to the book at all the major online bookstores, including separate links to Kindle stores in the U.S., Canada, Britain, and Australia.

She announces that her next book, *Fatal Threat*, will appear next month and that advance reader copies are available to members of her "Fatal Series Reader Group" on Facebook. The book is also available for presale, and there's a list of links to that as well.

She also encourages fans to check out another series that's different from her usual work, but her fans had been reluctant to try. She publishes a letter from a reader testifying to that, and how she loved them after reading one. To encourage others to do the same, Force offers a free copy of the first book.

Force's newsletter is the opposite of Stinnet's. She is all about the marketing. Her newsletter is long, but crisply written. Her fans want answers to these questions: "What's new?", "What's next?", and "What have I missed?" That last question is important to answer because Force has six series and more than 60 books!

While these are two different marketing styles, they share a common goal: to engage with readers and to sell books. Without knowing anything about them, I would assume that they did not deliberate long over how they would write their newsletters. It's a natural extension of their personalities and how they approached the business side of their job. This means that *you* shouldn't be too concerned about it, either. Just do it and see how readers respond.

2. Graphic Design

The design of your newsletter can range from plain to elaborate. It can have a banner headline or nothing at all. Your mailing list provider will offer templates to get you started. A good practice is to settle on a design and save it as a template. It will make the mailing process faster.

News from Marie!   Inbox x

Marie Force author@marieforce.com via cmail2.com   Jun 15 (5 days ago)
to me

○ Marie's Blog   🛒 Online Store   👥 Reader Groups

Thank You for a Great Release Week!

I'm so happy to hear from so many readers that you've loved Patrick and Mary's story in *Can't Buy Me Love*! Your reviews, emails and comments have made me smile a lot in the last week. Here's a sampling of some of my favorite comments:

- Marlene said: "Marie did it again! Every time I read one of her books, it is better than the last one. This book was fantastic. I loved it. I know the characters in the book. They are my friends."

- Connie said: "Marie has done it again!! How she continues to come up with awesome story lines I have no idea!! I love how she makes a secondary character a headliner!! You find yourself always wanting more at the end of her books!! Very well done Marie!!"

- Another reader wrote: "Marie Force has done it again and drawn me so far into her world that I forgot about anything other than sweet, sweet Mary and Patrick Murphy! I might have even burnt dinner while I devoured this book while standing next to the stove. I thoroughly enjoyed this addition to the wonderful world of Butler and can't wait to read more!"

And thank you, lovely readers, for making *Can't Buy Me Love* a *USA Today* bestseller!

Have you read *Can't Buy Me Love* yet? If you're in the suddenly sunny Northeast, grab your copy and take it to the beach or pool today!

Ebook

- Kindle US
- iBooks
- Nook
- Kobo
- Google
- Kindle CA
- Kindle UK
- Kindle AU

Marie Force's newsletter is focused on informing readers about her many books, new and upcoming. Notice how she engages her readers by quoting them by name.

3. Email Newsletter Service

There are plenty of reputable services that offer plans with different features and prices.

Many authors start with MailChimp because it's free up to 2,000 subscribers. Some authors, once they reach that level, switch to MailerLite because it's cheaper, but I have heard that their templates are more difficult to use.

There are other providers out there as well: Constant Contact, SendinBlue, ConvertKit, and AWeber. There are others as well as new ones that will show up after this book is published. And StoryOrigin, while it's not a newsletter provider, can help you set up your landing page and funnel subscribers to your provider.

Time is money. The amount of time it takes to move to a cheaper service may cost you more in the long run than staying with a good service that's more expensive. I found myself in that situation when my three-year contract with my website provider was about to expire. Should I move to a cheaper service? I ran the numbers, and while it would be cheaper, I would have to spend a lot of time overseeing the site transfer and changing the information with the company I bought my URLs from. I stayed put.

4. Frequency

Probably the most optimal frequency is monthly, because it reminds subscribers you exist. But there are authors like Craig Johnson, traditionally published, who only sends an email when he has news of a new book, a book tour, or before the "Longmire Days" event in Wyoming. He also makes it a habit on Christmas Eve to send subscribers a short story, which he publishes later in a collection.

The most important thing is to *be consistent* in your publication schedule. You don't want your audience to forget you.

5. Reader Magnet

You don't have to offer something to get people to sign up for your newsletter, but offering a reward will increase sign-ups. You can use anything: from a short story or a few chapters of your first novel to a free novel or more. Nonfiction authors can offer ancillary material, such as charts, case studies, or a booklet. This is a place where you can be innovative and creative.

There are several funnels you can build:

• **On your website.** This can be a sign-up box set to one side of the blog (in a place called the sidebar). It can be in a blog post pinned to the top of the blog (WordPress has an option that allows you to pick one post and make that always appear at the top of the blog page). Or, it can pop up when a new

A landing page is set up on your website and can only be reached when someone clicks on a link to join your mailing list.

Landing pages can be built using WordPress plug-ins, or with help from your email newsletter service. Companies like StoryOrigin and BookFunnel can take care of sending ebooks to your subscribers.

visitor shows up at your website (warning: this can annoy people into clicking away), appear when a pre-set condition is met, such as x amount of time has passed, or after they click on a link that will take them away from the site. You set this up within your website, depending on the blog's software or theme.

The signup usually appears as a simple form: first name, last name and email address. Some have the email only. You can choose to offer something for signing up, such as a free book, the free first couple of chapters of a book, or something else, or nothing at all. The visitor types in their information, clicks a button and sends it to the mailing list. The company sends a confirmation email, the customer clicks the "confirm" link on the email, and they're good to go.

- **In your books.** Whatever format your book is in — print, ebook, or audio — should include a funnel for your newsletter. Include a mention of it in the front and back matter.
- **As part of an ad campaign** on Facebook or Instafreebie to encourage sign-ups.

Other Tactics

Giveaways

Readers like getting free stuff, but this shouldn't be done too often — else they'll expect it and even feel entitled to getting your work for free.

I've seen authors hold a contest where the prize is a signed copy of their book or an unsigned copy of someone else's (they buy the book on Amazon and ship it to the winner's address). I've seen them offer in advance the first couple of chapters of the next book as a PDF. Giving material away in advance of an online promotion can make people on your list feel special.

If you lower the price on a book for an ad campaign, be sure to tell the members of your mailing list, as well as subscribers to your blog, Facebook page, and other social media outposts! However, I have heard of authors limiting a sale to their newsletter subscribers, and encouraging everyone else to sign up.

Cross-Promotion

If you know of another author with books in your genre, offer to trade promotions with them. If they have a book they're discounting or giving away the same time as you, this form of cross-promotion exposes readers on both lists to someone new.

Be careful with who you enlist as a ally. If you have read their books and liked them, you can throw your support behind them. Don't foist bad books on your fans.

Cecil Graham: What is a cynic? *Lord Darlington:* A man who knows the price of everything, and the value of nothing. *Cecil Graham:* And a sentimentalist, my dear Darlington, is a man who sees an absurd value in everything and doesn't know the market price of any single thing.
Oscar Wilde, *The Importance of Being Earnest*

Selling or Trading Subscriber Lists

There's cross-promotion, in which you're advocating on behalf of someone else's book. Then there's selling or trading your mailing list with another author.

I do *not* recommend doing this. Corporations and charities frequently sell their mailing lists, but that's not a good reason for you to do it.

First, you're doing it without permission, unless you say so in the small print, in which case you're welcome to all the bad karma that'll come your way. We may be habituated to clicking on the "terms and conditions" for submitting our email to someone online, but it doesn't mean we have to like being spammed by a stranger.

Don't do it.

Chapter 12
Amazon

Key Points to Remember

- An effective book description and relevant keywords will get your book before the right readers.
- Fill out the Author Page! You'd be amazed how many authors neglect this simple feature.
- Be wary of book marketers offering to sell you the "secrets" behind Amazon's algorithm.

We've had three big ideas at Amazon that we've stuck with for 18 years, and they're the reason we're successful: Put the customer first. Invent. And be patient.

Jeff Bezos

Like it or not, Amazon is the big dog in indie publishing. Sure, there are authors who do well putting their books wide, but they still rely on Amazon for a good share of their income. Authors win with Amazon by making use of all the opportunities they provide to display their books and them to their best advantage. So we're putting the tools they use to make their book descriptions sizzle, their pre-orders profitable, and their promotions pay off, into its own chapter. We also have some answers to the problems you may encounter with them.

You'll have two portals through which this work will be done, your KDP account and Author Central (*https://authorcentral.amazon.com/gp/home*).

Keywords

The biggest concern authors talk about when publishing on Amazon is finding the right keywords for their book. They're right to be concerned, because the seven series of keywords (up to 50 characters per line, in any order, remember) tells Amazon's algorithms where to display your book in search results.

The key here is *relevancy.* Do your keywords convert to sales? Amazon keeps track of this, and the more relevant your keywords, the more they'll serve them up in search results.

To find your book's keywords, try to think like a customer. What would they search for to find your book? The keyword section allows for about 40 words, so you have a lot of room to play with.

First of all, don't use the title or author name. They're already in the mix, and adding them to keywords won't do anything but waste space. Think of the nouns that describe your book. For *The Complete, Annotated Mysterious Affair at Styles,* discussed in Chapter 9: Producing Your EBook, it included Edwardian, British, English, doctors, country homes, poison, and strychnine. Think of the era your book is set in, historical, contemporary, or post-apocalyptic. The types of characters that inhabit it. Omit categories like romance or science fiction. They're already covered in your category choices.

TIP

Use Amazon's search box to help you find keywords. Once you type in a word, Amazon autofills the search box with suggestions. They based them on customers' actual searches. This gives you a leg up on finding popular searches that will lead them to your book!

As you gain more experience and information, you may want to go back and change your keywords. This is why there's a space for them on the metadata sheet.

Book Description

Authors mistakenly call this a blurb, which is a brief review from a prominent author or reviewer. A book description appears at the top of your book page, next to the cover. It can be any length, and its function is to sell the book.

Authors sometimes don't understand that. They write a description of the book's contents. This is fine, but this space is for advertising copy. This is where you sell the sizzle, not the steak. Describing the book without selling it is like serving salad without dressing; it's still good for you, but it can be more flavorful.

Writing effective ad copy is a talent that can be learned like storytelling. Think of it as a condensed form of storytelling, because you're packing in the feels your book will give the potential buyer in a couple of paragraphs, as well as the warning signs that will deter readers who won't appreciate your story and leave a 1-star review.

Probably the best way to learn how to write ad copy is to read a lot of it. Look at the top sellers in your genre. Note what catches your eye.

Here's an example that caught my eye: *White Out* by Danielle Girard. I'll underline the points that make this a successful book description:

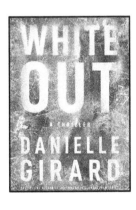

From the bestselling author of the Annabelle Schwartzman series comes a chilling story of a woman with a forgotten past and a town with dark secrets.

After surviving a car accident on an icy road in Hagen, North Dakota, Lily Baker regains consciousness with no idea where or who she is. Scattered Bible verses and the image of a man lying in a pool of blood haunt her memory.

The same night of the accident, a young woman is murdered and tossed in a dumpster. Kylie Milliard, Hagen's only detective, doesn't immediately recognize the victim, but Kylie soon discovers that Lily and the dead woman share a dark past...if only Lily could remember what it was.

<u>Lily and Kylie</u> both want answers. But Kylie has to play by the book. Lily has to play it safe. And the more Lily learns about her identity, the more she fears the truth.

From: This sentence is in bold, which catches the reader's eye. Shorter statements can be set in large type with the help of Kindlepreneur's free book description generator (*https://kindlepreneur.com/amazon-book-description-generator/*).

Bestselling author: If you earned the designation, declare it as soon as possible. It's social proof, especially if you can add "USAToday" or "New York Times" to it. Calling yourself an "Amazon best seller" is a risky move. Amazon gets nervous if it feels you're using its trademark to promote itself. The rule for this has changed over time, so look for the latest guidance before calling yourself one. If they call you on it, you may show them proof such as a screenshot of your book with Amazon's best-seller flag.

Dark secrets: This single-sentence description is called an elevator pitch or a logline. Boiling your story down to this level takes a lot of work at first, but it's a skill worth learning.

Who she is: Another single sentence that supplies the who (Lily Baker), inciting event (car accident), location (Hagen), sensory data (icy, cold), and her problem (amnesia). Two verbs and five major nouns.

Haunt her memory: In an effective book description, each sentence builds on the previous sentence. This one does it by adding a mystery, asking questions — who was the man? is he injured or dead? and what do Bible verses have to do with it? — that demand a solution.

The same night: Before introducing the main character, another mystery is created. If the writer had jumped to a new character, we would have been puzzled by her relationship to the story. Yes, it's only for a sentence, but why create a bump even for that long? Customers are easily distracted online, and making them work to put the pieces together risks them cutting away to another tab.

Lily and Kylie: Look at the short sentences. Each one describes a character's dilemma, and the obstacle facing them. By the end, among the several questions raised, you know which one is the big question that the book will answer: Who is Lily Baker? You also know that there will be plenty of danger and suspense along the way until you learn the answer.

Here's another example, this time from an enemies-to-lovers romance called *Hate the Player* by Max Monroe, the pen name for two women writers. This one is written in the first person by the novel's heroine, with the bolding and italics intact:

"Roses are red, violets are blue, stay away from Andrew Watson's *ahem* because no other women ever do."

That's quite the way to start a conversation at a casual lunch, huh? *Grilled chicken, French fries, and pelvic-fatigue, oh my!*

And that's not even the worst of it.

My friend Raquel didn't pull any punches when she warned me about my brand-new costar and his notoriously player-esque ways. Apparently, my most important mission on my first role in a feature film is to stay immune to his charms.

Are you kidding me? Production costs on this movie are in the hundreds of thousands a day, and staying away from a panty-whispering, vajayjay-charmer is supposed to be at the top of my list? *Pfft. Puh-lease.*

It doesn't matter that he's annoyingly attractive, uber rich, crazy famous, and lusted after by ninety percent of the female population; Andrew Watson is trouble with a capital T — especially for a woman like me.

As a preventative measure, I've decided to go ahead and hate him.

Don't worry, you guys, I'm completely in control. There's absolutely no way I'm going to do something stupid like fall in love with him.

I can hate the player but still secretly love his addictive game.

I'm sure of it.

I don't have as much to say about Max Monroe's book description, except writing in the lead character's voice works on the logic that if you like her here, you'll like her in the book.

Then there are authors for whom the phrase "less is a bore, so more more more" describes them perfectly. This one is from *Strawberries & Crème Murder*, a long series (60 books in this one alone) by Susan Gillard, recreated with the irregular large type, bolding, and underlining:

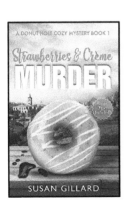

ATTENTION: This #1 Best Seller is <u>back</u> with a Second Edition Release of Book 1 in the Donut Hole Series.

"This book is a culinary delight! I really enjoyed all the donut descriptions and Heather, the amateur sleuth, is a very likable character."

We've made some MAJOR updates to the book that new and existing fans will definitely enjoy.

<u>Here's what you get:</u>

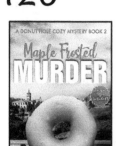

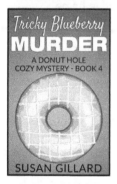

- **Finally, discover what Memorable events transpired before the murder** of Heather's deceptive ex-assistant with **a riveting new Prologue from Christa Fordyce,** the Murder Victim.

- **Instantly learn exactly what sticks in the craw of Stan Dombrowski about his reluctant arch-rival Heather** & her "Delightful Donut Shop" with an **insightful exclusive Epilogue from Stan Dombrowski; the book 2 Murder Victim.**

- **Enjoy an unbeatable reading experience** with enhanced formatting, **crucial continuity updates and dozens of typo fixes** thanks to our new professional editor!

- **Make Heather's recipes at home:** We've included a FREE offer for **4 of our most tasty Donut Recipes w/ pictures and easy to follow step-by-step instructions.**

Could a workplace disagreement lead to murder?

Donuts, deceit and the potential murder of a former assistant find master donut backer Heather Janke at the center of a mystery in which she is a potential suspect and possibly the only one capable of discerning the truth.

Was her former assistant Christa murdered and if so, why?

Follow Heather as she searches for clues to get to the bottom of this sweet caper.

Praise for Strawberry Cream Murder:

"This book is a culinary delight. I really enjoyed all the donut descriptions. Heather, the amateur sleuth, is a likable character. As a former Texan, I am glad the book takes place in Texas." - ★★★★★ Ms. Loves To Read

"I really loved this book and couldn't seem to put it down." - ★★★★★ Joyce C

"… this book is well done. The characters that are introduced are fully fleshed out, and the reader will not be overwhelmed by too many people too quickly. A solid mystery, with a satisfying conclusion. Looking forward to the next in the series." - ★★★★★ Stephanie Jones

"Nice clean cozy series. I plan to read the entire series. "- ★★★★★ Sandy

" I think you'll love this book like I did. Can't wait to start book 2" - ★★★★★ Cheryl

Satisfy your inner bookworm. Pick up your copy today by clicking the BUY NOW button at the top of this page.

Visually, this description is a mess, but the writing is energetic and enthusiastic. Going back to add more material to the book is an interesting way of setting yourself apart, and if you have to have your books reedited to fix mistakes, this is a good way to frame it as bonus material. However, Amazon frowns on you reprinting its reviews in the product description.

Here's a better book description, from *Glad One,* the first book in the humorous mystery series by Margaret Lashley:

Best Seller in Eight Mystery & Humor Categories! Rednecks, Romance, and a Last Shot at Redemption. Solve this Twisty Mystery Before You Die Laughing!

After being duped out of her life savings in Germany, Val Fremden retreats home to Florida with more than just her pride in tatters. Broke, jobless, divorced, and forty-five, she knows starting over won't be easy. But when her only friend suddenly turns up dead, Val begins to wonder if the world is out to get her.

Maybe it is ….

The sugar-white sands of Sunset Beach attract weirdoes like mosquitoes to a bug zapper. So when the will of Val's friend makes the local newspaper, lunatics and con artists stumble from their beach shacks scuffling for a piece of the leftover pie.

Determined to find her friend's true heir, Val reluctantly turns to three crackpots for help — a drunk, a redneck, and a snarky beach bum. Working at odds with each other, their bumbling investigation attracts the attention of a hot cop. He quickly gets into the fray and under Val's skin. Whether it's in a good way or bad only time will tell ….

Love your mysteries with a side of snide? Get set for a heaping helping of Southern-fried screwball action in this hilarious accidental thriller! Grab your copy now!

If you love funny, twisty mysteries that put gaffs over gore and laughs over legalese, the Val Fremden Mystery Series is for you! Part Bridget Jones, part My Name is Earl, each book in the series is packed with crazy characters, zingy dialogue, hilarious similes and rip-roaring situational humor, making them a laugh a minute!

Like many readers, if you love Janet Evanovich's Stephanie Plum or Jana Deleon's Fortune Redding, you'll probably find yourself resonating with Val Fremden, too. She's a lovable, hot mess who's a bit older, a tad more jaded, and a ton more experienced in big-time failure. Life's been tough for Val. Still, she always manages to find her way with sardonic humor and an intrepid spirit. A gin and tonic now and then helps, too.

Life's a beach and then you die. If you're ready for a good laugh and a great mystery, check out *Glad One* and its crazy cast of characters today. Funny Florida mysteries don't get any wackier!

Amazon #1 Best Seller in Amateur Sleuths, Cozy Mystery, Humor & Satire, Women's Detective Fiction, Comedy, Humorous Dark Comedy, Men, Women & Relationships Humor, and Love, Sex & Marriage Humor!

P.S. If you love humorous, page-turning mysteries like those by Deborah Brown, Lucy Quinn, Tricia O'Malley, Gemma Halliday, Karen Cantwell, Tara Sivec, Liliana Hart, Libby Howard, Chelsea Field, Jana Deleon, Gina LaManna, Janet Evanovich, Denise Grover Swank, Amy Vansant, and Stephanie Bond, you just might love *Glad One*, too!

Praise for *Glad One:*
"A funny, frenetic, fantastic read! Every bit as entertaining and maybe more so that Stephanie Plum at her best."
"Margaret Lashley has a great imagination for weird."
"Hooked like a fish. OMG Margaret Lashley is the best! Val could be Stephanie Plum's double!! Phenomenal writing."
"Fans of Evanovich have a new author to fall in love with."
"Her characters are real and full, her situations believable, and her dialogue marvelous."
"There's a mystery at the heart of this book – a few of them – that will hook fans of Janet Evanovich and other comic mystery writers."
"Margaret writes with a "smirk" of a Cheshire cat. Fantastic read."
"Full of twists and turns as only Margaret Lashley can write!"
"If you like Anne George's 'Southern Sisters' don't miss Margaret Lashley!"
"The characters are great – so many laugh out loud moments…"
"Glad One is a funny, witty and entertaining book."

This book description goes on probably far longer than it should, but if you're laughing throughout, it doesn't matter. Note how Lashley interweaves other popular authors in her genre, in hopes that her book will appear on their search pages as well.

IDEA

At the bottom of their description, some authors spell out exactly what to expect. Here are two examples culled from the best-seller lists:

• "A light, cozy mystery read with a dog loving and donut shop owning female private investigator, in a small town setting with quirky characters. No cliffhanger! No swearing! No gore! No graphic scenes!" (*Tangerine Dream and Murder* by Susan Gillard).

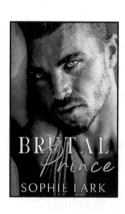

• "*Brutal Prince* is the explosive first act in the epic 'Brutal Birthright' series. It's a stand-alone Dark Mafia Romance, complete with HEA and no cliffhangers. It contains blazing hot bedroom scenes for mature readers only!!!" (*Brutal Prince: An Enemies To Lovers Mafia Romance* by Sophie Lark).

Author Page

Setting up your Amazon Author Page should be obvious, but you'd be amazed how many people don't.

That's a shame because it's easy to do and establishes your credibility as a writer. Without it, customers see a search page based on your name, and that can make them wonder who you are if you can't be bothered to show them.

Once you have a book for sale, you can set up your Author Central

A reclusive author can still have a decent photo taken with an appropriate setting, such as Skye Kingsbury's for her *Dictionary of Flowers and Gems.*

account. Visit https://authorcentral.amazon.com/ and sign in using your Amazon account information.

The Author Page feature is accessible through Author Central. You can set one up for each name you write under. Four names can be linked to one Amazon account, consisting of your real name and three pen names. If you don't publish books under your real name, you're still limited to three. If you need more, you can open another Amazon account.

At the minimum, you need at least two things to set up the Author Page:

• **Author bio:** It can be of any length and even include a list of your books and your author website.

An author bio is not simply a list of facts about you. It's a piece of creative writing that's as important as your book description. Written properly, it should reflect the type of books you publish. The tone it will take varies depending on whether you're writing sweet romance, gritty noir, financial advice, or self-help. The information you reveal should reinforce your ability to tell stories in that genre, or your credibility to give advice.

• **Author photo:** The same reasoning applies here. Your picture should signal the genre and tone of your books. You can't sell romance novels if your author photo (male, in the one we saw) looks like someone who stalks convenience store parking lots.

Some authors, for security, prefer using a piece of art. If you do this, make sure it can be easily read at thumbnail size.

Your Author Page gives you more options to share your message to your readers:

• **Blog feeds:** If you blog, you can add the RSS feed from your blog, so when you post there, it will automatically appear on your Amazon Author page under the row of books at the top of the screen.

If you don't know the URL for your feed, here's one way to find out if you have a WordPress website:

1. In your browser, bring up the page your blog is on.

2. Anywhere on the page, right-click on your mouse. A menu should appear.

3. Click "View page source"

4. Hit Control+F (Windows) or Command+F (Mac)

5. Type "feed"

6. Your RSS feed URL is found inside the href="" attribute.

7. Copy the URL (right-click and choosing "Copy Link Location" should work).

8. On your Author Page, click on "add blog" and paste the saved URL. Click "OK."

• **Photos and videos:** Adding photos and videos give readers an illusion of intimacy and help define your image.

● **Choose your author page URL:** The URL assigned to your page can be changed to something easier to remember. Bill's, for instance, is *amazon.com/author/billpeschel*. Odessa Moon's page is at *amazon.com/author/odessamoon*.

TIP

Each time you publish a book, Amazon adds it to your Author Page. But they slip up sometimes, so add a reminder to your tickler to check. If it's still missing, head to Author Central and click on the Books tab. Under the "Are we missing a book?" subhead, click the [Add more books] button, and follow the procedure.

TIP

Your Author Page is also where you can contact Amazon. At the bottom of each page is a "Contact Us" link. You can choose to email the customer service department, or have them call you. One of the most common reasons to contact them is to make sure the latest book in your series has been added to the series page. Even when you fill out the information correctly, the book is not added immediately.

Kindle Unlimited Features

Once per a three-month enrollment period, you can run one of two promotions: a Kindle Countdown Deal or a Free Book Promotion. Authors typically promote a promotion by announcing it on their website and newsletter, or spread the word with a third-party service such as Freebooksey or BookBub, or through ads on Facebook or other social media sites.

Kindle Countdown Deal: This is where you discount the price of the book for a limited period of time, from 1 hour to 7 days. This can be a one-time price drop, or you can increase the price in increments until it's back up to the full price. During this deal, your book will still earn its regular royalty rate of 70%, even when the book is priced at 99 cents.

Note: You can't run the promotion during the first 30 days your book is in KU. The price must not have been changed for 30 days before the deal, and it can't be changed for 15 days afterwards.

So for example, you can run a campaign that reduces the book's price to 99 cents for two days, then return it to its regular price. Or, run a four-day promotion in which the price drops to 99 cents the first day, rises to $1.99 the second, $2.99 the third, and $4.99 on the fourth.

Another thing to keep in mind is that the deal is limited to customers of the U.S. and U.K. stores. This can be a problem if you land a BookBub international slot; people in those countries won't get access to the deal, which will greatly upset them.

Amazon lists Countdown Deals at *amazon.com/Kindle-eBooks/b?ie=UTF8&node=7078878011*

Free Book Promotion: Every enrollment period, you have five free days to spend. You can break them up or run them consecutively. You won't receive royalties for sales during this period, and your book's rank will appear on the Kindle Free book chart instead of the regular one.

Although you can break up the promotion, the best practice is to run one five-day promotion. Because Amazon has not been consistent with dropping the price on the first day, many authors don't run a discount promotion that first day. You can choose to take a risk — perhaps using a service that doesn't charge as much as BookBub to reduce the financial risk — but you still have four days to schedule promotions.

Editorial Reviews

Author Central: According to Amazon's terms, this is where book reviews go, although some authors place theirs in the book description section. This is against Amazon's terms of service, and they may ask you to remove them.

Foreign Author Pages

Did you know Amazon has Author Central portals for its other major bookstores? You can log in there and format them to your liking.

The site for Great Britain (*https://authorcentral.amazon.co.uk/*) is easy to use, since it's already in English. But if you access the other international sites using Google's Chrome browser, it will translate the page for you.

France: *https://authorcentral.amazon.fr/*
Germany: *https://authorcentral.amazon.de/*
Japan: *https://author.amazon.co.jp/?locale=ja_JP*

TIP

Pre-Orders

Amazon allows you to put your book up for preorder. This special feature should be done only as part of a marketing campaign, because if mishandled it can cost you in reputation and lost sales.

The procedure is simple. You set your book up as usual, and upload a cover and interior file. The difference here is that these don't have to be the final version. Yes, you can upload an interior file that consists of "All work and no play makes Jack a management consultant" and a cover that you did in five minutes with Canva. Before the publication date, you would upload the finished version of the cover and interior files.

I think you can see a potential problem there. If the book is not done before publication date, you will have to cancel the preorder. You lose your sales and your reputation takes a hit, plus Amazon bars you from putting another book on preorder for a year.

But there's more. Authors who wait until the last minute to upload their book discover Murphy's Law. The new file might not overwrite the old file, or you get on your computer, head over to KDP, and discover the system's down. Even if it's not your fault, you suffer the same punishment for missing the deadline.

So should you let your fans preorder your book? Only if you:

- Have a launch plan in place.
- Have a lot of fans or you're famous.

If you have both, you will get the benefits from preorders. You'll get a lot of sales, and a lot of follow-on sales from fans who missed the preorder window but want your book anyway. The book's sales rank will rise and stay up there, and Amazon's algorithms will continue to put your book before people who like your kind of book.

If you don't have both, then you'll be taking a big risk for little reward. Worse, from the moment you put your book up on the site, Amazon's watching to see what it is doing. If it's not getting many orders, it will conclude your book is not popular. It will not move it up in the search rankings.

Seven Things To Know About Amazon

Both the devil and success are in the details. Amazon is such a massive beast that there are things you should know, small details, that make a big difference in your sales, such as finding out about the niche categories your book can be placed in that makes it easier to earn that best selling tag. Or learning that one tell that will warn you away from a marketing scammer. These things are so important that I decided to break them out to make it easier to learn.

- **The wrong portal.** Amazon appears to let you alter a book description through both the KDP account and Author Central portals, but it will work only in the KDP account. On the other hand, you can display book reviews only by using the Author Central portal. There's no rhyme or reason for this disparity; it's a bug Amazon never fixed.

- **Selling Amazon's "secrets."** You may run across book marketers claiming to know the "secret" of Amazon's A9 algorithm. There is no such thing as one A9 algorithm. There are many algorithms, each pertaining to a particular part of the site. You may even see claims that there's an A10 algorithm, and they'll offer to sell you the solution to cracking its code and using it to sell books. Except that the A10 algorithm doesn't exist. They're selling you air.

- **The power of a series.** Writing books in a series is a powerful tactic, because Amazon groups books in a series on its own page, with a [Buy Now] button for the entire series. This lets you create a marketing campaign

pointing customers to this page. And you know what's not on a series page? Competing ads!

● **Be consistant in naming a series.** If you're putting your books in a series, the spelling must be 100% the same. Don't use "The Dresden Files" for book 1 and "the Dresden Files" for book 2. Yes, the difference in capitalization tells Amazon they're not part of the same series! The names must be identical.

● **Categories.** Amazon lets you pick only two of them when you publish your book, but they leave room for 10 categories total. They'll also move your book in and out of categories, sometimes in unexpected ways.

You can also ask them to place your book in more categories. Do your research by looking at where your competitors' books have been placed, or enlist the help of Publishers Rocket (*publisherrocket.com/*) to find them. Note down the breadcrumb trail leading to the category you want (e.g.: "Kindle eBooks > Mystery, Thriller & Suspense > Mystery > Cozy > Culinary"). Call or email Amazon through Author Central and give them the breadcrumb trail for each category. Keep your message simple. Most of the time, they'll be happy to comply.

● **Also Boughts.** You publish your book and check it out a week or a month later, and there are no Also Boughts that show the books your customers purchased. What gives? They appear only after your book has sold 50 copies.

● **Amazon delays reporting sales.** Sometimes as much as four days. You could run a massively successful ad campaign, and not immediately see a change in your book's rank. Nothing you can do about it; just be patient.

Seven Ways To Hurt Your Career on Amazon

So you've got your books up on Amazon. You put some of them in the Kindle Unlimited program, so you'll get paid if someone reads them. Great! Now all you need to do is sit back and earn that promised five-figure income.

Until you get an email from Amazon saying you're toast. Your books have been pulled from Kindle Unlimited, or from the website altogether. Or maybe you were part of Amazon Associates and you did something there.

In any event, you're in for a baaaaad day.

Perhaps you cut a corner and bought a dodgy review service. Or you didn't read the Terms of Service (TOS) and missed a critical rule. Or, worse of all, you didn't do anything but be in the wrong place at the wrong time.

Here are seven scenarios that could kill or damage your career on Amazon. Or at least give you a few sleepless nights.

1. Putting in your book description your website, email, or book reviews

Yes, I've seen it done. I've seen one author urge readers to visit his website

for free books. Another put in his book description reviews from Lee Child and Gillian Flynn. Then there's the author of a 45-book mystery series, whose book description contains links to the 44 other books on Amazon. While that appears to be legal, I've heard of one author who had to take his links down after a customer complained.

Remember, just because you see someone else violate Amazon's Terms of Service doesn't mean you should it.

The inclusion of any of the following information in detail — page titles, descriptions, bullet points, or images — is prohibited:

- Pornographic, obscene, or offensive content.
- Phone numbers, physical mail addresses, email addresses, or website URLs.
- Availability, price, condition, alternative ordering information (such as links to other websites for placing orders), or alternative shipping offers (such as free shipping).
- Spoilers regarding Books, Music, Video, or DVD listings (information that reveals plot elements crucial to the suspense, mystery, or surprise ending of a story).
- Reviews, quotes, or testimonials.
- Solicitations for positive customer reviews.
- Advertisements, promotional material, or watermarks on images, photos, or videos.
- Time-sensitive information (i.e., dates of promotional tours, seminars, lectures, etc.).

The violation might earn you only a nastygram telling you to take it down, rather than expulsion from the garden, but it is a risk.

2. Including a KU book in someone else's box set, even if both are in KU.

So you have a free book in Kindle Unlimited, and another author asks you to contribute to a box set that would be available through KU as well. You're thrilled! What a chance for cross-promotion.

The set goes up … then comes down, along with a note from Amazon saying you violated their TOS. What the heck happened?

The answer is that Amazon gives one publisher the right to put a book in KU. That's all. If you serialize a novel in KU, and then offer it as an omnibus, then you should be all right. But if two publishers have the same book, the bot's gonna catch you.

The problem here is that Amazon did not announce this. It simply started pulling books, leading to a lot of upset authors emailing for details and much gnashing of teeth.

Another problem is inconsistency in actions on Amazon's part. Sometimes, the box set is pulled. Sometimes, it's the author's book. Sometimes both.

Welcome to the world of algorithms and bots. To police their bookstore, Amazon has to rely on artificial intelligence to make decisions, followed up by human intervention when they get it wrong.

Look at it this way: Amazon's looking for scammers who steal content, repackage it and sell it for cheap. They're trying to protect their customers from a bad book-buying experience.

3. Using a dodgy book promotion service

This is one that can catch unwary authors. They hire a promotional service that promises to get reviews for their book, but the service uses fake accounts to flood the Amazon book page with ineffective five-star reviews.

If you're caught with these types of reviews, hope that the worst that happens is that they disappear and not your account.

4. Joining Kindle Unlimited without pulling your ebook out of every retail vendor.

Sometimes, it's because you didn't notify all your vendors. Sometimes, the vendor didn't check all its sites. Sometimes, it could be a pirate site that Amazon doesn't recognize as such.

No matter how it happened, you're responsible for getting it fixed.

5. Misusing Amazon Associates links

The Amazon Associates program is designed to encourage you to link to their products on your blog or website. If a reader clicks on one of those links and buys something, you get a percentage of their spend.

For example, say I create an ad for my website to publicize Amazon's romance books. I like romances. For example, I blitzed through Mary Balogh's two books in her latest series: *Someone to Honor* and *Someone to Romance*. If you're a Regency romance fan, I highly recommend getting them.

So I figure I'll recommend her books to you. I can create a link, like I did above, that takes you to her two books. If you click on it and buy her books, I'll get a percentage of the purchase price. Neat, huh?

The problem comes if I try to insert Amazon links into, say, my newsletter, which is not the same as my website. Or if I insert it in a comment on someone else's blog.

Amazon doesn't like that, and you could get kicked out of the program if they catch you.

6. Amazon detects an unusual spike in your KU reads

This is serious. It could be you found an ad that really worked. Or it could be sheer dumb luck.

To Amazon, a sudden spike in page reads could mean you hired someone with a link farm or bots to read your books on KU.

Worse, some of these spammers try to hide their tracks by reading books from authors who have nothing to do with the scam. Too bad; Amazon will still yank your account.

The only thing you can do is get on the horn to their customer service department and try to work it out. Whether you want to or not, *you must do this.* You are the only advocate for your career. If you don't take it seriously, who will?

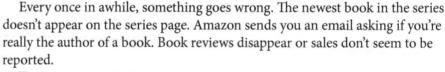

LOGROLLING IN OUR TIME

"Cheever continues to do what the best fiction has always done: give us back our humanity, enhanced."
— John Updike on John Cheever's *Falconer*

"Superb — the most important American novel I've read in years." — Cheever on Updike's *Rabbit Is Rich*

"Remarkable ... Powerful ... Mesmerizing ... Lyrical" — Susan Cheever on Paul Theroux's *O-Zone*

"A terrific novel about the way we live now." — Theroux on Cheever's *Doctors and Women*

"A beautiful book, and worthy of those mountains he is among."
— Paul Theroux on Peter Matthiessen's *The Snow Leopard*

"Sharp-eyed, honest, and exceptionally well-written."
— Matthiessen on Theroux's *The Old Patagonian Express*

"He is, to say the least, a mature and wise writer." — Anthony Burgess on Robertson Davies's *The Manticore*

"A delight to read." — Davies on Burgess's *Little Wilson and Big God*

— Howard Kaplan

7. Swapping reviews with authors

In the literary world, this is called "logrolling." It's long been a part of the literary scene, so prevalent that in the 1980s, the edgy humor magazine *Spy* magazine made it a regular feature.

These are illegal under TOS, even "circle jerk" reviews, in which several authors each review another's work, but there's no direct trade involved.

If you want to use an author's blurb, put it in the Editorial Description.

Dealing With Amazon Customer Service

Every once in awhile, something goes wrong. The newest book in the series doesn't appear on the series page. Amazon sends you an email asking if you're really the author of a book. Book reviews disappear or sales don't seem to be reported.

Time to contact Amazon.

To do so, sign into Author Central. At the bottom of the page, click the "Contact Us" link. You can either email them or have them call you.

How you act depends on the problem, so here are some practices to consider.

1. If you're asking them for a favor, provide the information that will make their job easier. If you're asking them to add your latest book to a series, give them the title of the book, the book's URL, and the URL of the series page.

2. Keep your email brief. There's no need to describe your author journey, or what-all happened. They need to know what it'll take to make you happy and solve the problem.

3. Focus on satisfying the customer. Amazon is all about customer service (by the way, you are not the customer, you're the supplier). If you can frame your request in a way that, by fulfilling it, customers would have a better experience on the site, chances are it'll be granted.

For example, we publish annotated editions of Agatha Christie's early novels that are in the public domain in the U.S. Our books were on their own page. Then, something happened, and Amazon lumped our annotated editions with the thousand other versions. Our unique books vanished, and our sales plummeted. In our request to give our books their own page, we stressed that customers looking for our deluxe editions could no longer find them easily. Amazon restored the pages. It took several calls, and one rep "elevated my request" to someone who could make a decision.

Amazon and Bookstores

Two of our favorite bookstores in central Pennsylvania, where we do signings and never, ever, discuss ebooks.

Bookstore owners understand that you have to work with Amazon. They get it.

This doesn't mean they have to like it, especially if you rub it in their face.

So when you're in your author persona in a bookstore, follow one simple rule.

Never. Mention. Amazon.

Do not stand up in front of an audience and say, "My ebooks are available on Amazon." I know of one author who did that during a public appearance. That author will not be invited back for a second.

When talking to readers off the stage, it's all right to say your books are available online, especially if someone asks. You don't have to play coy and delicately drop a hint. We're adults here.

It's about acting like an adult and being considerate of your host's feelings. Indie booksellers already operate on a slim profit margin. They need every sale to stay in business. They've invested their blood, sweat, and tears into keeping their business going. Because they love books, they love stories, they love readers, and they want books in their lives. Don't send business to Amazon when it could stay in your local bookstore.

Amazon doesn't care about indie bookstores. In fact, they've worked against indie booksellers who sold their books through Amazon.

If you want to know more, the next time you're talking with your local bookseller, ask them what they think about Amazon. Listen to them. You don't have to agree with them or argue with them. Just listen. Pay attention. Learn.

Chapter 13
Advertising

Key Points to Remember
- Book advertising is effective because you can see the effect on sales from your ads.
- Some authors prefer advertising on Amazon and some on Facebook.
- Advertising is most cost-effective when it is spread out over a series.

The man who does not advertise is a dead one, whether he knows it or not. Life is too short for you to hide yourself away mantled in your own modesty.
Elbert Hubbart

Like it or not, advertising works. Many authors feel reluctant to engage in it, partially because of bad experiences, advertising's shady reputation, or a reluctance to seem like they are bragging or begging.

But it's true: advertising works, and it works even better online, where you can target your ads at people who are genuinely interested in your books.

Terms

Before we begin, let's go over a few words you might be unfamiliar with:

- *Auction:* The format Amazon and Facebook use to determine who gets a particular slot on a page; an automated auction is held and the highest bidder wins.
- *Keywords:* A list of words and phrases used in customer's searches; your book will be placed before people using them.
- *Bid:* The price you're willing to pay in an auction for a slot on a product page.
- *Ad spend:* The amount of money you're spending on a campaign).
- *Relevancy:* A number that shows how aligned an author's book is to the needs of the customer. Amazon and Facebook want to place high-relevancy ads before customers and their algorithms will "punish" low-relevancy ads, either by showing them less, or, in Facebook's case, charging more for them.

Amazon Advertising

One of the two most popular advertising platforms — Facebook is the other — Amazon has numerous advantages for authors.

First, it places ads in front of readers, either as part of the search results, or on the book page.

Status	Keywords	Match	CPC Bid	Impr.	Clicks	ACPC	Spend	Sales	ACoS ▾
Enabled ⇕	kate parker	Broad	$0.50	4,092	34	$0.19	$6.37	$20.99	30.35%
Enabled ⇕	donna leon	Broad	$0.50	28,841	32	$0.19	$5.95	$19.96	29.81%
Enabled ⇕	rhys bowen	Broad	$0.50	23,741	65	$0.18	$11.90	$39.92	29.81%
Enabled ⇕	anne cleeland	Broad	$0.50	6,368	32	$0.18	$5.79	$19.96	29.01%
Enabled ⇕	karen charlton	Broad	$0.50	3,117	11	$0.26	$2.85	$9.98	28.56%
Enabled ⇕	julia spencer-fleming	Broad	$0.50	2,417	7	$0.20	$1.40	$4.99	28.06%
Enabled ⇕	james patterson	Broad	$0.50	23,487	16	$0.26	$4.14	$14.97	27.66%
Enabled ⇕	david baldacci	Broad	$0.50	12,289	9	$0.28	$2.48	$9.98	24.85%

Above: Amazon's ad dashboard for a single campaign. The columns show each keyword, your bid, the number of impressions, how many times it was clicked on, the average cost per click (ACPC), how much you spent, and the sales traced to that click. The AcoS (Advertising Cost of Sale) is the ratio between what you spent on that keyword and what it earned. Anything under 100% means you earned more than you spent, and the lower the percentage the better. (*Source: Reedsy https://blog.reedsy.com/ amazon-ads-for-authors- case-studies/*)

Second, the ad dashboard is easy to use. To create a campaign, you choose the book you want to promote, set the amount you want to spend per day (which lets you set a maximum budget for your campaign), list the keywords that you think your readers will use, set a price you're willing to pay for each keyword, and you're good to go.

There are optional decisions you can make, too. You can choose how strict you want your keyword to match the search word, from Exact to Broad. You can choose your bidding strategy, letting Amazon bid more for a slot — up to 150% more — if it's on page one of the search results. You can also tell Amazon to bid higher or lower in other circumstances. But Amazon will make sure your daily budget is not exceeded. For example, if you want to spend only $300 a month on ads, set your daily budget to $10, and Amazon will not go over this amount.

After that, you'll want to look at your dashboard to see how your ads are performing and the number of sales they've made. You'll want to download the information into your Excel spreadsheet and analyze the data. You can make midcourse corrections to a campaign, turning off underperforming keywords and changing the bids.

This ability to see your ad spend compared to the amount of estimated sales gives you a pretty accurate idea of the effectiveness of your campaign. Even better, Amazon, in July 2020, added a new category showing the effect of your ad on Kindle Unlimited reads. It's only an estimate, but a vital one for authors with a lot of books in KU.

One strategy authors use to generate a high income is to advertise the first book in their KU series. It goes like this: write five books in a series that's written to market, like thrillers, and make it available in KU. Advertise the

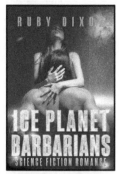

first book (price doesn't matter here, because you're targeting KU readers). Whale readers who love the first book go on to read the remaining four books.

If the author makes $2 per book in KU reads, an ad for the first book that cost the author a buck could return $10, which is an excellent return on investment.

That's an extreme "if everything goes right" example with the math simplified. Not every reader will race through the rest of the series. But one major indie author estimated that about half of the readers who read Book #1 will move on to Book #2, and of those who read Book #2, eighty percent will move on to #3, and so on. That's still a significant income potential. This is why there are best-selling authors you've never heard of (unless you've read their books), like Jessica Beck (*The Donut Mysteries*, 50 books); L.L. Muir (*Ghosts of Culloden Moor*, 53 books); Ruby Dixon (*Ice Planet Barbarians*, 21 books).

Facebook Advertising

There's a friendly argument going on in the indie world over which platform is better, Facebook or Amazon. It will probably never be resolved.

Here's the skinny on Facebook: it's a tricky platform to use, it can be heartless in taking your money and not showing results, but it also has the potential to place your books or newsletter before millions of potential readers who have expressed an interest in your genre.

My advice: Cut your teeth on Amazon ads first. Move to Facebook only when you're comfortable with Amazon.

Target your fans' favorite indie authors instead of the trad-published big dogs. The price per click for thriller author Lee Child is higher than Mark Dawson.

Other Ad Platforms

The best practice today is to focus on Amazon and Facebook advertising, with an occasional BookBub ad that appears at the bottom of the newsletter (which is not the same as a BookBub deal). The other advertising options — Google AdWords, Goodreads, and other social media platforms — have not been effective. Considering how much time it takes to learn how to use Amazon and Facebook ads effectively, it's a better use of your time and resources to focus on them first.

Chapter 14
Reviews

Key Points to Remember
- Even reputable journals such as *Kirkus* and *Publishers Weekly* offer paid review options.
- If you get a good review, particularly from a name author, display it everywhere you can.
- Soliciting top Amazon reviewers requires the author to find contact info online.

James Patterson has mastered the art (if you can call it that) of writing mindless, page-turning bestsellers that sell millions of copies, then disappear as quickly as last night's fast-food meal.

Chicago Sun-Times critic, which a Little, Brown publicist changed in its promotional material to "Patterson has mastered the art of writing page-turning bestsellers."

Reviews are an important tool in building credibility about your book. Readers like to see someone else's opinion about your work before buying, but soliciting them is not enough. You have to place it before them on your website, Amazon Author's page, and your Twitter, Facebook, and other social media feeds.

They come in two flavors: reviews and blurbs. A blurb is a short hit, praise for your book that you solicited from a (preferably) famous or authoritative person. If you write horror, it could be a blurb from Stephen King or Clive Barker. For a work on current affairs, a blurb from Megyn Kelly or Anderson Cooper could carry weight.

Before the age of self-publishing, traditional publishers sent copies of new books to reviewers, who would pick and choose according to their taste, the buzz behind the work, their knowledge of the author, and other factors.

Now that newspapers and magazines have slashed or eliminated book reviews, a new class of reviewer has appeared, this time with their hands out. Some of them are noted names, capitalizing on their reputation such as *Kirkus Reviews* or *Publishers Weekly*. Even the so-called influencers on Instagram are demanding authors to pay them to display their books to their fans.

These services operate on similar lines. You submit your book and pay a fee. They review it and send it to you. If you approve it, it is released. They put it up on their website and you use it any way you like. Rejecting it buries the review, but they keep the money.

Are these pay-for-play services worth it? That depends on these factors:

1. The quality of the blurb. A look at Kirkus' indie reviews shows what you can expect:

"Relishable lead characters front an enthusiastic, jaunty adventure." (*Landfall* by Jerry Aubin)

Review Services

These services offer to review your book for a fee. *This is not a recommendation.* Visit their sites and review their policies before deciding. Read their reviews to get an idea of the quality of their writing, and if you would be happy to see their words on the cover of your book.

• **PW Select** (*booklife.com/about-us/pw-select.html*)
• **IndieReader** (*indiereader.com*)
• **Kirkus Indie Reviews** (*kirkusreviews.com/indie-reviews/*)
• **Self-Publishing Review** (*selfpublishingreview.com/*)
• **BlueInk Review** (*blueinkreview.com/*)
• **Foreword Clarion Reviews** (*forewordreviews.com/*)

"A promising first effort — filled with strong characters — that shines despite its ponderous writing style." (*Calypso Sun* by Clay Alexander)

"A well-researched and enjoyable, if flawed, historical novel of American pioneers." (*The Promise Seed* by Jody Glittenberg)

Are these useful blurbs? Will they convince a reader to pick up your book?

2. The chance of getting a good blurb. Reputable outlets have some stake in giving an honest review. It's on a continuum: an average book getting a great review might not cause much damage, unlike a terrible book. And isn't one person's "average" book another person's "must read"?

Still, everyone can agree that if you can't get a usable blurb for your book, you've wasted your money.

3. How you will exploit the blurb. You can't influence #1 and #2, except by writing a great story. The only thing more useless than a bad review (unless you're Norman Mailer who displayed the slams for one novel in an ad in *The New York Times*) is a great review that doesn't appear anywhere else. If you're considering paying for a review, make sure you display it everywhere, such as your Amazon book page, your Amazon Author's Page, prominently on your website, in ads, your Goodreads page, etc.

You will find plenty of arguments on both sides about the value of paid reviews. There have been best-selling indie authors who do not use them. Genre authors, as a whole, will probably not benefit from them, at least not as much as enthusiastic Amazon reviewers.

Soliciting

One tactics for getting reviews has been to ask Amazon reviewers who have liked books similar to yours. This process was short-circuited by Amazon when they removed their contact information from their website. But reviewers are still out there, and the process for soliciting reviews successfully hasn't changed.

Do NOT use automated services that spam reviewers on your behalf. I used to receive numerous requests from one such service. They were easy to identify because they came from "Fantasy Author" or "Mystery Author." The text is the same, as if the author filled out a form and included a paragraph with their book's description.

I kill these emails without looking at them. Why? Because I don't like spam. I know that the author does not know my work.

If you want a reviewer to look at your book, do your research. Pick a number of them to approach. Read a few of their reviews to get a sense of their work and if you want them to read your book!

Write them a personal email. Tell them you've seen their work and add details to prove it. Don't make it a long email, make your point, give 'em your

• **US Review of Books** (*theusreview.com/*)
• **San Francisco Book Review** (*sanfranciscobookreview.com/*). This company also publishes in Manhattan, Seattle, and Tulsa, Okla., and offers a "sponsored review" program, which charges for reviews, profiles, and interviews.

> When I was writing my first book, my editor advised me to put everything I wanted the review-reading public to know in the first and last chapters, because those are the only chapters that most reviewers read. In the years since then, I have discovered that indeed most of the quotes pulled by reviewers from my books have come from the first and last sections.
> **Michael Lind**

pitch, offer them a copy of your book, and stop.

After that, if you don't hear from them, it's all right to ask again, mentioning in the first paragraph that you had sent them a request but hadn't heard back. After that, leave them alone. Clearly, the answer is no.

Because the purpose behind this is not to get a hundred meaningless reviews, but several very good reviews.

Handling Bad Reviews

It's bound to happen. Someone doesn't like your book, and they tell the world.

It's easy to feel hurt. Your book is your baby, and no one wants to be told their child is ugly. The impulse to lash out is difficult to control.

Resist the impulse. It's best not to feed the trolls. What are they? They're shit-stirrers. They're out to cause trouble. Wrestling with them risks getting muck on you. Plus, it wastes mental energy better put to other uses.

Don't confuse them with a good-faith judgment of your book. The difference between the two can be found in the review itself. If it is long, detailed, and accompanied by quotes from the book, it was not written by a troll. If the opinions are short, misspelled, crude, and even personal, it was.

What can you do about a bad review? If countering them with your own opinion doesn't help, you'll need to step up your reviewing game. The tactic is called "flooding the zone," and consists of getting positive reviews for your book that can counter the negative. A potential reader who sees the 1-star review will be more likely to discount it when he sees a number of 5-star reviews.

It's not a perfect or ideal solution, but it's the best one possible. Meanwhile, shake it off and work on your next book.

And if nothing else will sooth your anxieties, we'll leave you with what some writers (and one reviewer) have said about book reviews:

> I've never learned anything from a review. I'm sensitive enough to reviews that I don't read them. The good ones don't make me any happier, and the bad ones, so many of them, they haven't paid attention, or they get things wrong. It's irritating.
> **Pete Dexter**

> It's like anal sex. If that's what I want to do to you and you're not into it, then go away, because that's what will keep happening.
> **A.L. Kennedy,** about reviewers criticizing her books' edgy tone.

> I have lost count of the number of dull books I have hailed as masterpieces, rather than trouble myself to finish.
> **A.N. Wilson**

Chapter 15
Public Appearances

Key Points to Remember

- Public appearances are not for everyone; plenty of writers make a living without them.
- It builds your reputation locally and could lead to speaking engagements.
- You may have said your pitch a thousand times, but it's the first time to the person hearing it.

> A new book is like a new brand of detergent. You have to let the public know about it. What's wrong with that?
> **Jacqueline Susann**

> My life isn't of interest — my books (I hope) are. I'm sick to death of chatty bits about authors, & LOATHE this form of advertisement.
> **Georgette Heyer**

Should you do bookstore signings, convention talks, or book club visits? Do they help your sales? Is it worth the time and effort?

The answer depends on your career goals and your desire to make a fool of yourself in public.

The answer is easily "no" if you're uncomfortable sitting behind a table at a craft show. If the thought of walking across the stage toward a podium makes you feel like you're riding NASA's Vomit Comet at 40,000 feet, same answer.

(Note, that feeling is different from the mildly queasy and anxious feeling I got recently before sitting in on a book club discussion of *The Complete, Annotated Whose Body?* at my favorite bookstore. One is debilitating, the second is nerves.)

The answer can be "yes" if you love going out in public, meeting strangers and fans, and getting to talk about books. If most of your life, like mine, is spent behind a desk in the basement, you welcome getting out in the fresh air and sunshine.

If you're wondering if it's worth pursuing this type of publicity, then ask yourself: are you a "genre filler" author or do you aspire to more? Do you want to write meaningful books, books that readers can return to like a friend, that become a part of their lives?

I'm not sneering at genre-filler authors. They are competent storytellers. They know their genre and its tropes and what readers expect from them. They deliver. The stories are consumed, enjoyed, and forgotten.

They're the Macdonald's® of publishing. The Campbell Soups®. The Ford Prefects.*

* A reference to *The Hitchhiker's Guide to the Galaxy*. The researcher who came to Earth from Betelgeuse chose this name because he believed it was inconspicuous and totally forgettable.

> "
>
> What can you say about how you write books? What I mean is, first you've got to think of something, and when you've thought of it you've got to force yourself to sit down and write it. That's all. It would have taken me just three minutes to explain that, and then the Talk would have been ended and everyone would have been very fed up. I can't imagine why everybody is always so keen to talk about writing. I should have thought it was an author's business to write, not talk.
> **Ariadne Oliver**
> (aka Agatha Christie)

Genre-filler authors are colorless, both in their persona and in their prose. There is nothing distinctive about them or their work. Whale readers read their books, but they don't remember who wrote them, or seek their next book unless it's announced in the back of their last book as a pre-order.

The number of genre-filler authors used to be limited by the size of a publisher's list. Not anymore. Indie publishing makes it possible for there to be tens of thousands of genre-filler authors.

Again, I'm not criticizing genre filler authors, believe me. They provide entertainment in the same way as the writers of *The Big Bang Theory* or *Everybody Loves Raymond*. These shows were hits that ran for many seasons, but do viewers know who wrote them? Do they remember memorable episodes? If you were around when *Seinfeld* ruled the airwaves, you'd recall Jerry Seinfeld and Larry David and episodes like "The Contest," "The Soup Nazi," or "The Puffy Shirt." I recognize those episodes, yet I've never seen a complete episode! That's how much influence the show has on popular culture.

In fiction, James Patterson is a genre-filler author. Does that sound like an insult? He publishes reliably entertaining fiction, sells a cajillion books, and when he's gone he'll be remembered in the same way in the same way people remembered Marie Corelli and Thomas B. Costain. He'll be forgotten and his books will pile up on tables at library book sales while people will still be reading Stephen King and J.K. Rowling.

So now that you understand the difference, I'll ask again: which type of writer are you? If you're a genre-filler author, you can dispense with seeking publicity and making public appearances. It'll give you more time to relax on the lanai of your beach house in Kauai.*

Why Do Public Appearances

Even if you're a genre-filler author, it's worth trying a few local events to see what happens.

There are four major advantages to appearing in public:

- **To build a relationship with booksellers.** Your presence is a one-day thing, but if the bookseller likes you, the store will promote your books to the right customers. This could mean hundreds of sales a year from that store.
- **It builds social proof that you're an author.** This is broadband publicity that turns you into a public figure.
- **It leads to more public speaking offers.** If you publicize your events, if you put footage of you at an event on your website and YouTube, if you

---

* "Beach house in Kauai" is our phrase at Peschel Press for authors who are anonymously killing it with well-marketed, multiple series of books.

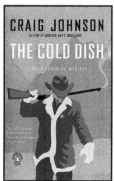

No one knew me. I was sitting in a department store and people would ask me where the lingerie sales were.
Mary Higgins Clark

update your media kit with your appearances, and if you announce your availability for speaking engagements, you open yourself up to more of the same. This is especially true if you are speaking on big-picture subjects (think TEDTalks) or willing to share your knowledge of the publishing business at writing conferences.

● **It turns readers into fans.** Think about Chuck Palahnuick, who engaged with his audiences by reading from his creepy stories, sharing a particular type of story and asking for more of the same, and giving out amazing swag (like bloody stumps signed by him). Think of Stephen King, who one time signed books for *eight hours straight*, despite a bleeding hand wound. In fact, the crowd demanded that he smear his blood on their books, and he compiled!

Those are over-the-top examples, and I'm not saying you should get weird to succeed. If you're writing books that connect emotionally to your readers, being there is enough. I had the pleasure of meeting Terry Pratchett in Washington, D.C., on his tour for *A Monstrous Regiment*. He told funny stories, answered questions, and signed books. Same thing with Craig Johnson, who comes through Mechanicsburg, Pa., twice a year to promote his latest book in the Longmire series. He sells several hundred copies each time, too.

Test the Waters

Probably the best reason for doing a public event early in your career is for the knowledge you'll gain from the experience.

You may discover that you love being onstage. If you rehearse what you're going to say and do, you might like entertaining the audience. Many stand-up comedians said they were surprised at their response to getting their first laughs. Some likened it to a drug high, and they found it equally addictive. But unlike comedians, you'll be in a safer space. You were invited to appear. The audience is there because they want to be. They'll be rooting for you to succeed.

So let's look at the types of public appearances with their risks and rewards.

Get help: Enlist the help of a supportive spouse, friend, or child to help with setup, organize the table, run errands, and sell books while you run off and play Author. They can even photograph you for your promotional materials!

Book Signings

Pros: Meeting fans, schmoozing with booksellers, enjoying a day in a bookstore.

Cons: No fans, no sales, and a day around books you can't touch, directing

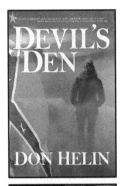

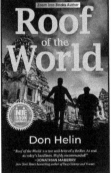

A Brief History of Book Signings

Book signings have been around for only a century. In the 1920s, stores held "book signing teas" for authors. Wanamaker's Department Store in Philadelphia went further than that with its annual "Book Week" where authors gathered to speak and sign books.

people to the bathrooms.

The success of a book signing depends on your comfort level with selling. Unless you're a nationally known figure and can expect a line of people waiting at the table when you sit down, you're going to have to take the lead in marketing your book.

That means stepping out from behind the table and talking to customers.

Don Helin, a Pennsylvania-based writer of military thrillers, is a master at this. We were at a Saturday morning book signing at a bookstore. His table was closer to the entrance than mine, and he was up on his feet. Don dresses like a relaxed college professor: scruffy beard, glasses, corduroy jacket with the elbow patches. His voice is genial and warm, and he doesn't walk so much as he ambles.

So when he approaches customers asking "do you read thrillers?" they don't react as if he was shaking a dead cat in their faces. If they say "no," he genially wishes them a good day. If they say "yes," he tells them about his books, briefly mentioning that the villains in one book are white supremacists, and that Vietnam figures heavily in the other.

Don is a smart man. He emphasizes characters and history in his novels, not Tom Clancy-style hardware. Most of his audience is made up of women. Using this approach that morning, he hand-sold several books that morning and gave away cards and bookmarks to many more. He got shot down many times, but like any good salesperson, he didn't let that stop him. He made it look so easy that anyone could do it.

Judge Your Success By Your Reach

Don't judge a book signing by how many books you sold. It's self-defeating and not the goal of your appearance.

Do you buy a book sight unseen? Probably not. You look at the cover, read the back copy, check out the first few pages to see if the prose engages you. Why should you expect a stranger to do the same thing with your books?

If a sale happens, that's wonderful. Enjoy the moment. But a more accurate measurement of an event's success is how many people you connected with.

How can you reach people? Here's how:

● Offer a sign-up sheet for your newsletter. If you have a premium to offer, such as an ebook, state that clearly at the top and mention it in your spiel.

● Hand out swag: business cards, postcards, and bookmarks that list your books, sales text, and website.

● If you have a lot of books, hand out flyers or catalogs. We made ours using Microsoft Publisher and printed it on our laser printer. The only extra expense was to buy a long-armed stapler.

● If it's a good fit for your genre, create a chapbook containing excerpts from all your books. This lets customers test-read your work in private.

Speeches and Presentations

Pro: Scripted event, attendees drawn to subject and not to you

Con: Pain in the tuckus to prepare and rehearse, possibility of technical problems, fear of large audience

One disadvantage of a book signing is that it relies on people knowing who you are to come out. Even if they know who you are, they may not be interested in buying something you wrote. Even your mother.

What to do? Create a presentation in which the focus is not on you but something of value to the audience.

I ran into that situation when the Mechanicsburg Mystery Book Shop asked if I wanted to do a signing. I offered instead to give a talk about Agatha Christie. At the time, I had researched and published annotated editions of her first two novels, so I knew a lot about her. There was far more to her than the image of a genial elderly woman whose life revolved around her books and her trips to the Middle East with her archaeologist husband. She grew up in a lonely dreamworld of a childhood where she read voraciously and told herself stories. She married quickly, was challenged to write a novel by her sister and inadvertently created a mystery icon that hung about her writing life like an anchor. When her husband decided to leave her, she fled, disappearing for 11 days that riveted Britain's attention and affected her for the rest of her life. Quite a spirited young woman, our Agatha.

So before a packed house at the Mechanicsburg Mystery Bookshop, I told Agatha's story, accompanied by a PowerPoint slideshow of family photographs, maps, book covers, and photos of Poirot and Miss Marple. The audience got an enthralling story, I sold a number of books, and the bookstore owner invited me back the next year to give a talk about Sherlock Holmes.

The show was a lot of work to put together. I wrote a script, found the artwork and learned PowerPoint to put it together. I rehearsed with the script several times and cut and rewrote anything that sounded awkward. I wanted to avoid Harrison Ford's critique of George Lucas' script to Star Wars: "You can write this s***, George, but you sure can't say it."

The preparation paid off. A few years later, I was invited by a group of Agatha Christie fans to talk about her. All I had to do was print a new script, run through it a couple of times, and I was good to go. And, yes, I read my script during the presentation, but I knew the material well enough that I could go off on tangents if I felt like it. Rehearsal builds confidence which eases your worries about speaking.

> What I tell kids when I make commencement speeches at colleges is, "The only person who can kill your dream is yourself." Those aren't just words. They're true. Some people who want to act brilliant would say they're too simple, but the truth is usually simple. You keep hold of your dream, you work hard, and you've always got a chance of getting what you wanted. I believe that. I had to believe that. And it worked for me.
>
> **Tom Clancy**

But When Things Go Pear-Shaped ...

It's bound to happen. Nobody shows up. The projector you need for your talk blows a bulb. The room is too small. The room is too big. The bookseller didn't get your books in time.

Every author who has held a book signing will have a story like that. Best-selling mystery writer Lawrence Block could tell about the signing in Charlotte in which the only attendee was some kid who brought one of Block's books on writing to sign, and then pity-bought a paperback for him to sign as well. (Hint: That was me.)

If you do enough events, something will go wrong. When I was giving a PowerPoint talk about Agatha Christie, the batteries in the remote went wonky. I'd push the button for the next slide; nothing. Press again and it moved two slides.

After the third time, I abandoned the clicker, walked to the center of the audience next to the computer and continued talking, using the keyboard to keep the slides coming. I was doing theatre in the round, referring to my script, tapping the space bar, and keeping eye contact with the audience. If nothing else, the prospect of disaster kept all of us attentive.

So when it happens, take a deep breath and find your sense of humor. Explain the situation, apologize, laugh about it, and carry on. They'll love you even more for handling it and giving them a story they can tell their friends (who might be impressed enough by your *sang froid* that they'll check out your books, too).

Media Interviews

Pros: Easy to do, just answer questions!

Cons: Quotes taken out of context, or worse, being quoted accurately. Did you really mean to say that about your brother-in-law?

Once you've done enough events, you might get the call. Someone with a printing press, a podcast, or a TV camera wants to interview you. Or, you discover that a local TV or radio station hosts segments about authors and you offer yourself as a willing sacrifice.

Congratulations. You've crossed another threshold, because someone else who didn't know you from Adam or Eve has decided that you are useful to them. It may be because of your personal story in your memoir. It may be because you have in-depth knowledge of a particular subject, like I have of Agatha Christie, Dorothy L. Sayers, the Victorian era, or Sherlock Holmes. Or, maybe you live in the area the media covers, which makes you of interest locally.

So before you find yourself on the receiving end of questions like "where do you get your ideas," here's some things to remember.

This business of writing about writers is more ambivalent than the end product normally admits. As a fan and reader, you want your hero to be genuinely inspirational. As a journalist, you hope for lunacy, spite, deplorable indiscretions, a full-scale nervous breakdown in mid-interview.

Martin Amis

- **Come up with three points to get across.** Usually, it'll be your book's title, the pitch, and your website.
- **Keep your cool.** Always be polite, no matter how provoked you feel. If it becomes too much for you, say, "I have to go, thank you very much," and hang up.
- **Don't overshare.** Interviewers range from barely competent to experts at getting you to drop your guard. The former can be easily handled; they'd be happy to fill their notebooks with quotes to dump into the story. What do you do with the latter? Stick to your talking points and leave gracefully.

So enjoy the moment, then forget it, because chances are the publicity won't affect your life or your sales.

Take the case of Elissa Stein, who wrote a social history of menstruation, *Flow,* that came out in 2010. The book was launched with a starred review from *Booklist* and a rave from *Publishers Weekly.* The publicity campaign called for interviews by Dr. Oz, NPR, Martha Stewart, and *The View.* There was even interest from *The New York Times.*

What happened, as Stein wrote on her blog, was "anticipation, mind-blowing thrills, bone-crushing disappointment." An hour-long audio interview with Dr. Oz produced a seven-minute snippet that surfaced at Oprah.com. A major snowstorm forced cancellation of the NPR interview. It was never rescheduled. Martha Stewart canceled. *The Times* ghosted her. Her interview on *The View* made for great television, but all in all, she sold less than 300 copies.

Conventions

Pros: Fun to attend

Cons: Expensive, tiring, and exposes you to "con crud"

Another way of promoting your books is by attending conventions as a merchant and/or panelist. Nearly every genre has such gatherings: mysteries (Bouchercon and Malice Domestic); thrillers (Thrillfest); science fiction and fantasy (Dragoncon); romance (Romantic Times); and literature and poetry (Association of Writers & Writing Programs). There are also conventions devoted to sub-genres such as horror, Sherlock Holmes (Scintillation of Scions), Doctor Who, and superheroes.

Conventions need authors to act as keynote speakers, luncheon speakers, and to lead workshops and staff panels. They also need authors to act as moderators; this takes a particular skill at introducing the guests, leading the discussion, and keeping panelists from gassing on too long. Books and other products are sold in the vendors room.

Conventions invite authors to headline the main events in return for paying their travel and other expenses. They may even kick in a stipend.

Compensation for the rest varies from convention to convention.

When you're starting out, it's guaranteed that no one's going to ask you to give a keynote address. You can volunteer for a panel, or submit a proposal for one that plays to your books. If you know authors in your genre going to the same con, consider offering them as a package deal (with the authors' approval of course). Making someone else's life easier by doing the work for them is a good way to get where you want.

Convention Conduct

Conventions can be great fun, but mixing people, long hours, and alcohol is a recipe for bad behavior. This isn't Spring Break in Cancun, but a business trip. Each time you step out of your room, you are on stage. Every encounter with a fan, bookstore owner, fellow writer, the bartender, will leave an impression on them.

But success can excuse a lot of bad behavior. Science-fiction writer Harlan Ellison left behind a long trail of stories that are told and retold until they have taken on the status of myth. At Aggie Con at Texas A&M University in 1969, he referred to the university's Corps of Cadets as "America's next generation of Nazis," nearly making the first Aggie Con its last. The damage didn't last long: he was invited back as guest of honor five years later.

Bad Behavior

There is a downside to public appearances. Every bookseller, librarian, book reviewer, and conference visitor have met the Author From Hell.

• I had interviewed a popular mystery writer by phone and published not only a profile, but a positive review of her novel. At the signing, she berated me in a loud voice for writing that she "was not just a mystery writer." In a voice that carried throughout the bookstore, she informed me that you never, never identify someone by what they were not; you did it by describing what they were. Shell-shocked, I stammered an apology. She grumpily signed my book, and I quickly fled.

The rant made a deep impression on the bookstore staff, who apologized to me afterwards. The publicist was so mortified that she sent me a fruit basket to my newspaper (she later dropped this popular mystery writer as a client). I donated the book to the local library and struck the author off my review list. I will admit that the writer had a point; I never made that mistake again.

• Then there was the bookseller who met a best-selling romance author at a Romantic Times convention. Perhaps she felt it was beneath her to make an appearance at a convention, so this author walked through the convention surrounded by her assistants — yes, assistants — and armed with an attitude that made it clear she was not thrilled to be there. Her behavior was so

Our booth at Hershey ArtFest on the lawn of the Cocoa Beanery in Hershey.

distasteful that the bookseller returned to her store and removed her books from the table near the cash register. She stopped hand-selling her books, costing our best-selling writer 50-100 sales a year. "I have plenty of other authors I like to promote," she said.

• An indie author came into the Hershey Public Library with his book in hand, hoping to donate it to the collection. The librarian gave the standard noncommittal answer, and he informed her that it had been accepted by the library system in the next county. He implied that if the head librarian there thought it was good enough to accept, she should as well.

Dumb move. Librarians, like booksellers, love to talk to each other. After he left, she called that head librarian. She was told, yes, indie author had paid a visit, and, no, they did not accept the book.

• There was the author who appeared at the mystery bookstore who told the audience that they could buy his cheaper ebooks at Amazon. This was true, and the bookseller didn't mind that he had other versions available, but did he have to remind the audience whose money was going to keep the bookstore open? His first appearance there became his last.

Art, Book and Specialty Shows

Another way of promoting your book is by buying table space at shows and festivals and selling your books to the public.

Don't reject the idea out of hand. Mark Twain formed a company to sell his

books, with salesmen fanning across the country on his behalf. John Grisham sold a thousand copies of his first book *A Time to Kill* out of the trunk of his car. Irma Rombauer sold the first edition of *Joy of Cooking* out of her apartment.

When you sell a book, you get both your royalty and the bookseller's markup. A book you buy from KDP for six dollars could be sold for $12 or $15. It's also an effective way to build a fan base. You get the chance to talk to readers and watch them react to your works, sign up for your newsletter, and leave with a great impression of you.

Being at a show lets you connect with readers who might not go to bookstores, or non-readers who know that a signed book makes a great gift for readers.

Books on certain subjects or genres, such as kids' picture books, cats, antique autos, fantasy, and superheroes can be a big hit at shows. At many of them, you would be the only author selling books.

On the other hand, retailing is a lot of work and requires organization and salesmanship skills. You can develop your equipment list and ability to schmooze your customers a little at a time, getting better and more efficient with each show. Even if the show provides a table and chairs, you'll still need books, a cashbox, and a receipt book. As you grow more experienced, you can add promotional material and a way to accept credit-card payments. Outdoor shows require a 10'x10' canopy, tables and chairs, and a vehicle large enough to carry them.

Peschel Press has appeared at dozens of events, including library events, arts and crafts shows, and book expos. We've appeared at Scintillation of Scions and the Malice Domestic mystery convention.

To help you get started, here are four lists: the basic necessities for an indoor show where chairs and tables are provided, an expanded list; a list of additional items for use at outdoor festivals; and the contents of your equipment box.

Basic Necessities

- **Your books:** Our books are niche products, so I don't bring more than six of each title, and a few more for *Writers Gone Wild* which has a wider appeal. Try a minimum of a half-dozen of each title, and throw an extra box of books in the trunk. You can always retrieve them at the site as needed.

- **Cash box, change, and receipt book:** How much cash to begin with depends on how you price your books. We've run "show specials" where we sold books for as low as $12, and at other times closer to our list price. While it seems ideal from a marketing standpoint to charge $14.99, I avoid making change, so it's round numbers for me! Use a receipt book that creates a carbon copy to keep track of your sales and income.

● **Pens and Sharpies:** To record your sales and sign your books. Think of a good line to add to your signature, perhaps something related to your books. I use "Go wild!" for *Writers Gone Wild* and "Bottoms Up!" for the books about Victorian poisoner William Palmer.

Test your signature in your book before the signing! I used Sharpies until I discovered they easily bled through the page.

Advanced Necessities

A way to accept credit and debit cards: One popular method to accept a credit card payment is to get a free account with Square (*squareup.com*). They'll send you a card-reader to plug into the headphone jack of your smartphone or iPad. Square takes a small percentage of each sale.

● **Bookstands:** Leaning a copy against a stack of your books could bend the back cover and makes it easy to be knocked over. Stands can position your books so those expensive, eye-catching covers can be appreciated.

● **Marketing materials:** Bookmarks, business cards, brochures, tri-fold or half-page catalogs, buttons, magnets, postcards. You are limited only by your imagination, savings, and inclination.

But start small at first. A business card or bookmark with the book cover and your website info might be all they'll need to remember you. Other types of swag I've found to be a waste of money. Giving away badges with your book cover on it might seem like a good idea, but would anyone but a hardcore fan wear it? They may be more likely if it was a cool design and not an obvious piece of advertising. It also might be popular swag at a science-fiction/fantasy convention, but not at a mystery convention. When looking at an idea, imagine what a customer would do, not what you think they would do.

Here was a lesson I learned the hard way. For my first book, *Writers Gone Wild*, I ordered 500 postcards and bookmarks. Six years later, I'm nearly out of the postcards, but only after sending a hundred of them to a mailing list of writing teachers I bought, and passing them out repeatedly, including throwing them into boxes of stuff I sold on eBay. I also bought business cards featuring two other books, and another postcard with three books on it. Already they're outdated, and I still have plenty of them left.

We've pared down our offerings to a business card and a black and white catalog, 8.5 inches by 5.5 inches, featuring all of our books. I laid it out in Microsoft Publisher, printed them on my laser printer, and folded them over. I only needed a long stapler to finish the job.

Test laying out your display before the event to iron out unexpected problems.

We also have the cookie flyer. Teresa developed a wonderful recipe for Butterscotch Crunchies. These addictive sweet treats are designed to never tire your taste buds. We bake a batch of them for shows and pass them out (check first to make sure it's allowed). Many people stop, and when they do, we give them the recipe. We also make sure our major offerings are printed on the back. As my Teresa puts it, "People throw away sales material, but they never toss recipes."

- **Holders for your materials:** There's nothing more unsightly than papers spread across your table, especially when the wind sweeps them off the table. Clear plastic acrylic holders are very inexpensive and give your table a professional look.

- **Signs:** A table can support a six-foot-long sign displaying your name, book covers, and website. Hanging banners can display your book covers. Believe me, you haven't seen people stop and stare until they've seen a half-naked man showing off your latest romance novel! Signs can be printed at office-supply stores or at online printers such as GotPrint (*gotprint.com*) or VistaPrint (*vistaprint.com*). Most services have templates that you can download and design your signs on.

- **Camera:** Take pictures for your blog and to capture other writers' great marketing ideas. The best way to learn is see something you love and figure out how to make it work for you.

- **Plastic bags:** Recycle. Clean grocery bags can be reused to hold purchases.

Outdoor Events

An outdoor arts festival requires specialized equipment that can handle wind and rain.

- **Canopy:** My first event was an arts and crafts show with a dozen vendors held outside the local coffeehouse. I came armed with my cardboard table, a folding lawn chair, my books, an envelope of cash, and my own sweet self. Hatless.

The view from Bill's unshaded table at his first outdoor event. On top of his to-do list the next day was "buy canopy."

Within an hour, I deeply regretted my lack of planning. By the end of the day, I was exhausted and demoralized. A look at the other vendors impressed on me the amateur nature of my presentation. Changes had to be made.

Now, we own a portable 10'x10' canopy that one person can raise, yet fold into a bag the size of a large golf bag. Although it came with spikes and guy lines steady it, it can't resist high winds. It needed anchors, in the form of four heavy-duty bags designed to be filled with sand or river pebbles and Velcroed around each leg. Our model also came with large plastic sheets that can be Velcroed to form walls. I highly recommend these as a defense against afternoon rain storms that can drench your stock and send catalogs and bookmarks flying across the field (remember those clear acrylic holders? This is where they earn their price).

- **Chairs:** Foldable lawn chairs are ideal, although you can buy tall director's chairs that elevate you nearly to the customer's eye level.

- **Water bottle and snacks:** A cheap alternative when you can't get away from the table, or you don't have enough money to spend on food. Make sure your snacks are easy to consume. You don't want to be dealing with keeping a meatball sub from decorating your shirt when a customer comes up. We prefer Belvitas. As long as your packing, throw in some pain relievers as well.

The Art of the Spiel

We did fabulously at our third appearance at the Winter Arts Show at Hershey High School. We underestimated the number of cookies and recipe flyers to give away. Teresa had made a double batch of her Butterscotch Crunchies, and we had more than a hundred flyers printed up. We were cookie- and recipe-free after five hours, with an hour left to go. We also sold books, to a crowd not known for buying books.

The reason why we were so successful was we used scripts.

This was a lesson we learned after three years of doing shows, so I want you to learn this out of the box. No one told us this. We didn't learn how to engage with customers consciously. But after talking to hundreds of customers, we subconsciously worked on our spiel. We refined and streamlined our chatter. We learned when to close with an invitation to pick up a catalog or a flyer, or smile and wave goodbye.

We learned the art of the spiel.

Preparing Your Script

There are three parts to the spiel:

1. The Opener: If they're passing by, it could be as simple as "Hello!" followed by a remark about the weather (Hershey in early November is a beautiful time; the leaves are turning, the air is crisp, and Christmas is coming). Most of the time, they'll be equally happy to respond. If they move on, let them.

Teresa showing off A Dictionary of Flowers and Gems *at Cupboard Maker Books in Enola.*

If they pause to look, we'll thank them sincerely for coming to the event. I'll follow with a self-introduction: "I'm Bill Peschel, and this is Peschel Press." I like to joke about it: "I named it after myself because I couldn't think of anything better." Or, "I named it after myself because I have a huge ego." An obvious joke, but they laugh. Most people want to laugh.

2. The Pitch: If they stopped, they want to hear you. I repeat: *They want to hear about your products.* It doesn't matter why. They could be readers; they could be shopping for others; they're bored and hope you'll entertain them.

We describe our books in general, using our slogan "The history behind the mystery." We describe our books in detail, focusing on interesting facts and stories, and convey the emotional feel you would get reading each book.

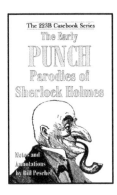

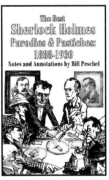

So while talking about *Writers Gone Wild*, I'll emphasize it was published by Penguin. This gives me credibility because Penguin is a well-known publisher. Even if they never heard of it, they'll understand that I am a professionally published author. I give them the elevator pitch ("200 short stories about famous writers and the trouble they got up to away from their desk" or "stories that you never heard in English class"). I'll give examples. Teresa likes to tell about the mystery writer who was a "teenage lesbian murderess." She isn't in the book, but it's so salacious that Teresa tells it anyway. I'll mention Virginia Woolf punking the Royal Navy, Ernest Hemingway throwing meat at his first wife, Sylvia Plath biting the ear of her future husband until it drew blood, and whatever else comes to mind.

Moving on to the Complete, Annotated series, I'll highlight the authors (assuming that while Dorothy L. Sayers is not known to them, Agatha Christie is). I'll show them the inside pages, pointing out the beautiful illustrations and original essays. Mentioning that these would make great gift books for mystery readers plants the idea in their minds and leads to sales.

Then I'll move on to the 223B Series, calling them "fanfiction from Conan Doyle's lifetime." I'll mention that there are famous figures who wrote these pieces (Mark Twain, J.M. Barrie, adding "the creator of Peter Pan" in case they didn't know,) as well as anonymous newspaper reporters. I'll also warn that some of these stories aren't very good, but they all show how Sherlock spread like a virus through the culture. Then I'll mention the "best of" collection that collects the cream of the stories.

With a combination of humor and stories, we try to engage and entertain shoppers.

3. Call to action (CTA): I'll mention our show special and the discounted price. I'll pause and gauge their reaction. If they seem not interested, I'll point out the catalogs and/or cookies. If they change the subject, I'll go along, and we'll have a nice chat. If they leave, I'll thank them again.

Sometimes, they'll make a purchase. Or they'll look at the tote bags (which Teresa makes at home) and we'll chat about that.

As CTAs go, it's not very emphatic, but it works for us.

Write Your Own Script

I'm not saying my script is the best, nor should everyone use it. Develop your own, based on your strengths and the type of books you're selling.

Also:

1. Be pleasant, but not overbearing. Back away if they're not interested. People's body language — not looking at you, moving quickly, pre-occupied with a map or smartphone, walking as far from you as possible — will make it clear they're not interested. Leave them be.

2. Don't let a glum face keep you from approaching them. I've seen faces light up when I say "Great day, isn't it?" If nothing else, the sight of a cheerful face leaves them feeling better. That's a win in my book.

3. Keep it fresh. Be conscious of what you're saying and avoid sounding robotic or monotone. Vary your pace and intonation. Experiment with dropping the tone or volume and see the result. Change the script when you feel like it, or try out new jokes.

4. Never, ever be rude back. Even if you think you're being dissed. Other shoppers can hear what you're saying. Don't give them a reason to avoid you.

5. Don't take it personally. I've had customers tell me they don't read books. "That's all right. We all like different things." Maybe I'm oblivious, but I never had anyone be downright rude to me. Nor should you obsess about what they think of you. You're a moment in their busy life, and unless you do something outrageous, they'll forget you.

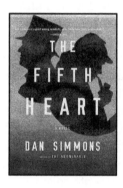

6. Treat selling like improv. This is where it gets fun, when you go "off the script" and enjoy talking to people. I've fawned over a man's beautiful suit (really, it was stunning), commiserated over a woman's cranky baby, and discussed a customer's visit to William Gillette's castle (he portrayed Sherlock on stage and in a movie). If you don't know what to say, ask "have you read anything good lately?" At one show, a customer told me about the works of Dan Simmons, who writes books in all kinds of genres and has won awards in each of them. I loved *The Fifth Heart,* in which Henry James was paired with Sherlock!

Some rewards can't be counted in dollars and cents.

Equipment Box

I have a Rubbermaid container stored in the basement so when a show comes along, it's ready to be tossed into the back seat. The contents of your box depends on your set-up and whether you're doing indoor or outdoor events. For example, a hammer is vital for pegging down a canopy but not necessary if you are doing only indoor events.

Here is what's in my toolbox. Note that they were packed for a particular use, but also because you never know when it might be needed. Prepare for the unexpected:

- Hammer for canopy pegs
- Packing tape to attach the banner to the table and to secure boxes
- Duct tape for emergencies
- Clothespins if the table banner needs reinforcement or to keep the tablecloth down in high winds
- Scissors to cut tape on boxes
- Binder clips in a jar to reinforce the table banner and other uses
- Packets of sunscreen taken from a hotel room and tossed in

Chapter 16
Publicity

Key Points to Remember
- Media producers will be more inclined to choose you if you do their work for them.
- It's easier to get local publicity first. Use those clips to pitch to regional and national outlets.
- Podcasts and video are inexpensive publicity outlets, but they demand time and tech skills.

> For artists, the great problem to solve is how to get oneself noticed.
> **Honoré de Balzac**

> There's no such thing as bad publicity except your own obituary.
> **Brendan Behan**

Publicity is an option.

There are high-earning writers — and I'm talking those making five- and six-figure incomes *a month* — who never needed to gin up publicity for themselves and their books.

They're successful by writing to market, publishing frequently in series, using ghostwriters, and taking advantage of Amazon's Kindle Unlimited. They're laser-focused on this goal and, frankly, the last thing they want is to tell anyone how much they're making and how they're doing it.

It's depressing when you realize that. It seems unfair, somehow. You can write the best book in your genre, but if you can't put it in people's hands, if you feel your book is getting hip-checked by Amazon's preference for KU titles and the big boys' monetary power, what's the point?

I don't have an answer for that, except to take the long view. The marketplace has always had these kinds of imbalances. It's built into the way we're wired as humans.

Rather than feeling overwhelmed, focus on what you can control. Your books. Your website. Your marketing. Because the market is so large, because the hunger for good stories is so intense, there will always be a need for stories.

Despite the inequalities in the system, you can succeed through online ads, your mailing list, and judicious use of marketing services such as BookBub.

So consider this chapter a way of rounding out your education as the owner of a storytelling business.

Types of Publicity

Publicity and marketing are two different beasts. Publicity is any technique used to get a media outlet to cover you and your work. Marketing is when you're paying others to do the same thing.

Placing an ad in *People* magazine is marketing. Getting *People* to profile you is publicity.

There are many different types of publicity, like planting signs by the side of the road or putting up flyers on grocery store bulletin boards, so this section will restrict itself to areas where an author can have an effect. .

Examples of publicity include (but are not limited to):

- Issuing press releases announcing a news tie-in to your book
- Pitching you and your book to the media: TV, radio, newspapers, magazines, podcasters, and vloggers
- Newsletters
- Posting material, podcasts, videos on your blog or guest-posting on other sites
- Producing ancillary material based on your work, such as excerpts from your book or articles based on your research
- Public appearances

Most of the above will be covered in their own section.

The Onion Model of Publicity

When considering your publicity options, it's helpful to think of it as an onion consisting of three layers:

1. The outside skin is *local* media outlets. Newspapers, radio, and TV stations. In our area, ABC27 interviews local authors as a regular feature. After the interview, you might get a small bump in sales, but you also get a video clip that you can put on your website. This is part of building your brand as an author and is still useful if you're writing nonfiction, particularly self-help.

2. The next layer is *regional* outlets. If you live in a major city, then your local and regional outlets are combined. For example, I live in Hershey, so my regional outlets include those in nearby Harrisburg, York, and Philadelphia. There are also regional magazines such as *Susquehanna Life*, *Pennsylvania* magazine, and *Philadelphia* magazine.

3. The *national* outlets are what you would expect. *The New York Times* and the *Washington Post*; the major networks and the cable channels; National Public Radio; and major magazines. This includes major websites such as *Slate*, *Huffington Post*, and *The Onion's AV Club*.

I created the onion model as a way of thinking about how you can move through the media world. It's possible to jump right to the national level if your story is compelling or your essays good. But if you're starting out, approaching local outlets and working your way up will teach you what you need to learn. By emphasizing your success at the local level, you reassure gatekeepers at the regional and national levels that you're worth considering.

One Example of a Media Onion

The Inquirer
DAILY NEWS philly●com

The Washington Post

Making your media appearances available on your website acts as your screen test to producers.

Think of what you're doing as creating a "sizzle reel." Actors and models do this. These are short videos, no more than a few minutes long, stitching together their best performances and/or images. Casting directors can get a quick idea how well a person registers on camera. Search for sizzle reels on YouTube and you'll find plenty of examples.

Your publicity clips generated locally act as your "sizzle reel" to a magazine editor considering you as the subject for a profile, or a bookstore owner thinking of having you give a talk.

How to Pitch Yourself

The process is simple: identify, observe, and serve.

Identify what outlets are available in your area. List newspapers, magazines, giveaway papers, and local TV shows with a segment about residents who do interesting things.

Observe them for openings into which you can see yourself or your book. Look at yourself from the media's point of view. Do they publish briefs about author appearances? Do they review books? What kind? Are there feature stories? What do they focus on: the compelling personal story, useful information the public needs to know, or a news hook on which your book can hang?

Serve them by making it easy to use you. Pitch your story to them, or have your spouse or friend step in if you're embarrassed about promoting yourself. Find out who to reach at the outlet and send them an email or a letter and promotional material you think they need, including your author photo and book cover.

Keep the pitch brief and to the point. Recast your pitch to match their tone and focus. The more you're in sync with their needs, the greater chance they'll say yes. Include a link to the "sizzle reel" on your website. Media people are human, and if you make it easy for them to do their job, they'll be more likely to say yes.

How to Do Their Job

• Can they find your book cover and author photos in a format they can use? Print media need images set in CMYK color format at 300dpi. Broadcast media prefers RGB color format and about 600 pixels wide.

• Can a writer find your biography, full of material they can draw on for a profile? I have two biographies available, a paragraph long version, similar to what I put in my books, and a long version that contains more personal details. I don't put that version online, but I tell them that it is available.

• Can TV producers find any video of your public appearances, so they can judge how you sound, how you answer questions, what you look like on camera?

Mind Your Manners

If they don't respond, try again a few weeks later. If they still don't respond, stop. Don't get snarky with them, or beg. Contact them again *only* if you have a new book coming out that you think would work, and don't remind them that they rejected you before.

Yes, it sucks being rejected, but don't take it personally. Only those who have worked behind the scenes know how many people are banging on their metaphorical doors seeking publicity. Even when I was reviewing books at a small South Carolina newspaper — 90,000 subscribers in a town few people had heard of — I was getting more than 30 books a week from major New York publishers to fill 1-4 slots per week in the Sunday book page. I had to turn down reviewing books by major authors because I had no space or time. The same will happen to you.

So keep trying. Keep your name in front of them. There may come a day when they need somebody, and that's when your efforts will pay off.

Press Releases

Press releases are overrated. There are plenty of free and fee services that suggest blasting your release to a thousand media sites will get attention, but I have never found that to be the case.

If you're absolutely determined to waste your time, your best chance is to figure out a news hook from your book that ties in with current trends or breaking news stories. You'll have a better shot at publicity than, "Author Jane Anonymous announces Monday the publication of her first romance 'My Heart Will Go On.'"

But unless your book really has a news hook, you're better off not bothering.

Exception: If you write a nonfiction book that seems made for politically liberal book buyers, it's worth pursuing an interview on National Public Radio stations. Each state has its own local public radio outfit, so you'll have to research where they are and who to send your press release to. Even if you snag a five-minute interview in the smallest NPR outlet, you can parlay that by putting the clip up on your website and make it part of your media packet. You can't buy this kind of credibility.

Famous On the Internet

An alternative to working with traditional media is going your own way on the internet. Podcasts and vlogs (video blogging) have grown in popularity, serving an audience seeking distraction, entertainment, or education through their smartphones.

But there is a big downside to this strategy. It can consume a lot of time and creative energy. There can be a steep learning curve. And you may discover you have a face for podcasts, or a voice for miming.

In either case, make sure that your production aligns with the type of books you write. A podcast on writing tips would work with, say, the author of *Career Indie Author*, but mystery or romance fans are rarely interested in your opinion of the Oxford comma.

Podcasts

Hearing a person's voice breathing in your ear is probably the most intimate feeling you can get with your clothes on. The human voice — breathy, sensible, earnest, comical or imitative — gets past our guards and can deeply move us.

That's what a good podcast can do. Like indie books, podcasts can be on any subject with no restrictions on length, content, or speech.

To succeed, you have to have a clear focus, an ability to stay on schedule, and be capable of creating good content.

The beauty of podcasting compared to vlogging is that you might already have all the equipment you need, or can acquire it at a low price.

● **Microphone:** Possibly the only thing you'll need to buy. I started with a cheap small model that I could clip to my shirt before graduating to my children's microphone from *Rock Band*. A top-quality Shure 87 microphone used by studio musicians costs a hundred bucks.

● **Pop filter:** A good microphone picks up your voice, along with sounds you wouldn't expect to hear, such as your breathing, or the sharp puff of air when you say words that begin with a hard "k" (kite or kitten) or "c" (can or coconut). These sound like explosions on an unprotected microphone. A pop filter can be bought online or made at home from a nylon stocking stretched over an embroidery hoop. A piece of foam slipped over the top of the microphone serves the same function.

● **Audacity software:** A free open-source audio recorder and editor (*audacityteam.org/*). It's easy to use and learn from the company's wiki and YouTube videos. It comes with filters to add effects and clean up the sound.

● **Computer:** Which you have already to record the show and edit the content.

As for the subject matter and recording, that's up to you. Download and listen to a few podcasts to get an idea of the possibilities.

Here are a few types of shows:

Interview Shows

What Is It: Two or more people having a conversation. It can be a combination of a Q-and-A with a general free-ranging conversa-

tion. It can also be held face to face, over the phone, or recorded through Skype or Zoom.

Examples: Marc Maron's *WTF*; *Gilbert Gottfried's Amazing Colossal Podcast*. Writing podcasts include Jami Albright and Sara Rosett's *Wish I'd Known Then … For Writers* and *Mark Dawson's Self Publishing Formula*.

Advantages: Minimal editing involved to delete dull bits or dead air, something the interviewer regretted saying out loud, or extraneous noises. Great way to cross-promote with someone more popular than you.

Disadvantages: A lot of work involved coming up with questions and arranging for guests, and just starting out it may be difficult to get the people you want.

Lecture-type Show

What Is It: One person in front of a microphone telling a story.

Examples: Dan Carlin's *Hardcore History*; *The Moth*.

Advantages: You're always available and willing to talk. Plus, you'll work cheap.

Disadvantages: It takes work coming up with a script. You may need to be more finicky about the production values. When two people are talking, you can get a natural rhythm going, with ups, downs, starts, stops, laughter, etc. A solo show needs to incorporate a rhythm that doesn't bore the listener.

Group Show

If you have people on the same wavelength, get them together and talk, combined with an interview format. You get the camaraderie combined with some comedy (if you're lucky) and insights into the subject at hand, whether talking about mysteries, politics, or Sherlock Holmes.

Examples: *The Baker Street Babes, I Hear of Sherlock Everywhere*.

Advantages: Having someone around to carry the conversational load; you might be surprised what someone else comes up with.

Disadvantages: Can be difficult getting people together; possible subject fatigue.

Let's Put On a Show

If you're a fiction writer, consider creating a show, or adapting your short stories.

Examples: *Welcome to Night Vale; The Bright Sessions; Limetown*.

Seth Harwood, after taking classes at Harvard Extension School and attending the prestigious Iowa Writers' Workshop, spent four years in a futile attempt to land a publishing contract for his writings, including a crime novel called *Jack Wakes Up.* He recorded an audiobook and in 2006 began posting

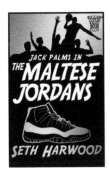

There is a basic principle that distinguishes a hot medium like radio from a cool one like the telephone, or a hot medium like the movie from a cool one like TV. A hot medium is one that extends one single sense in "high definition." High definition is the state of being well-filled with data. . . . Hot media are low in participation, and cool media are high in participation or completion by the audience. . . . The hot form excludes, and the cool one includes.
Marshall McLuhan

chapters on Podiobooks (now Scribl). He built up enough of an audience to interest a small publisher, and on publication the book hit No. 1 on Amazon's crime fiction list. He continues to post his audio fiction today.

Advantages: A show with a unique, personal voice has the potential to attract a large audience. A popular show could boost your visibility and profitability.

Disadvantages: The amount of work involved could hamper your regular writing.

Video Equipment

To have your own television show, you used to need an agent, a manager, a bunch of scriptwriters, a film crew, a director, and a network to pay for it all. Then you needed an audience to bring in enough ad revenue to avoid cancellation.

Not anymore. With YouTube acting as your network, you can put on a show of your own. So long as it's not too obscene or risque or infringes on someone else's intellectual property, your show will never be canceled. Even if YouTube goes the way of Friendster and BBS services, you still own the rights to your work.

The question is: What do you want to do? And can you do it?

One answer would be to look to YouTube for answers. The style and quality of the shows range from the basic — a person, a desk, and a camera — to elaborate productions with a script, different camera placements, music and sound effects, even acting!

As with everything else in the indie world, it's up to you.

Since we're talking about publicity and marketing, keep it simple. Unless you have a format already decided, treat your first video like a blog post. You have something to say that pertains to the book. Write a script. Make it short, punchy, and pungent. You want to be hot, in the Marshall McLuhan way, not attractiveness. You want to be a little hyper, a little over-caffeinated unless your shtick is to be understated; if so, do the full Buster Keaton.

Whichever way you go, go big. At least at first; you can always dial it back later.

Equipment: You'll need a camera, webcam, or smartphone for filming, a microphone for recording sound, and editing software. The products change from year to year, so rather than give an outdated list, it's best to search online for the latest recommendations.

After watching a couple of videos, you'll see a few things in common:

● Videos can be as short or as long as they need to be, but the cardinal rule is that there's no dead air.

● The face can be much closer to the camera than you'd think. A good part of the screen is taken up by your face.

• Note the cutting. Some videos make heavy use of "jump cuts," which is when you remove film from a single take. They're speeding up the pace to add excitement and also to remove those moments when they screw up a word or lose their place.

• Most videos don't begin or end with credits or theme music. They jump right in. (However, visit *incompetech.com/music/* for free, royalty-free music and see what Kevin MacLeod has. Highly recommended.)

INC►MPETECH

What about book trailers? When YouTube was launched, one popular type of video was the book trailer. Borrowing from Hollywood, these ads were designed to lure potential readers into the story.

Frankly, I don't think they work. Taking the elevator-blurb pitch and stretching it into a three-minute piece is Bohr-RING no matter how much drifting text and evocative public-domain art you use.

Before shelling out money for a book trailer, ask yourself: Would you want to see the trailer if you didn't know anything about the book or the author?

Livestreaming

In the past few years, YouTube, Facebook, and Vimeo have developed the technology to let you stream content live.

The plus side is that there's an excitement about livestreaming that uploading a video can't inspire. Anyone livestreaming their program will capture more attention than an author putting up another video of herself talking or a book trailer.

But there are several downsides:

1. Livestreaming is technically demanding. While anyone can stream content holding their smartphone in front of them, effectively marketing yourself demands a higher level of polish. Even if it's just you talking from your desk, you'll want a decent camera (not the webcam that came with your monitor) and even lighting that doesn't make you look like you're hosting a horror-movie show on late-night cable (unless that's your intention).

2. Livestreaming needs speed. Streaming high-quality video demands a fast internet connection to keep your face from jittering across the stream, or failing entirely.

3. Livestreaming is best done with help. Someone should be monitoring the comments coming in to feed you questions or fix a reported problem. You may even need someone standing by the camera to make sure you're still in the frame and in focus.

4. You need to plan ahead. Just like a real TV show, everyone needs to know what's going to happen ahead of time. If you fluff a line on a podcast or a video, you can still edit the mistakes out. Not so when you're livestreaming.

This is what movie stars do.

If you remember the great movie *My Favorite Year* (1982), when film actor Alan Swann (played by Peter O'Toole) is told he'll have to perform before a live audience, he panics and shouts "I'm NOT an actor! I'm a movie star!" When you're livestreaming, there are no second takes.

5. You need be yourself. It's the worst advice you can give an actor, but it's true for authors. You don't have to sound like an FM radio host with sweet, mellifluous tones or look gorgeous enough to host a TV news show. Your readers don't expect you to be anything but your authentic self.

Even if you're not sure this is what you want to do, it's worth making a few test videos to learn the process. You may surprise yourself at how much fun you're having. Also, look at how other authors do it and how you respond to them. If Debbie Macomber, below, can handle a livestream with her fans at her age, what's stopping you from showing readers your best self?

PART IV

Advanced Business

Some fascinating photos
might be also taken of me,
a burly but agile man,
stalking a rarity
or sweeping it into my net
from a flowerhead.

Vladimir Nabokov, to Life magazine

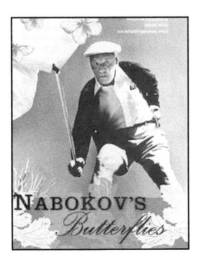

Chapter 17
Book Launches

Key Points to Remember

- An effective launch combines advertising, newsletters (yours and others), and social media.
- Discount newsletters play a big role, but they can be expensive.
- Coordinating price discounts with publicity campaigns requires planning and monitoring.

No, Virginia, there is not and never has been a Santa Claus in the publishing world, nor a time when editors were all like Max Perkins and the patriarchs were benign lovers of good books. The noses were as hard as they are today, though the manners were better. If writers are treated like cans of beans now, they were all too often treated like Bob Crachit then.

Mary Lee Settle

A book launch is the advertising, marketing, and publicity campaign designed to sell a book. That's it.

But behind this simple definition lies a lot of planning, thinking, and anxiety by the author. *What do I do? Where do I go? Do I hire a publicist? Do I set up book signings? Where do I even start?*

As owner of your business, you'll need to decide on the strategy behind your book launch. It can be a combination of online and real-world tactics. You can spend whatever you need, but remember your budget!

Unfortunately, I can't give you a book launch campaign you can pull out of the box and use. There are too many variables in play: your book's genre, your skill level, the amount of money you can spend, the number of fans you have following you already, and your relationship with local booksellers among them.

What I can do is show you the blocks that you can combine to build your campaign.

What Is the goal?

Because Amazon is such a big and influential bookseller, the optimal launch campaign takes into account how the Zon looks at your book. The company's algorithms support books that are steady sellers. It's a logical decision. They don't want to promote low sellers. They don't want to promote spiking big sellers; those may have been influenced by a big marketing push or sheer luck (a mention in a national magazine, for instance). Books that sell steadily, with occasional dips and rises, are the safest bets.

As for audience, this is where your keywords and book description come into play. Day by day, hour by hour, Amazon is looking over your book's virtual shoulders. It's seeing what happens when it is introduced to a customer whose search matches your keywords. Did the customer buy it? Sales are good; no sales are not good. Amazon's not expecting every customer to walk out with your book, but it is comparing your results with every other book on that page. If your book is sold to .02% of the shoppers who see it, it's still doing better than a similar book sold to .01% of shoppers.

Relevancy and pace of sales come into play when setting up a launch campaign as well. You want to place your book before audiences who are likely to buy it, and you want to spread out the campaign over several days so that sales are consistent.

Of course, you don't know which part of your campaign will work and what won't. You'll be making a lot of guesses along the way. If it's any help, your competitors will be making guesses about their campaigns as well.

Building Blocks of a Campaign

Advertising

AMS ads
Facebook ads
BookBub

Amazon

Kindle Countdown Deal (KU only)
Kindle Free Book Promotion (KU only)

Book Discount Newsletters

In 2012, BookBub opened its doors as one of the first book discovery services. Its business model was simple, gathering a pool of readers interested in free and discounted ebooks, and charging authors to advertise their books to them. By being careful in their selection of books, accepting indie books with a high number of favorable reviews or from traditional publishers, they built up to become the largest newsletter service, with more than 15 million subscribers.

Other services followed hoping to replicate BookBub's success. Some deliver their offerings through emailed newsletters, while others list books on their website or Facebook page.

One typical strategy involves authors stacking promotions. An author will plan next month to discount a book — frequently the first book in a series — and apply to the sites below. For example, an author setting up a five-day campaign will apply for a BookBub listing for Day #1, Fussy Librarian for Day #2, Robin Reads for Day #3, and a mix of smaller sites for Day #4 and Day #5. The goal is exposure to the largest audience possible.

The author knows that there's no guarantee that any of the sites will take a book (BookBub, as the largest service, has the highest rejection rate). The author will take these rejections in stride and apply to more services.

The list below are the reputable services I know of as of 2020. When researching these services, especially ones not on this list, be aware that some have unsavory reputations. David Gaughran's article is especially educational in this regard: *davidgaughran.com/2018/04/11/please-help-an-author-fight-this-crazy-court-case/*

Major sites

BookBub
BookRaid (charges per click)
ENT (EReader News Today)
Freebooksy
Fussy Librarian
Robin Reads

Smaller sites

Bargain Booksy
Bargain Ebook Hunter
BKNights
BookAdrenaline (Mystery/Thriller)
Book Barbarian (Sci-Fi/Fantasy)
BookBasset (no erotica)
Book Boost
Book Cave
BookGorilla
Book Rebel
Book Runes
BookDoggy
Booksends
ebookaroo
eBookSoda
EreaderIQ
FKBT (Free Kindle Books and Tips)
GenrePulse
Just Kindle Books
KindleNation Daily
ManyBooks
Pixel of Ink
Price Dropped Books
Prolific Works

Red Feather Romance (Romance/Erotica)
Reign of Reads
Romance Devoured (Romance/Erotica)

Mailing List Builders

BookSweeps
LitRing

Things You Can Do

ARC team and street team for reviews
Bookstore events
Facebook page campaign
Facebook takeovers
Goodreads Giveaway
Kindle Countdown Deal
Kindle Free Book Promotion
Newsletter tactics
Plea to readers
Newsletter swaps
Offer free book or prequel novella through BookFunnel, BookSweeps, or StoryOrigin

Book Reviewers

Booksprout
NetGalley co-op

Sample Campaigns

OK, so you have this list of resources, and you know you should use them in some way to sell books, but *how do you go about it?*

What do you do next?

Here are some examples of writers and their campaigns. Some worked, some didn't. I'm not saying you should copy these campaigns, because they may not work for your book, in your genre, in this phase of the moon. But it'll give you some idea of what they did, why they did it, and what results they got.

I think the big takeaway from this is to consciously know what you're doing and why. What is your goal? To sell books? To build preorders? To get people to sign up for your newsletter? To get the *right* people to sign up, who won't take your book and unsubscribe? If you know your goal, chances are you'll have a better chance of hitting it with these tools.

These examples are taken from the authors who are willing to share their information. For privacy reasons, I've deliberately obscured their names and book titles.

A Simple Promotion

Goal: To give away free books and score reviews.

Plan: This inexpensive campaign relied on getting Amazon to make the first book in the series free.

- Put the Kindle Unlimited Book for free for five days in a row.
- Announce the free book on five different discount newsletters.
- Make the first book in the series free, have the second book for sale, and the third book on preorder.

Spend: Nearly $400.

Profit / Loss: About four times the spend in profit.

Result: More than 15,000 copies given away, a top-ten rank in the free charts, a bunch of new reviews, mostly very good.

Comment: A very basic campaign. None of the promotional sites were very expensive, probably no more than $75 each, but well worth the result. This also shows, if you're looking to make enough money to support yourself, the long road you'll have to travel. While it's great to pocket, say, $1,500, that's still only about two week's salary in the U.S. Still, if you're trying to build up your fan base, this is a promising beginning.

A Series Launch

Goal: To promote sales of the newly released third book in the series.

Plan: This romance series is in Kindle Unlimited, so the author developed a two-pronged strategy:

- She scheduled a Kindle Countdown Deal for book #1, and reduced the price of book #2. She also arranged several newsletter swaps, and bought spots on several discount newsletters such as Freebooksey. She also bought ads on Facebook.
- For Book #3, she released the news on her newsletter, and networked with author friends to promote the release on their newsletters. She spent money on Facebook ads and a newsletter aimed at romance readers.

Result: Excellent. This author already has a fan base despite publishing only two books, so these promos helped put her book in Kindle's top 500 on Amazon overall. The cost was relatively small, perhaps $500, but spread over a three-book series.

A Failed Launch

Goal: To boost the author's income with a bigger ad budget. The author had successfully published a number of books. Each previous book paid for its expenses within a day or two.

Plan: The book would go wide, like the author's previous books. There would be promotions with at least two major book sites.

Result: Murphy's Law strikes! One ebook platform never confirmed the promotion, and problems with the paperwork on the second site led the author to switch to an aggregate to get the book on that platform.

The author also decided after publication to place the book in Kindle Unlimited. It took one major platform three days to delist the book, which meant the book wasn't selling anywhere during that time.

Comment: The author admitted that switching to KU in the middle of the campaign was a bad idea. She also confessed that the book did not meet all of the tropes the genre's fans expected. Many hated the hero for doing something that violated a major trope! The best she could do was pull the plug on the campaign, learn from her mistake, and move on to the next book.

A Trad-Pub Launch

Debbie Macomber is a longtime trad-published author. Her publisher takes care of some of her marketing, such as creating promotional material like bookmarks and book club lists, advertising on BookBub and Facebook, and arranging her publicity tour. But she also has a team of marketers who promote her books on social media using a variety of tools to create excitement and anticipation, and to remind readers of her next book.

Macomber described in detail her launch strategy for BookBub (*insights.bookbub.com/book-launch-checklist-marketing-timeline-traditionally-published-authors/*). It is tailored for her audience and the social media they use. None of this may be applicable to your book's genre, of course, but it gives you an idea of how one major author, along with her marketing staff and her publisher, promote her books.

I'll list the highlights here, but you should read the original article, which goes into detail about each part of the launch, and shows examples of her posts.

Six months before launch

- Post the cover to encourage preorders
- Add synopsis to website, promote it on social media
- Announce on mailing list
- Update author profile

Three months before launch

- Create photos of your book against appropriate backgrounds for social media campaigns.

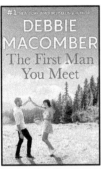

French edition

Ebook-only
edition from Spain

Manga edition
from Japan

- Create images with quotes from your book, the author, and blurbs for social media campaigns. Always add preorder link to posts.
- Run ARC giveaways on Facebook, with comment being the "cost" of entry. (Asking for shares on Facebook is a no-no.)

Create bonus content postable on social media. (In Macomber's case, it's recipes mentioned in her books).

- Share any early reviews.
- Send ARCs to major publications, along with a personalized note.

One month before launch

- Create countdown social posts
- Promote Pinterest board around the book
- Share book trailer
- Share glimpses of your author life and details behind your work on the new book.

Book launch day

- Send a launch day newsletter
- Update social media header images
- Post celebratory social media updates

After the launch

- Run multi-author promotions, marketing your title to each others' fans
- Run Q&As on Twitter, Reddit, and Facebook Live
- Run book tours and signings
- Continue running giveaways on fun themes
- Consider running seasonal tie-ins if the book calls for it
- Consider running tie-ins on special days
- Celebrate your success with your readers
- Recommend books to your readers on sites like BookBub

Again, I'm not recommending that you adopt any or all of Macomber's strategy. She has been writing novels since 1988 and has built up a large fan base. What works for her type of books — wholesome stories about family, friendships and love — might not work well with your reverse harem shifter series. Or, maybe it would!

The point is that, behind the novels that appear on the "New Releases" table at the front of the bookstore, that are shelved on the "New Books" case at the library, that are profiled in *People* and *Vanity Fair*, there's a marketing engine pulsating behind it.

Even now, two years after BookBub published her article, the Macomber marketing juggernaut steams on. Her Amazon author page shows 12 books available for preorder, including reprints and Spanish and German editions. Her Facebook page displays about a post a day, including a 2020 reading challenge pinned to the top, a positive review for another author's book, an announcement that Shania Twain is producing a movie based on one of her novels, and a book giveaway post (with 3,200 comments!).

Chapter 18
Social Media

Key Points to Remember

- Engaging on social media can be rewarding, but it's difficult to proves that it sells books.
- It can raise awareness that you're an author over the long haul.
- Success lies in combining entertainment with marketing. No ads!

Social media is the ultimate equalizer. It gives a voice and a platform to anyone willing to engage.

Amy Jo Martin,
social media
business owner

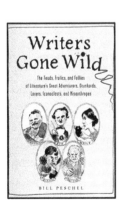

You hear it all the time. You need a platform of fans to attract a book deal. You need fans following you on Twitter, Facebook, YouTube, and Snapchat. You need to be online every day, meeting the public and selling yourself and your books.

We have been told that for years. When I sold *Writers Gone Wild* to Penguin in 2009, I received a book describing all the ways to become known before publication. Just reading it fatigued me. I'm expected to post everywhere, to engage in selling my books one by one? What was my print run again ... 20,000?

That's a lot of talking.

It turns out that nobody knew what to do with social media. The people giving the advice didn't know what worked, except a lotta "likes" and a lotta "follows," that must be good, right? The more eyeballs, the more sales, right?

Wrong. Not all eyeballs were the same.

Let's pretend I have 100,000 followers on Twitter, reading my bon mots. You have 1,000 fans following your newsletter. Those are people who read your books, and want to know when you're publishing your next book.

Who do you think would get more sales: you with your 1,000 book-reading fans, or me with my 100,000 strangers who didn't know me except from Twitter?

In 2015, the Pew Research Center found that seven in ten American adults read at least part of a book in 2014. Among Americans, the median number of books they read was four. That means half the adult American population read less than four books, half read more than four. (The average was seven).

So, assuming that my 100,000 Twitter followers represented all Americans, only 70,000 read at least one book, and 35,000 read more than four books. Depending on the genre I write in — a lot more

romance readers than literary, for example — I'd have to convince 35,000 of my followers to devote some of their book-buying attention to my book. And that's only assuming that those Twitter followers mimic the national percentage of readers (and are not spambots, for example). Since the answer to "how many people on Twitter read books" is "we don't know," this doesn't give me confidence in my ability to sell books this way.

I'd rather take my chances on your 1,000 true fans than my 100,000 followers.

This is not to say that all newsletter followers are the same, either. Authors gain followers in one of two ways: "organic" followers who visit your website or read your books and sign up, and recruited followers who sign up in order to get a free book. It's well-known that most of those in the latter category are "lookie-loos" who take the free book and never buy one. In fact, there are some who live to simply collect free books. It's a digital version of hoarding, like people who save bags of their poo or empty prescription medicine bottles.

It's easy to get caught up in the social media whirl, expressing your opinions and humor, getting into conversations about the things you're passionate about. But if none of that gets you closer to your goal of getting them to buy a book, sign up for your newsletter, or follow your blog posts, as far as CIA is concerned, you're wasting your time.

That's the key issue. What is your goal? To find your true fans, your readers.

With that in mind, social media can be an effective ally to finding those fans. With them, you can create online communities where you can share whatever you create. It can be knowledge that you've gathered in your researches, your unique take on news stories and trends, stories about yourself, your family, and your writing life. In short, anything that aligns with the type of books you publish.

This is what fantasy author Garrett Robinson discovered. After building a large audience on YouTube with videos about Marvel superheroes, he discovered that his fans there didn't buy his books.

So whatever you tweet, Facebook, or Instagram, it should be with the goal of a) creating a community of people interested in certain subjects, b) getting them to visit your website, sign up for your newsletter and/or buy your books.

By the way, I do not mean that you should advertise your books. I've seen many writers fall into this trap on Twitter. Tweet after tweet, nothing but a picture of their book and a demand that you CHECK THIS SWEET BOOK OUT, now 99 CENTS!!! followed by stars, comets and emojis, and hashtags. Or they'll move from Facebook group to Facebook group, dropping their little spam bombs. They've done it on groups that have a strict "no self-promotion" rule, leaving behind angry moderators and annoyed members.

I'm not angry at the author, but I am seriously peeved at whoever was paid to tell them that. It saddens me that months will pass and the author will wonder why their sales haven't moved the needle. That's because they've been muted, blocked, and unfollowed from here to next Christmas.

Instead, you want to fish for readers. Not tens of thousands of minnows, but one whale at a time. A reader interested in your genre, interested in your subject matter interested in you, and therefore likely to buy your books.

Building Your Net

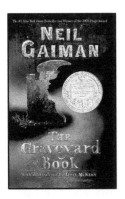

What you want to do is build your sales funnel. You're a fisherman. You want to lure someone to your website so they can get to know you, and receive an offer to sign up for your newsletter.

I can feel you cringing already, but this is not a scam. You're not lying, nor are you tricking anyone. They'll see you coming, know why you're there, and they might still be willing to come into your net.

Why do potential readers do this? Because you're offering entertainment and/or enlightenment. They want to be entertained. They want to be enlightened. If they like you, they'll *want* to hang around and see what else you can give them.

Think about your favorite authors. If Neil Gaiman invites you to sign up for his newsletter, would you? How about J.K. Rowling; wouldn't you like to know what she's going to do next with her Harry Potter world? How about James Patterson. I wouldn't, but *somebody's* buying those books.

You're doing the same thing with your world. You're sending out feelers so that people who would love to spend time with your characters discover you. How bad is that?

So you want to write posts that reflect your world, your stories, your interests where they intersect with your stories.

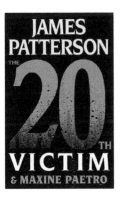

Here's where your imagination has to take over and draw the connection between what you write and what you can tell your future fans. If you write historical fiction, you can use your research and talk about why French noblemen had colorfully decorated tick boxes to keep the little buggers they picked off their clothes (ew!). If your field is contemporary thrillers, you can write about the favorite weapons your Spec Ops heroes use. Romance writers? How about praise for your fellow authors who write in your genre? Their fans would love to hear your thoughts, and consider looking at your books as well.

A post a week, spread out over social media with the right hashtags so they could be seen, is one way to get your message out without exposing you to the sometimes toxic environment and arguing that pervades social media.

Establishing Your Outposts

It can take only one idiot to make your life hell online. On the internet, no one cares who you are, and an alias gives people license to expose the worst part of themselves.

But it is possible to use social media for your purposes without exposing yourself to most personal attacks. It requires building a few defenses, and that means establishing outposts.

By that, I mean that you post your material on your blog and your Facebook fan page (not your personal page. Use that to talk to your family and friends, and keep it private). Then you use the other social media sites to broadcast your post, with proper art and hashtags, so that people can *discover* you there, and visit you *here*.

Is Social Media For You?

What are your goals? Do you want to be a public figure? Do you want to jump into the public debate on politics, sex, and religion? Do you have a thick hide? Your controversial takes expressed in tweets, blog posts, and guest posts on sites like *Salon*, *Slate*, *Medium*, and the *Huffington Post* will test your resistance to abuse.

Just ask conservative fantasy author Larry Correia, who posted about the reaction he receives [WARNING: foul words]:

> "Three days ago I put up that post refuting the meme about the RNC [Republican National Committee] speakers. By the time it got shared a thousand times, off the top of my head I think that thread got me an insane healing power of crystals hippie, five morons calling me names who were so incoherent that I couldn't actually tell what they were upset by, a couple Common Internet Shit Gibbons, a Socialist Lemming, some pseudo-intellectual gotcha attempts from people who aren't smart enough to pick up dog turds in the park for a living, and one incredibly boring dope who babbled about his asinine philosophy on EVERYTHING for THREE DAYS STRAIGHT. By the end I was reading all his posts in the voice of Colin Robinson."*

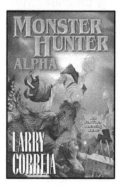

* "About My 'Tone' On Social Media," *Monster Hunter Nation,* https:// monsterhunternation.com/. Colin Robinson is an energy vampire character on the FX horror comedy series "What We Do in the Shadows."

There's nothing like taking controversial stands to draw attention.

When it comes to your social media choices, go where your readers hang out.

Do you want to promote a cozy series based on a hobby such as quilting? You might find a home on Pinterest.

How about a YA series? Reaching out on more youth-oriented sites such as Instagram might be the way to go.

If you're writing nonfiction on, say, economics, answer questions on Quara or LinkedIn.

General principles no matter what social media you're using: Build your material to suit the platform; do it regularly; get feedback to learn what worked and what didn't.

Beware the danger of focusing too much on social media. It takes time and diverts you from your primary focus, which is to write books.

The power of feedback: To judge what you're doing, learn what feedback is available for each platform. At the end of the week, at the same day and time, capture that data.

Posting Advice

If you're certain that you want to post on multiple sites, the trick is to be efficient about it. There are several ways to post material to social media sites:

- **Directly.** You visit each site, call up the entry screen, type in the material and upload any photos, and send. If you have several sites, this can be time-consuming and you can't schedule posts.

- **Through WordPress.** If you activate the Jetpack software in WordPress, there's an option called Publicize that lets you send a note to various social media platforms about your website post when it appears. You can edit the message to make it more SEO-friendly and even add hashtags. On the other hand, it sends the exact same message and the same piece of art to each social media outlet. It won't let you tweak it to take advantage of each social media's unique capabilities. For example, the way Facebook displays a link looks different from the way Twitter and Instagram does it. Plus, you have no way of sending more messages; you're limited to one per post.

- **Through third-party website or software.** The most popular of these is Hootsuite (*hootsuite.com*). The free version lets you post to three social networks and schedule messages. A monthly fee allows you to add more networks and access to more features. All of the accounts can be seen and posted to from one dashboard, letting you read incoming messages on them in real time while you're writing, creating, and scheduling posts.

Competitors to Hootsuite include Sendible (*sendible.com*), SocialPilot

---

> There are two ways to be a female novelist: play the game and ply everyone you encounter with sugar, or be a cool, distant ice queen, ideally ensconced for much of the year at some remote liberal arts college, disseminating your opinions only to your rapt students and never to, say, Facebook.
>
> **Emily Gould**

(*socialpilot.co*), Buffer (*buffer.com*), ContentStudio (*contentstudio.io*), Smart Post (*smartpostapp.com/*), or SocialOomph (*socialoomph.com*). For more alternatives, google "hootsuite alternatives."

● **Post design:** Each social network has its own rules and best practices for designing posts. Here, let's talk about the best way to design and write a compelling post.

The first restriction depends upon the social network. A 144-character post for Twitter imposes a restriction not seen in a Facebook post.

● **Hashtags:** A hashtag is a word that begin with the pound sign (#) that is used on social media. It acts as a keyword that people use in searches. Its use began on Twitter and has spread to Instagram, Facebook, and Pinterest. They are not used on LinkedIn or Goodreads.

Learn which hashtags are commonly used for each social media. Writers on Twitter, for example, use #amwriting to encourage everyone to continue writing. Book marketers use #bookmarketing and #bookmarket. If you post often, create a hashtag of your own and use it regularly, so people interested in your work can look up your other posts. Make it short and easy to remember and spell.

To learn more about popular hashtags, the #tagdef website (*tagdef.com/en/*) lets you search for hashtags and phrases.

Where Should You Post

Facebook is by far the dominant social media platform. With 1.5 billion users, 190 million of them in the United States, it should be the first place to set up a social media outpost.

If you're looking for younger users, head over to Instagram and Snapchat. A research study from Statistica (*statista.com/statistics/250172/social-network-usage-of-us-teens-and-young-adults/*) found that the two sites attract 79% of U.S. teenagers.

Chapter 19

Facebook

Key Points to Remember

- If you want a social media presence, make Facebook your first choice.
- Don't mix your personal life with your professional life.
- Overdoing the self-promotion will drive away readers.

> Readers are looking for three main things from authors on Facebook.
>
> 1. Behind-the-scenes glimpses into the writer's life and writing process.
>
> 2. Inside scoops on new releases, sales and upcoming events.
>
> 3. Access.
>
> **Jane Friedman**

*F*acebook should be your major social media outpost.

That's because Facebook, like it or not, is the dominant social media platform. Founded in 2005, it boasts 1.5 billion users and ranks second in usage after YouTube. According to a survey by Pew Research, of those who use Facebook in the U.S., 74% visit the site at least once a day. More than half its members visit the site several times a day.

Facebook's appeal among all age groups is wide as well. More than three-quarters of people aged 18 to 49 use Facebook. Of those age 50 to 64, 68% use the site.

The number of Facebook users is large as well. India dominates with 290 million members, followed by the United States (190 million) and Indonesia (140 million).

It is true that Facebook has disadvantages. Its user interface is unfriendly, and it can be difficult to grow your readership organically. They prefer to profit from your presence, and throw obstacles in your way to encourage you to send them money.

Still, the prospect of reaching millions of visitors is enticing, and the only way to find them is to get on the platform and start posting.

About Facebook Pages

First, you need to know that Facebook lets you create three types of pages, each with a few critical differences.

Your *profile* page is your personal page. It's supposed to have your real name, and while you're free to put your business information on it — such as identifying yourself as an author and linking to your business website — it's not supposed to be used for self-promotion. The occasional mention of your book may be fine, but out-and-out self-promotion is not.

In addition to your profile page, you can also create one of six types of *Pages*:

- Artist, band or public figure, including authors, athletes, doctors, or actors

• Company, organization, or institution, including publishing houses, non-profit groups, or churches

• Local business or place with a physical location

• Brand or product, such as clothing, cars, appliances, or toys

• Entertainment surrounding a particular product, such as a book series, album, TV channel, or movie

• Cause or community

Each type comes with different features and options.

The third type of page is *Groups*. This is for small groups of people centered around a shared interest, such as a book club, writing group, or family reunion.

Because Facebook changes how it does things frequently, I can't provide instructions on where to find and what to click. Instead, I'll point out the parts of the page that you should fill out, and list topics to write about.

Optimize Your Page

Once you've created your Facebook page, you'll need to fill it out.

• **Banner:** Facebook has changed the size of the banner several times, but currently it is 820 pixels wide by 312 pixels high. On phones, however, the banner will be 640 pixels wide by 360 pixels high, and your design will be cropped to fit, so don't put important information near the left and right edges.

• **News Feed Photos**: This is the photo which accompanies your posts. It should keep to a 4:3 ratio, meaning that if the width is 1200 pixels, the height should be 900 pixels. (This is calculated by dividing the width by 4 and multiplying the result by 3.)

There are other size limits for photos used for events and ads (both regular and carousel ads that rotate among up to 10 images and videos). Since those are advanced applications, it's best to look them up online to find the latest rules for them.

Now you're ready to update your page's information.

• **Category:** You can have up to three. Most of you will probably choose (like I did) author, writer, and publisher.

• **Username**: People will tag you using this, so use your author name instead of a business or nickname.

• **Interests:** Filling this out gives readers an idea of your hobbies and personal interests.

• **Email address:** Make it easy for people to contact you.

• **Website link**: If you don't have a website,link to your other social media accounts.

> A Facebook page again allows you to set up a following and communicate with your followers. There are also several features that allow you to sell your books on Facebook. Although this sounds perfect it is Facebook's practices that let it down. Daily they contact you and ask you to place an advert for your site. They never let up, if it is not messages and notifications, it is posts asking you on your timeline. These are so frequent they become spam. To research how effective these were I paid for one advert for £8. I got 123 views and 23 likes, not exactly the high statistics they publish.
> **Sam H. Arnold**

- **Biography:** If you have your metadata form already filled out, this should be a snap. If you've won any awards or have best-seller status, be sure to highlight them!
- **Privacy policy:** If your website has a page with a privacy policy on it, link to it here.

What to Post

First, the one type of post you shouldn't put up: self-promotion. In other words, an ad for your book. I can't think of a better way of chasing away potential readers.

I saw this a lot on Twitter. I'd get a notice that an author followed my feed, and I'd follow back, only to see that his Twitter feed was an uninterrupted stream of ads for his book. Quick unfollow.

Yes, readers would like to know your book exists, but it doesn't follow that they want to see an ad. If they did, wouldn't they watch TV instead? Plenty of ads there.

Instead, people want to visit your page to be informed and entertained. To show you what I mean, I visited 14 best-selling authors and pulled a sample post from each.

Other Topics to Write About

- Behind the scenes of your writing life: research, editing, your library
- Downloadable resources
- Invitations to join your launch team, beta readers team, or ARC readers
- Media you consume: books, movies, TV shows
- Personal photos and memories
- Quotes you live by or inspirational quotes
- Sneak peeks from your next book, including a cover reveal
- Snippets from your website blog

Is There a Best Time to Post?

There are a lot of opinions, but not much light to be shed on the subject. A study conducted by social media software producer Buffer suggests the period between 1 p.m. and 3 p.m. EST from Monday to Saturday is an optimal time. Engagement rates rise during this time, especially on Thursday and Friday.

But other studies have reached different conclusions. The answer seems to be to find the best time to post to *your* audience. Start by posting regularly, and then visit Facebook Audience Insights (*facebook.com/business/insights/ tools/audience-insights*) and learn more about who's visiting your page and when. Adjust your posting schedule and see what happens.

Advocate for Charity / John Green

> **John Green** ✓   •••
> December 9, 2018 · 🌐
>
> We're entering the last hour of the Project for Awesome.
> Thank you to everyone who has donated, supported,
> and voted! Live now in the 48th hour with Hank Green
> at http://projectforawesome.com/live. Perks still
> available at projectforawesome.com/donate.

$145,454 total donated

P4A'18

YOUTUBE.COM
Project for Awesome Kick-Off!
Donate on Indiegogo: http://projectforawesome.com...

Advocate for Politics / Amy Tan

> **Amy Tan** ✓   •••
> August 3 at 9:50 PM · 🌐
>
> 9-year-old Gio and I read about activists a couple of
> times week. We live in a dual household compound and
> it's great we can share meals and reading time in this
> new era brought on by the pandemic. Gio added
> —"and also because of Trump." After reading, our habit
> is to draw something inspired by what we learned.
> Today he chose a chapter on environmentalist Rachel
> Carson, who helped to get DDT banned. We learned
> about harm to the ecosystem and that many living
> creatures w... **See More**

Announce An Upcoming Book / Jodi Picoult

> **Jodi Picoult** 😊 feeling excited with **Random**   •••
> **House**.
> Paid Partnership · 🌐
>
> The countdown begins! I can't wait for you to read THE
> BOOK OF TWO WAYS on 9.22.20. Pre-order a copy
> today from your favorite retailer: https://bit.ly
> /2OQ2mRK

COMING IN 2 MONTHS!

Jodi Picoult

#1 NEW YORK TIMES BESTSELLING AUTHOR OF
SMALL GREAT THINGS

ON SALE
9.22.20

the
book of
two ways

Preorder today | JodiPicoult.com

Ask for Help / Rainbow Rowell

> **Rainbow Rowell** ✓   •••
> November 19, 2019 · 🌐
>
> PLEASE VOTE FOR 'WAYWARD SON' ONE MORE TIME!
> Thank you for helping it reach the Goodreads Choice
> Award finals!!

OTE IN THE FI

reads
OICE
ARDS
019

Final Round: Vote for the Best
Young Adult Fantasy & Scienc...
Discover the Best Young Adult Fanta...

Final Round: Vote
Young Adult Fanta
Discover the Best You

👍❤ 73   5 Comments 3 Shares

Celebrate Release Day / Danielle Steel

Danielle Steel ✔
July 28 at 11:40 AM · 🌐

CHILD'S PLAY is out in paperback today! The lessons our children teach us are the hardest ones. What do we do when they don't pursue our hopes for them? This riveting new novel explores how families can evolve and grow in unexpected ways. It's about learning to accept each other as we are, and learning to let our kids fly on their own wings, which is not so easy to do . . . with tears and laughter, and lessons to be learned on all sides!!! A slice of real life!!! I hope you l... **See More**

PENGUINRANDOMHOUSE.COM
Child's Play by Danielle Steel: 9780399179501 |...
NEW YORK TIMES BESTSELLER · The lessons our children teach us are the hardest ones. What do we do when our children don't pursue our hopes for them? In this riveting new novel,...

Display Your Cool Photos / Patricia Cornwell

Patricia Cornwell ✔
July 25 at 11:33 AM · 🌐

Together from a distance

Display Your Cool Videos / Paulo Coelho

Paulo Coelho ✔
July 29 at 9:38 AM · 🌐

Heart made of salt, by Christina Oiticica Bulgari @Gallery Elle

0:09 / 0:14

Cute Pet Photos / Rick Riordan

Rick Riordan ✔
July 1 · 🌐

Current mood. Zzzzz.

Humorous Posts / Nail Gaiman

Neil Gaiman ✔
July 28 at 7:24 PM · 🌐

I found myself wondering what that superhero for the Age of Trump, Florida Man, was doing these days. So I googled...

Google

🔍 florida man tries

🔍 florida man tries **to pawn his baby**
🔍 florida man tries **to run to bermuda**
🔍 florida man tries **to kill neighbors with kindness**
🔍 florida man tries **to barbecue sex offenders**
🔍 florida man tries **to attack neighbor with tractor**
🔍 florida man tries **to shoot puppy**
🔍 florida man tries **to rob gamestop**
🔍 florida man tries **to run over son**
🔍 florida man tries **to**
🔍 florida man tries **to blow up chickens**

Mini Blog Post / Zane Strebor

Zane Strebor
June 19, 2019 · 🌐

When I woke up this morning, lying in bed, I asked myself, "What are some of the secrets to success in life?" I found the answer right there in my own room. The fan said, "Be cool," the roof said, "Aim high," the window said, "See the world," the clock said, "Every minute is precious," the mirror said, "Reflect before you act," the calendar said, "Be up-to-date," and the door said, "Push hard for your goals."

👍😊😍 419   36 Comments 74 Shares

Praise Another Author / Junot Diaz

Junot Díaz ✔
May 3, 2018 · 🌐

Ali Wong is so fucking LIT. "After she finished her set to loud applause Ms. Wong drove home, pumped some milk for her baby, went to sleep and woke up at 7 a.m. to breast-feed, while her husband, Justin Hakuta, took care of their 2-1/2-year-old daughter. In her new special she raises the question of work-life balance and explains her secret. "I have a nanny," she said. "That's it."

It infuriates her that more celebrities don't acknowledge this. "It's unfair to the hard-core... **See More**

NYTIMES.COM
The Strategic Mind of Ali Wong
Thanks to sharp bits about gender roles, she's on the ...

Self Portrait / Mindy Kaling

Mindy Kaling ✔
August 2 at 5:48 PM · 🌐

Testing this whole vitamin D theory

Share Interesting Article / Lisa See

Lisa See ✓
August 2 at 3:00 AM · 🌐

We're deep into summer now! Here's a fun list of novels to read during these long, hot, and truly strange months. I love the title of the list, because it's sure appropriate these days: Nine Escapist Reads That Will Make You Feel Like You're Traveling Even Though You Can't. Ha! I love it! So happy and honored to see The Tea Girl of Hummingbird Lane included. Have you read all of these? Do you have others to recommend?

Link: bit.ly/2EhT1An

FORTUNE.COM
9 escapist reads that will make you feel like you're traveling even though you can't

Share Intimate Moments / Anne Rice

Anne Rice ✓
20h · 🌐

This is Christopher. Anne asked me to share the following message with you all.

"Today is the day our family mourns the passing of my daughter Michele Rice, lost to leukemia on this day in 1972. She was the inspiration for the beauty of Claudia in INTERVIEW WITH THE VAMPIRE. In this painful moment my heart goes out to all people who are suffering grief during this time of COVID-19."

Chapter 20
Goodreads

Key Points to Remember

- Authors have found it difficult to market their books effectively to Goodreads members.
- Linking a Goodreads account to your Facebook account risks losing reviews from FB friends.
- Since the service is free, set up your author page and make sure your books are listed.

This passion for wanting to meet the latest poet, shake hands with the latest novelist, get hold of the latest painter, devour … what is it, what is it they want from a man total that they didn't get from his work? What do they expect? What is there left of him when he's done his work? What's any artist but the dregs of his work? The human shambles that follows it around.
William Gaddis

Goodreads was founded in 2007 and acquired by Amazon in 2013. It is designed to appeal to readers. They can manage their reading list, create a virtual library of their print books, leave reviews of books, and talk about their favorite books on the site's bulletin boards.

Demographics

With 45 million visitors a month, 20 million from the U.S., it should be the ideal social network for authors. It skews heavily toward women, so writers with books written for them will find a home.

The problem with Goodreads is that there's not a lot for authors to do there. You can set up your author profile and list your books. You can route your blog through the site. You can participate in book giveaways (for a fee), but nothing I've seen shows that it's worth doing, including the one time I tried it.

Optimize Your Page

The first thing to do is to sign up for a Goodreads account. Search for your pen name and click on it. This will take you to the basic author page. At the bottom of the page, click on the link "Is this you? Let us know" and send a request to join the Author Program.

Warning: Don't log in using your other social media accounts, especially Facebook! This lets Amazon, which owns Goodreads, look at your Facebook information. If it discovers that a friend or relative of yours on Facebook also gave you a five-star review of your latest book, it will remove that review! (Thanks to Dave Chesson, the Kindlepreneur, for discovering this one amazing trick!)

Instead, create your account using an email address that is not connected to Amazon.

Like other social media accounts, you can fill out your author page with a nice photo, a brief biography, and your bookshelf of books you like.

What to Post

There's not a lot of opportunities to post. You can list your upcoming events. It will let you link your author page to your websites' RSS feed so that what you post on your blog will also show up on your author page. Goodreads also has an Ask the Author feature that let's you answer generic questions such as "What are you working on next?" But Goodreaders aren't likely to ask you questions unless they already know who you are, like Margaret Atwood (who answered 36 questions before shutting off this feature).

Trouble Spots

Goodreads does not moderate its reviews, so it attracts a high number of people who delight in anonymously savaging books and authors. The problem has gotten so bad that authors repeatedly advise each other not to engage with the site. Set up your account page, make sure your books are on there, link up your blog to it, and walk away. And don't read the reviews.

Authors Killing It Here

None. When you search for "authors killing it on Goodreads" and get a link to a review of a book on killing during wartime, your site has a problem.

One low-key alternative to Goodreads is Litsy (*litsy.com/web/home*), which bills itself as a place "where books make friends."

Readers have a loyalty that cannot be matched anywhere else in the creative arts, which explains why so many writers who have run out of gas can keep coasting anyway, propelled on to the bestseller lists by the magic words AUTHOR OF on the covers of their books.
Stephen King

I have no fans. You know what I got? Customers. And customers are your friends.
Mickey Spillane

A woman came up to me the other day and said, "You're the kiddie-book man!" I wanted to kill her.
Maurice Sendak

Chapter 21

Twitter

Key Points to Remember

- Twitter is excellent for building your profile but requires regular posting.
- The site was among the most visited but visits have declined against Facebook and YouTube.
- It can be a drain on your time and energy and a distraction if your tweets cause controversy.

> The real key to success in the self-publishing field seems to be drive and dedication, if you're the shy, mousy sort you're probably safer sticking with commercial publishing.
> **Stephen Goldin**

If you want to be noticed on the internet, say something controversial or stupid on Twitter. If you want to sell books … that's tougher.

Founded in 2006, it is among the top 50 most-visited sites on the net. Once in the top 10, it has dropped to #43, according to web traffic analysis site Alexa, while two sites favorable to authors rank much higher: YouTube (#2) and Facebook (#6).

While regular posts on Twitter can sustain or broaden your appeal, it requires putting out high-quality material, and it doesn't connect directly to sales of your books. But if you want to be a public figure, for better or for worse, Twitter is the place to be.

Demographics

Twitter's 63 million U.S. members favors males and skews toward the 18-to-30 demographic.

Optimize Your Page

On the next page is the Twitter page of Gary Shteyngart, which we'll use to illustrate how you can flesh out your page.

- **Banner:** Your header image should be 1500 pixels by 500 pixels. Your profile image (author photo) should be 400x400 pixels.
- **Pinned tweet:** One tweet can be pinned to the top of your tweetstream so anyone visiting your page can see it. Use this space to further deepen the depiction of your brand or announce an upcoming book.
- **Media Gallery:** Off to the right side is a media gallery where your last six photos or videos are published. Fill it early with tweets with visually striking images.
- **Contact settings:** Link your website.
- **Biography:** You're limited to 160 characters. If you have the short bio filled out on your metadata form, you may need to compress it further. Highlight awards or best-seller status!

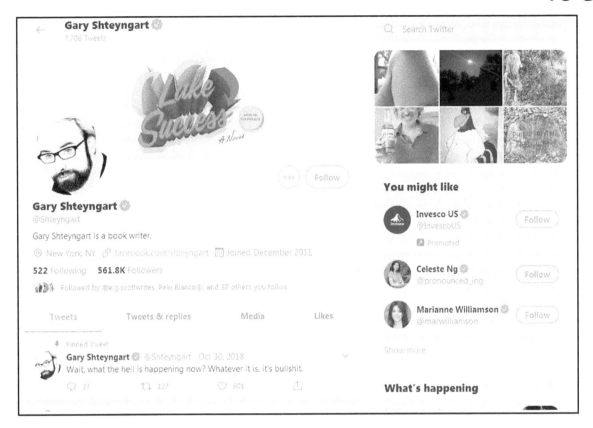

What to Post

Advocacy / Margaret Atwood

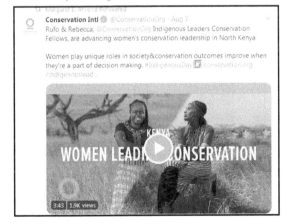

Author Shoutouts / Joyce Carol Oates

Cover Reveal / Harlan Coben

Excerpts From Your Book / Alain de Botton

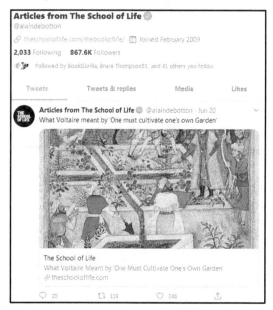

Facebook Posts / Paulo Coelho

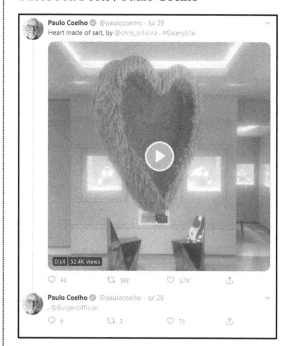

Note the added link to @Bulgariofficial, to let them know he filmed their sculpture. Good example of networking!

Humor / Gary Shteyngart

Illusion of Intimacy / Susan Orlean

Leaving / Teju Cole

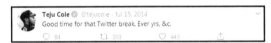

Politics / Augusten Burroughs

Quote Your Genius / Anne Lamott

Self Promotion by Others / Roxane Gay

("NBD" = no big deal)

Twitter Fan Retweets / Chuck Palahniuk

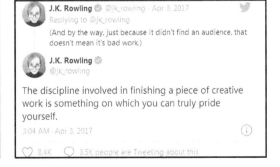

Writing Advice / J.K. Rowling

Other Topics To Write About

- Ask for book recommendations
- Behind the scenes in your writing life
- Create and answer fan or general questions
- Conduct a poll
- Highlight great reviews
- Hold a Twitter chat for a limited time
- Join trending conversations
- Promote sales and specials
- Recognize holidays and special events
- Share articles relevant to your audience

Best Time of Day to Post

You can post 24/7 from your smartphone without having to prepare art or carefully curate content. But the best time for engaging people seems to be 8-10 a.m. and 6-9 p.m. EST, presumably when people are preparing to go to work or coming home in the evening.

Noon or 5-6 p.m. have also been identified if your goals are retweets or clickthrough.

Chapter 22

Pinterest

Key Points to Remember
- Pinterest favors beautiful or provacative images over prose.
- Its membership skews heavily toward women between the ages of 18 and 49.
- One major feature is that it allows you to build multiple boards around a single subject.

Pinterest is not about connecting and chatting with people, which makes it more business-oriented and saves your time. If you stop interacting on Twitter and Facebook, people might drop you and turn away. But [on] Pinterest, nobody really cares if you leave comments or engage.

Roy Emmerson,
social media expert

This image-sharing service opened in 2010 and boasts more than 400 million monthly users, the majority of them women. In fact, the Pew Research Center estimates that 42% of all women online use Pinterest (compared to 15% of men). There are 87 million U.S. members and the site skews between 18-49.

Optimize Your Page

● **Banner:** This is not one you create yourself, but one Pinterest forms from pins you choose. It can be chosen by the latest pins, from pins other people saved from your boards, or from your favorite board.

● **Author photo:** Unlike other social media, Pinterest makes the banner image optional. So if you're not using one, your author photo predominates. Make sure it's sharp and on-brand.

● **Description:** Unlike other social media, Pinterest gives you a large footprint for your board's description. I've seen boards with a four-sentence-long description. Take advantage of it.

● **Website link:** A piece of art can have a link attached to it that leads back to your website. I've seen a bookseller link a book cover to their Shopify store.

What to Post

Pinterest is unique in that you can build multiple boards around various subjects instead of a single page centered around you.

Blog Post Promotion / Marissa Meyer

Book Covers You Love / Celeste Ng

Book Marketing Tips / Jane Friedman

Book Promotion / Meg Waite Clayton

Book Recommendations / Shana Galen

Character Inspiration / Megan Erickson

Fan Appreciation / Sylvia Day

Free Fiction / Kellie Coates Gilbert

Historical Photos / Evangeline Holland

Inspiration / Rachel Thompson

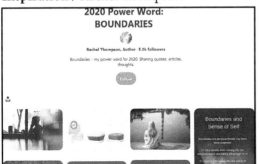

Interviews and Profiles / Elizabeth Gilbert

Personal Interests / Debbie Macomber

(The leftmost book links to Martha Stewart Living; networking!)

Podcast Promotion / Reese Ryan

Writing Advice / Sarah MacLean

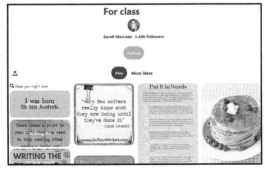

Create boards in a theme around your writing. If you write science fiction, for example, create some boards that have to do with science fiction – remember you want to draw like-minded people to you – people who may be interested to buy and read your books. It is not hard to create a theme park of boards to engage people who may like you and your books.

Karen Lotter,
social media
manager

Other Topics To Write About

Because Pinterest primarily shares pictures, it's possible to build a board on any subject. Look at your core interests as they align with your books, and use that as a starting point.

Best Time of Day to Post

Timing is not nearly as strong here as it is on Twitter or Facebook. But there are studies out there that suggest these times where viewership is at a peak: 8 to 11 p.m., 2 to 4 a.m., and 2 to 4 p.m. EST.

Chapter 23

Instagram

Key Points to Remember

- This Facebook-owned site has a high percentage of 18-24 year olds.
- Like Pinterest, it demands compelling photos, but inspirational words work too.
- Instagram offers a business page where you can access tools to boost your posts.

This Facebook-owned photo-sharing service has become popular among YA authors as a way of connecting with readers and fans. Users have found the rate of engagement is higher than on Facebook, it's easier to use, and the business page gives you access to metrics and tools to help sell books.

Demographics

The service skews more towards the under-30 crowd, with more women than men accessing the service, sometimes several times a day. It's particularly popular among the 18-24 year olds, with 75% of them using Instagram versus 57% of 25-30 year olds. The U.S. tops the list in number of users with 116 million versus India (73 million) and Brazil (82 million).

Optimize Your Account

- Connect to your Facebook business page. Post to Instagram, and it will automatically post to your Facebook page. However, there's an argument about whether this is a good thing, so check to see how your posts look in Facebook. You may need to post separately anyway.
- Create a business page. There are a thousand categories to choose from, including "author."
- Use hashtags, like #amreading, #bookstagrams, #bookish, #currentread, etc.
- Get Linktree, which allows you to store more links to your Instagram bio page.

What to Post

Photos! Lots and lots of photos! Family photos, places you've visited, evocative photos.

> Instagram is another platform that has a real writer community. It is also important to use hashtags on Instagram. Many of the same hashtags work, although, I would also use #writersofinstagram. Many writers state that using the story feature, results in more followers.
>
> **Sam H. Arnold**

Announce an Event / @jerralea

Author Selfies / @prisoliveras

Curated Photos / @foldedpagesdistillery

foldedpagesdistillery What are some ways you're satisfying your travel bug during shelter in place? My daughter and I have a continuous game on our evening walks where we pretend to be bazillionaires and plan out over the top dream vacations from every angle and detail. (Its fun and hilarious) We've watched several documentaries on different places in the world (and welcome any documentary recommendations!) and of course, all the arm chair traveling that happens when we escape into books.

I was recently gifted this beautiful copy of "Jane Was Here" from

1,648 likes

JULY 27

Launch Day / @stephaneeneee

stephaneeneee • Follow
Greensboro, North Carolina

stephaneeneee 🎉IT'S LAUNCH DAY! 🎉

it's official!

"You Were Worth the Wait" is ready to GO!

👇👇👇a sentence I still can't believe I'm saying!!!

you know this has been a LONG time coming + I'm absolutely speechless as we announce this launch!😭.

I never in my life believed that this would be a reality, but my lifelong dream has come true + today I am absolutely honored to share this part

575 likes

12 HOURS AGO

Personal Photos / @kristenkill

Question Your Audience / @bookworms.mk

Share a Video / @ramid.caliphh

Share Your Poetry / @_maledetto

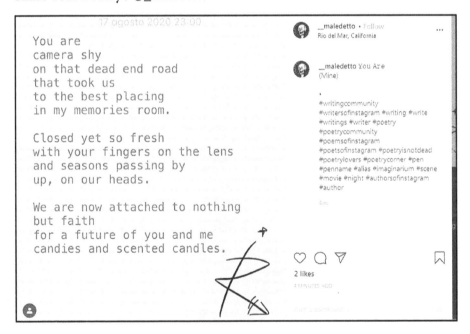

Share Your Writing / @moriah_jane

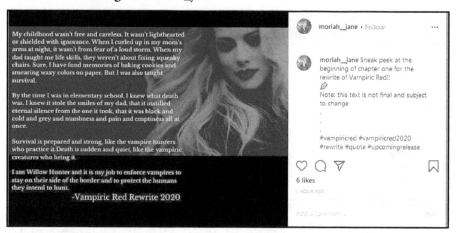

My childhood wasn't free and careless. It wasn't lighthearted or shielded with ignorance. When I curled up in my mom's arms at night, it wasn't from fear of a loud storm. When my dad taught me life skills, they weren't about fixing squeaky chairs. Sure, I have fond memories of baking cookies and smearing waxy colors on paper. But I was also taught survival.

By the time I was in elementary school, I knew what death was. I knew it stole the smiles of my dad, that it instilled eternal silence from the one it took, that it was black and cold and grey and numbness and pain and emptiness all at once.

Survival is prepared and strong, like the vampire hunters who practice it. Death is sudden and quiet, like the vampiric creatures who bring it.

I am Willow Hunter and it is my job to enforce vampires to stay on their side of the border and to protect the humans they intend to hunt.

-Vampiric Red Rewrite 2020

moriah__jane • Follow

moriah__jane Sneak peek at the beginning of chapter one for the rewrite of Vampiric Red!!
Note: this text is not final and subject to change

#vampiricred #vampiricred2020 #rewrite #quote #upcomingrelease

6 likes
1 HOUR AGO

Share Weird Things / @rooopecore

KEEP IT IN MIND!

rooopecore • Follow

rooopecore "I am convinced I have been programmed to function like a machine with purpose
Sometimes I cannot differ between making a choice and being convinced I'm making one
Life is a command chain of real misery and imaginary happiness drenched in gasoline
And the instruction manual is just a guide on how to light the matchsticks"
RooopeCore//

1h

rooopecore #words #wordgasm #writer #author #poet #poem #writings #writing #writersofinstagram #writersofig

16 likes
1 HOUR AGO

Tweets / Read It Forward

Best Time of Day to Post

Early in the morning, like 6 a.m. EST from Tuesday to Friday, noon to 4 p.m., and noon Saturday. This is usually when people have time to check their phones for a little distraction.

Some authors use Instagram to keep their fans and followers updated. In fact, you can keep your readers up-to-date on your entire writing process, from jotting down ideas all the way to publication. This way your book will be more top-of-mind when it becomes available for purchase — that's a good thing.

Dave Chesson

Chapter 24
Organization

- Work is done by breaking big tasks down into small tasks and doing them one by one.
- Setting up a production list ensures nothing is forgotten and critical details are remembered.
- Keeping good records demonstrate to the IRS that you're running a business.

You don't actually do a project; you can only do action steps related to it. When enough of the right action steps have been taken, some situation will have been created that matches your initial picture of the outcome closely enough that you can call it "done."

David Allen,
author of *Getting Things Done: The Art of Stress-Free Productivity*

Children have this amazing ability to dive into anything without thinking about the consequences. There's no restraint, no second-guessing, just do it.

Your writing may seem like that at first. You're firing on all cylinders, putting it down on paper. You're publishing stories, networking with authors, following up on emails, getting editors and cover artists in line, and checking your ads. And you're keeping all the details in your head.

Eventually, you'll run into a wall. You'll miss deadlines, or forget crucial facts. You read about an interesting marketing technique, vow to try it, but never do.

When that happens for the umpteen time, you realize that day has come.

It's time to get organized.

Master To-Do List / Week's To-Do List

There's a debate in the self-help and productivity world about to-do lists. Some like them, while some contend that seeing a long list of endless chores hampers creativity and encourages you to stall.

Which system is best? I have a rule for that, and it applies to everything, whether it involves organization, dieting, saving money, even plotting stories:

"The best system for you is the one you use the most."

In my case, I'm a to-do list fan. I love keeping track of important tasks on paper and not my smartphone — which I don't carry — or a computer program.

Compared to our ancestors a century ago, our lives are much more complicated. I come from a long line of farmers in northeast Ohio. For generations, their lives revolved around the seasonal cycle. They grew

crops, raised animals, kept their family safe, and attended church. They lived simple lives that required a deep knowledge about a few vital subjects.

Today, we have to do all that, but we also need to know how to maintain our cars, computers, and smartphones. We have to manage our investments and savings, taxes, and health care. We have to quickly master tasks that come up suddenly, such as helping your teen apply to college, teaching them how to drive, or figuring out how to squeeze more bookcases into a crowded house.

Add to that running your writing business, and you need a system to keep track of your tasks.

Which brings us to to-do lists. I use several kinds.

Permanent List

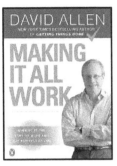

In his *Getting Things Done* system, David Allen suggests reducing the drag on your mental energy by emptying your head of every task you need to perform, no matter how small. Maintaining a list of tasks that you can review weekly, he argues, frees your mind of the mental effort needed to remember them, energy you can devote to more creative and productive work.

List-making is especially useful for long-term projects. When we moved to Hershey, we bought a home that needed renovations. A lot of them. We drew up a list with subheads such as "landscape," "outside house," "living room," "kitchen," and "dining room." Every time we came across something that had to be painted, replaced, cleaned, or repaired, we added it to the list. Major jobs such as stopping the basement from leaking water during rainstorms were broken down into tasks, such as applying Dry-Loc to the walls, rebuilding the front sidewalk, and attaching elbows to the downspouts.

The master list was pinned to the bulletin board in the kitchen. As each task was completed, it was lined through. This gave us instant positive feedback — "look at what we're accomplishing" — as well as reminding us what still had to be done.

Weekly To-Do List

Having a permanent list provides a useful place to start, but you may find it easier to add a shorter second list to use during the week.

Each night, I sit down and write in my small notebook the next day's list. Exercise at the top, followed by work on the next book. Social media posts in the afternoon, followed by smaller tasks that I'll try to squeeze in.

On Sundays, I'll sit down with my notebook, go over the list, cross off completed tasks, write in new tasks, and renegotiate the existing tasks. Do they still need to be done? Can they be put on the backburner for some mythical later?

> Every human being has exactly the same amount of time, and yet consider the output of Robert Louis Stevenson, John Peabody Harrington, Isaac Asimov, Ray Bradbury, William Goldman, Neil Simon, Joyce Carol Oates, Agatha Christie, and John Gardner. How did they accomplish what they have? They weren't deflected from their priorities by activities of lesser importance. The work continues, even though everything else may have to give. They know that their greatest resource is themselves. Wasting time is wasting themselves. When people ask them, "Where'd you find the time?" They wonder, "Where do you lose it?"
> **Kenneth Atuchity**

Succeeding at 90% (or 60%, or 30%)

It used to bother me. I'd adopt a new system, only to find that I couldn't do everything it demanded. I'd work through the to-dos, but I couldn't do it all. It was discouraging.

Over time, I realized something. Even though I didn't get everything done, I did more than when I didn't have a list or a system in place.

Understanding that I made progress gave me the confidence to keep going, and not be discouraged when I fell short of my goals.

Time Management

If we focus on the task at hand instead of fretting about how much work we have to do, we get more done. (That's also an argument *against* using to-do lists; they force us to confront what we have to do instead of bearing down and doing them.)

But it's also true that you only get 24 hours in a day.

In the end, you have to do what works for you. But it is useful to remind yourself that worrying never accomplishes anything, and that we can be surprised at what we can accomplish if we get out of our own ways. Twenty-four hours: never more; never less.

This means you'll have to make tough decisions: push hard to finish your next book, or get that website up

Time management at its best

Courtesy Jeff Bacon and Broadside Cartoons, www.navybroadside.com/

and running? When will you find time for social media? And what about advertising on Amazon and Facebook?

Fortunately, your books are always fresh. Unlike traditional publishing, which gives your new book six weeks for it to hit and then it's over, you can relaunch your books. You can put new covers on them, or launch an advertising campaign that will boost your sales a year after it came out. There are authors who have seen their books become best sellers years later.

If you've got a day job and you're raising your kids and you don't have much time, use what you can to create a great series of books. Start slow. Bootstrap your way up the ladder. There are sales strategies you can employ later that will help you find your audience. Be patient.

Project Management

Once upon a time, traditionally published successful writers had it easy. They'd spend their mornings writing, and when they had achieved their word count, devote the rest of their day living their lives. Maybe do a little research, submit to an interview about their latest book, or do some light editing over a cocktail.

At least, that's the image put out by writers like Lawrence Block, Mary Higgins Clark, and Anne River Siddons. Sure, getting there was a tough road, but once you were inside the publishing world and selling books, it seemed like a pretty good gig.

Block: "Some days the writing flows and I can do my five pages in one glorious hour. When that happens, I'm free to do as I wish with the rest of the day."

Clark: "Typically, she has a cup of coffee in her office in the morning, then writes or edits until lunch."

Siddons: "Each morning, Siddons dresses, puts on her makeup and then heads out to the backyard cottage that serves as her office. And each night, she and her husband edit the day's work by reading it aloud over evening cocktails." †

To be honest, these writers worked hard to get to that level of success. They worked long hours to hone their writing and editing skills. They battled personal problems familiar to every family: the death of a spouse, multiple marriages, and alcohol problems. But at least the majority of their job involved writing and editing.

Indie writers never had that option. Even if they don't do social media or have a website, high-income writers have to publish fast and hone their marketing chops, and keep it up.

This is where project management comes in.

What Is Project Management?

When corporations decide to do something, whether it's to launch a new product, create and sell a piece of software, or even move the offices to a new location, they form teams, make plans, assign responsibilities, and create a schedule with deadlines.

You, the indie author, won't have nearly this big a task. But if you're

---

† *Block:* Block, Lawrence. *Writing the Novel*, p. 124. *Clark:* Kalb, Peggy Edersheim, "Murder, She Word Processes," *The Wall Street Journal*, Sept. 4, 1998, pg. W11A. *Siddons:* "Peachtree Road," *Powell's City of Books*, http://www.powells.com/book/peachtree-road-9780061097232

SALES

TASK	TARGET DATE	OWNER	STATUS
1) Letter to advertisers communicating new pub dates/deadlines	12/14	AC/JL	•
2) Business cards to printer for both LMG + ACS	12/14	AC/JL	LMG ACS
3) Sales collateral ready for use	12/14	AC/JL	
4) List of New York activities for Kim	12/20	DO/All	•
5) Update Machine w/ new territory structure	1/6	AC/JL/DM	

PRODUCTION

TASK	DATE	OWNER	STATUS
1) Setup monitors in PubHub	12/28	JL	•
2) Conduct 2nd pageflow/Plate Test	12/28	AC	
3) Resend pageflow doc	12/27	AC	•

CONTENT

TASK	TARGET DATE	OWNER	STATUS
1) Ensure all styles and libraries are final	12/21	AC/JL	•
2) Summarized defects + outstanding issues from 12/12 Dry-run	12/13	AC/JL	•
3) Review page flow schedule and approval/post mortem mtg	12/21	AC/JL	•
4) Follow up on agate decision and next steps/ramifications on other groups	12/13	AC/JL	
5) Review automatic flows onto page	12/13	AC/JL	•
6) Document Plan B for CMS	12/28	AC/JL	
7) Confirm page flow test plan	12/13	AC/JL	•
8) Complete final Style Guide	12/26	AC/JL	
9) Complete testing of Event Tracker	12/17	AC/JL	•
10) Validate photo workflow and communicate changes to the broader team	12/27	Ashwin	
11) Follow up on Newsletter development and delivery	12/19	AC/JL	•
12) Test Newsletters	12/28	AC/JL	
13) Develop BCS pageflow schedule for 1/7	12/28	AC/JL	•
14) Finalize Folder structure	12/21	AC/JL	•

Project management at Bill's last newspaper job when they moved from daily publication to three times weekly. I hope nothing you do will be on this level of complexity.

developing a book series, for example, you'll potentially have a lot of interlocking components to manage:

- Plot and write the books.
- Get the books edited, whether through an editor you find and hire, or from your spouse, friends, fellow writers, or beta readers. You'll have to create the PDF or ebook, send them out, set a deadline for comment, then revise based on their notes.
- Maintain a series bible to keep track of characters, place descriptions, customs and other world-building elements. (Yes, George R.R. Martin doesn't use one. He relies on two hardcore fans to answer his questions. When you're a best-selling author, you can do that too.)
- Hire a cover artist and supply him with a brief.
- Write the book description and ad copy.
- Create and run advertising and marketing campaigns.

- Keep track of your daily work. If you deduct your expenses and the IRS comes calling for an *whisper* audit, you'll need proof that this is a full-time job and not a hobby. A daily work diary proves your intent.
- Track your expenses, income and number of books sold. The IRS wants to know.
- Record statistics you need to review, such as the results of your advertising campaigns, the number of visitors to your website, and the number of times your newsletters are opened. Use this feedback to determine which strategies are working and where improvements need to be made.
- File your correspondence, research materials, drafts and outlines, and any other material passing across your desk worth saving. Organization counts, and will pay off the moment you can get your hands quickly on a vital piece of paper.
- Determine a publishing schedule for next four quarters. This could be as complex or a simple as you like. Start by deciding what books are you publishing in each quarter. Set a date, then work backward, taking into account your productivity, including how many days a week you're working.

In the end, if you know how many words a day you can produce, you'll get a good idea when the book will be ready for the editor, when to schedule a cover, when to develop an ad campaign, and the lag time between ordering print copies and receiving them.

To help fill out your production checklist and business plan, here are some online resources that I found useful as a source of ideas:

- Jane Friedman provides a self-publishing checklist with estimated times it would take for freelancers to do their jobs. (*janefriedman.com/self-publishing-checklist/*)
- IngramSpark's simpler checklist breaks the publishing process down into segments. (*ingramspark.com/blog/book-production-schedule*)
- Carla King wrote an excellent book production checklist covering the construction of your book including front and back matter and cover templates. (*sfwriters.org/wp-content/uploads/2019/02/bookproductionchecklist.pdf*)
- Best-selling author Denise Grover Swank wrote a three-part series about her business plan used during the production of two series:

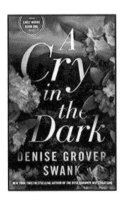

- Part One (*denisegroverswank.com/a-business-plan-for-indie-authors-part-one/*)
- Part Two (*denisegroverswank.com/a-business-plan-for-indie-authors-part-two/*)
- Part Three (*denisegroverswank.com/a-business-plan-for-indie-authors-part-three/*)

Book Production Checklist

As the production guru behind Peschel Press, I found that I needed to automate as many of my processes as possible. Because I can't remember all the details, I created this Production Checklist to guide me. The Word file sits on my hard drive, and I print it out and write the book's title on it as soon as I need the form.

Here's my current checklist. I deleted information specific to the functioning of Peschel Press, and replaced names with [Generic Types of Information].

Generic Book Production Checklist

Title: _____

☐ Finish manuscript draft! Before you start; think. Did you revise everything you wanted? It's easier to do it now than after you create two Word files for the ebook and trade paperback editions.

☐ Copy edit manuscript

☐ Copyright page

☐ Chapter titles against table of contents

☐ Numbered chapters for correct sequence (1,2,3)

☐ Series of words for parallel structure

☐ Proper names for consistency, accuracy, checkmark as you go

☐ Parentheses to ensure they're paired

☐ Quote marks to ensure they're paired and no doubles w/in doubles

☐ Paragraph indents. First paragraph in chapter and after line space is not indented.

☐ Spellcheck manuscript

☐ Grammarcheck manuscript

☐ Get Bowker ISBN

☐ Contact Library of Congress Preassigned Control Number program (no closer than two weeks to publication) to receive number for copyright page.

☐ Proof manuscript file on Kindle before splitting into two formats.

☐ Fill out METADATA file from Peschel Press folder.

Create Trade Paperback

☐ Flow text into interior template file. Code original MS by finding italics and bold and coding them (like %%% or @@@). Save as text file, delete words in template file. Reopen text file into Word, cut and paste into interior template.

☐ Create EBOOK file. Delete MANUSCRIPT TPB file. Corrections made

---

Discipline is never a restraint. It's an aid. The first commandment of the romantic school is: "Don't worry about grammar, spelling, pronunciation, vocabulary, plot or structure — just let it come." That's not writing; that's vomiting, and it leads to uncontrolled, unreadable prose. Remember: Easy writing makes hard reading, but hard writing makes it easy reading.

Florence King

Ill-fitting grammar are like ill-fitting shoes. You can get used to it for a bit, but then one day your toes fall off and you can't walk to the bathroom.

Jasper Fforde

after this will be made to the TPB's interior template file and the ebook file.

☐ TABLE OF CONTENTS: To add leaders, either assign a leader to the first line, then update the TableOfContents style, or if you're using a previous template already modified, use the style.

☐ Format text using Styles

☐ Format poems, messages (telegrams, notes)

☐ Add back matter

☐ Add section breaks

☐ Style display heads.

☐ Add interior art. Greyscale if needed. Make sure final versions are kept in separate folder, and that all are the right size by adding horizontal and vertical resolution columns in windows explorer. Art must be 300dpi JPGs except for line art, which must be 600dpi BMPs.

☐ Add header

☐ Add page numbers. Make sure first page of each chapter does not have them.

Proof Trade Paperback

☐ PROOF START: Print PDF pages and cover and edit

☐ Proof cover, back cover text, spine

☐ Proof captions

☐ Check for widows and orphans (single words only)

☐ Check excessively tight or loose lines

☐ Paragraphs have ending punctuation

☐ Wrong-word errors

☐ Run Spellcheck and Pro Writing Aid PROOF FINISH

☐ Before making PDF, decompress all artwork (do not save)

☐ Print PDF using Save As PDF in Word or Nitro extension

☐ Check PDF to make sure chapter titles are at proper place

☐ Ensure styles are applied consistently

☐ Build cover / back cover

When TPB Is Finished

☐ Load onto KDP; set pages to CREAM

☐ When book appears at Amazon, claim on Author's Page Bibliography

☐ Update BookBub Author page

☐ Set up Goodreads page

☐ Send press release and b/w 300dpi of book cover to media outlets and groups that accept them (writers groups)

☐ Post to Facebook groups that accept them. DO NOT SPAM GROUPS.

☐ Copy book covers into "BUSINESS Book Cover" folder

> Self-editing is simply something people learn over time as they strive to make their comics better, people with the skill to know the difference. You need that skill, so don't be shy about it, look at your comic and think to yourself about what you like and don't like, and be honest about it. Then, like everything else, just keep working.
>
> **Kate Beaton,**
> cartoonist

□ Create book page at your website

Prep IngramSpark TPB

□ Update interior file before making a new PDF. Update copyright notice, check ads in the back of the book. Make sure that grayscale art is 300dpi saved JPG and line art is 600dpi saved BMP.

□ Submit information to Ingram for cover template (bookmark in My Other Accounts folder). Get PDF.

□ Visit https://pdf2jpg.net/ to convert PDF to JPG

□ Resize cover art on template.

□ Make sure document size is as stated in lower-left-hand-corner (for 6x9 it's 15x12).

□ Save as CMYK. Make sure it's not compressed.

□ Check file's horizontal and vertical dimensions in Windows Explorer.

□ Post to IngramSpark.

When We Receive TPB

□ File copyright with Library of Congress. Double-check spelling of title, author and other info. Send two copies to Library of Congress.

□ Send one copy to satisfy the CIP program obligation to Library of Congress; US Programs, Law, and Literature Division; Cataloging in Publication Program; 101 Independence Ave., S.E.; Washington, D.C. 20540-4283

□ Mail copies to friends / reviewers

□ Note on Free Book List File

□ Add book to Bookshop.org site

□ Announce in newsletter.

Create Ebook

□ Copy artwork into new folder

□ Check artwork for size (79dpi, 600px wide); cover (300dpi, 600px wide); and type (RGB).

□ Compare EBOOK file with TPB template file using the Word function.

□ Add End Page — Newsletter solicitation with CTA

□ Add catalog page, author photo, at end of main text and BEFORE footnotes

□ Ensure publication names are italicized/non-italicized where appropriate

□ Bold and underline footnote title

□ Underline footnote link

□ Add back copy text to front

☐ Move copyright to back.
☐ Add line: Ebook version by [company]
☐ Add ** links to artwork
☐ Modify Table of Contents as needed
☐ Proof captions
☐ Run Spellcheck
☐ Run Grammarcheck
☐ Create ebook, using Kindle Create for KDP, Jutoh for rest.

When Ebook Is Produced

☐ Proof ebook.
☐ Check footnote links by working back to front, front to back, then move down to next footnote and repeat.
☐ Check for correct placement of art and spelling/facts in captions.
☐ Check hyperlinks
☐ Load onto Kindle, Nook, Kobo, Google Play
☐ Load onto Smashwords (for iTunes and other sites)
☐ Announce on newsletter

When Ebook Has Appeared on Sites

☐ Update sales spreadsheet with new title
☐ Update website book page with links
☐ Update Amazon Author Page bibliography
☐ Update Goodreads
☐ Send announcement to groups
☐ Set up Google Alert for book's title

Organize Your Company

In Part 1 we did the minimum organization of your company, because at that point you were more interested in writing and publishing a book. Now it's time to think about your company's future, how it will be organized, keeping track of your data, and keeping the IRS off your back.

Warning: Before you make any decisions, consult with your accountant or tax attorney (I am neither). Do not rely on this information without double-checking it.

When Should You Set Up an LLC or Corporation?

When you're just starting out, when it's just you and the computer and your first book, a sole-proprietorship is all you'll need. As you generate income and turn a profit, you may want the advantages and protection of a more organized structure. A company gives you tax breaks, meaning you'll pay less in taxes. If your company goes bankrupt, the creditors can't go after your personal assets.

How much income? Somewhere between $25,000 and $100,000, with the exact point where you're not creating enough in expenses to offset against your income. When you're making a little profit, the tax burden won't feel like much. But as your income grows, you'll want to keep more of what you earn. Unless you *like* paying the state more taxes at your income level than everyone else.

Forming an LLC or a corporation would allow you to write off income in ways that you can't do as a sole-proprietorship, such as hiring your children or leasing a new car for business purposes.

But income is not the only reason to consider forming a company. Here are three more:

WARNING

• **Lawsuits:** You get sued because someone recognized themselves in your novel or tell-all memoir, or someone slips outside your tent at a craft show. An LLC shields your personal assets from any court judgments.

• **International partnerships:** This happened: You're the writer of a webcomic and you're working with an artist in another country, and you two agree to share the profits.

Ordinarily, this would call for a limited partnership or an LLC. But the artist is in Canada and the writer is in the United States. Congratulations! They get twice the paperwork to fill out and twice the tax forms.

They solved the problem by having the writer form the company, with the artist working as an employee, and the profits split according to a formula. They also agreed to make the writer the operator of the business. Not only did this simplify matters, but it freed the artist to work full-time.

• **Sales tax:** Peschel Press exists as a sole-proprietorship, with no official presence. However, it does have a tax ID number with the State of Pennsylvania. We sell books at trade shows, festivals, and conventions, so we're required by law to collect the sales tax and file a form twice a year. Pennsylvania required a business name, hence: Peschel Press.

Because we buy books for resale to the public, I also filed forms with Amazon and IngramSpark so I don't have to pay them sales tax. This was a pain, but it only had to be done once.

Note that when we sell books to bookstores for resale, I'm acting as a wholesaler. The bookstore is responsible for collecting and paying the sales tax.

Learning these details is part of acquiring the business mindset.

Three Business Models

You can organize your business in four ways, from easiest to most

> The reality is there's very few really fine agents, so if you don't learn about the business of publishing and understand the economics of how it works, you become a victim, and you can't protect your art that way.
> **Dean Koontz**

complex: sole-proprietorship, limited liability company, corporation, and S corporation. There are also nonprofits, cooperatives, and limited partnerships, but they are more appropriate for other types of businesses and will not be covered here.

Sole-Proprietorship

What it is: A business with no official recognition.

Cost: Free.

Amount of paperwork: Small, but pay attention to the laws at the local and state levels. Does your local government or homeowners association limit or forbid working out of your home? Are writers allowed in a residential zone (most likely, since you shouldn't have customers parking outside and tractor-trailers hauling books)? Do you need to file your business name with the state, commonly called "doing business as"?

Going forward, consider setting up a checking account in the business' name. It's much easier to track your income and expenses when they flow in and out of a dedicated account, and it'll keep your household money from mixing with business money. It will also show the IRS that this is a business and not a hobby.

Advantages: 1. Cheap to run and simple to dissolve. 2. Few paperwork hassles. 3. Your business income is not taxed separately, but appears on your standard tax form.

Disadvantages: 1. You can't sell stock to raise money and banks are reluctant to make business loans. 2. If you lose a lawsuit, you're personally liable for any judgments. 3. The IRS audits sole proprietorships far more often than LLCs and corporations. In fact, once you're earning more than $100,000, you are five times more likely to be audited than an S Corp.

Limited Liability Corporation

What it is: An official status that gives you the asset protection of an incorporated business. It can consist of one owner, two or more owners, or a combination of individuals, corporations, or other LLCs.

There are several subcategories of LLCs: sole proprietorship (the default choice made for you unless you choose otherwise), S Corporation, C Corporation, and disregarded entity, which will not be discussed here, but is mentioned for completeness' sake.

Cost: Varies. Some of the paperwork can be bought from legal sites, and filing fees vary from state to state (currently $125 in Pennsylvania).

Amount of paperwork: Substantial. You register your business name with the state, file articles of incorporation or a docketing statement that describes how your LLC is set up and who's involved and possibly an operating

> Until you've established a track record, it's unlikely you'll attract a skilled agent, and a bad agent — or a shyster masquerading as an agent — can do one's career far more harm than good.
>
> **Robert B. Parker**

agreement setting out the rules for how the LLC is run. Hiring employees requires more paperwork: employment taxes, workers' compensation insurance, and informational returns with the IRS. You may also consider opening a bank account and getting a credit card in your business' name. Separating your business from personal expenses will make it much easier to keep track of come tax time.

Rules for LLCs, and corporations as well, vary from state to state. Check your state's website and a consultant for further information.

LLCs' Advantages: 1. Your personal assets are shielded if the business goes belly-up. But it's a "limited" liability; you're not protected if you or your employees break the law. 2. There's more record-keeping than a sole-proprietorship, but less than a corporation. 3. The members decide how the profits are shared. 4. You pay less taxes than a sole-proprietorship, and your chance of getting audited is lower as well.

LLCs' Disadvantages: 1. In many states, the LLC must be dissolved if a member leaves it, unless there are provisions allowing it. 2. Members must pay the federal self-employment tax that finances Medicare and Social Security.

S Corps' Advantages: 1. An S corporation is not taxed; only the wages plus any distribution of profits, which is taxed at a lower rate. However, this varies from state to state. 2. Depending on the state, shareholders can leave without forcing the business to close.

S Corps' Disadvantages: 1. Paperwork and recordkeeping similar to that of corporations. 2. The IRS keeps track of the ratio between salaries and distributions and audits corporations with low salaries.

Corporation

What it is: A business, with shareholders, employees, and headaches. We'll get into this briefly, but unless you're planning on building a real company, you shouldn't worry about this.

Cost: Substantial. Legal Zoom, a business which sells templates for legal procedures, suggests $100-$250 for filing the articles of incorporation, $800-$1,000 franchise tax (unless you set up in Nevada; then it's free), $50-$200 government filing fees, plus attorneys fees that start at $500.

Amount of paperwork: Substantial: register business name, trademark it, acquire licenses and permits (if needed), and file articles of incorporation. You'll need people to fill the board and issue stock certificates. You'll also need a lawyer versed in the process to guide you.

Advantages: 1. Similar limited liability protection as in LLCs. 2. Easier to raise capital. 3. Tax advantages. 4. Easier to hire qualified help, especially if you offer stock in the company.

Disadvantages: 1. Depending on local, state, and federal laws, you'll need to keep track of filing forms and keeping accurate records. 2. It costs more money to administer a corporation, such as paying annual fees to the state. 3. Double taxation: Money flowing to the corporation gets taxed, and taxed again when it pays employees.

Data

Feedback is an important element in the business mindset. You need information at every stage of the publishing process. You need an editor or beta reader to look over your work, another eye on cover designs, someone to vet your book descriptions, and a way to record book sales and website visits.

The best data retrieval system is one where you can lay your hands on the information quickly. For example, if someone wanted to know our best-selling book last year, I can find the answer in a few minutes. If you can do that, you have a successful system.

Tracking Your Stories

In the beginning, it's easy to remember where your stories have been. But as you write more and more, it becomes harder to tell them apart. And if you write nonfiction essays, opinion pieces, and guest posts, it becomes easy to forget what went where.

In pre-computer days, efficient writers used index cards. That's what I'll describe here.

Here's what a sample file card looks like:

> "THE ADVENTURE OF THE WHYOS"
> Story, 9,300 words
> Written 2/3/11 – 2/8/11
>
> Submissions:
> *Ellery Queen* 3/5/11 Rejected 3/19/11
> *Alfred Hitchcock* 3/20/11 Rejected 3/27/11
> Published as ebook 4/11/11
> Published in *The Casebook of Twain and Holmes* May 4, 2018

This format could be adapted as an Excel spreadsheet. By adding category tags it'll be easy to find all your articles on a certain subject, like book reviews, how-to-write posts, or unpublished short stories of a certain length.

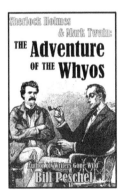

> "But you've written lots of books," said Joyce; "you make a lot of money out of them, don't you?"
>
> "In a way," said Mrs. Oliver, her thoughts flying to the Inland Revenue. **Ariadne Oliver,** Agatha Christie's author avatar in *Hallowe'en Party*.

You and the IRS

Before we go any further, know this:

I am not a tax attorney.

Do not accept any of this advice as gospel, final, or binding. Always follow the tax codes, local, state, and federal, that apply to you and your business. Tax laws change, and you should rely on competent help to handle your finances.

If you're going to deduct your publishing expenses on your income tax return, you need to keep track of them. At tax time, your accountant will apportion those expenses throughout your return. In other words, a deduction for gas mileage to your book event might be listed in a different part of the form than your marketing purchases. So you must list each expense separately, and then add them up. Don't give your accountant only the totals, such as X for publicity and X for meals and travel. You may find that some of your expenses should not be claimed, or that you don't want to claim too many deductions relative to your income.

Consistently keeping track of your expenses will also make your accountant's job easier. Tax time is the major season in a CPA's life. Every client has to file a return, and most of the time they come into the office at the last minute, bearing a shopping bag stuffed with receipts.

Don't be one of those people. The tax year ends on Dec. 31, and if you show up on Feb. 1 with your income and your expenses neatly laid out, not only will you get a major obstacle out of the way, but you'll ensure that your CPA will stick by you for life. Clients who are easy to work don't show up every day.

How to Keep Track

If you use Excel to keep track of your book sales, there's no reason why you shouldn't use it to keep track of your expenses. Set up a simple file for the year that allows you to list the date, type, and amount, with a separate column for income and expenses.

I've created a simple spreadsheet that you can download and modify for your own uses. Plus, I'll throw in another spreadsheet that's even more basic, that allows you to enter your expenses according to their type (research, advertising, legal services).

Recording Your Work

If you're going to claim business expenses on your tax form, get into the habit of recording your work each day.

It can be as simple as a computer file or a notebook. I carry a portable

	JULY		
Date	Income / Expenses	Credit	Debit
2-Jul	State Sales and Use Tax, 1st half of 2015		17.09
3-Jul	ABEBooks (Ill. His. Of Weapons, Swords, Spears, etc.)		12.47
9-Jul	CreateSpace (12 SH Edwardian I)		77.28
13-Jul	CreateSpace (7 Punch shipped to Mysterious Bookshop)		33.28
17-Jul	lulu	5.46	
18-Jul	Facebook charge to boost booksigning post (must be app. 24 hr)		10.00
17-Jul	7 Punch to Mysterious Bookshop 106 (Paid #29125/8/10/15)	67.13	
18-Jul	Cupboardmaker Books 1 Punch	10.15	
20-Jul	Kindle Worlds	2.72	
20-Jul	Nook	10.36	
20-Jul	Smashwords	14.95	
23-Jul	7 Victorian, plus 1 of rest from CS to Mysterious Bookshop		76.79
27-Jul	ABEBooks Across America on Emigrant Train		3.49
28-Jul	7 Victorian from CS to Mysterious Bookshop 107 (unpaid)	66.99	
29-Jul	5 Punch signed to Mysterious Bookshop 108 (Paid #29134; 8/12/15)	47.95	
29-Jul	CreateSpace	65.52	
Total		291.23	230.40

We use a more complicated version that divides expenses into categories,
but this is good if you're starting your writing career.

notebook to track my to-do list and record ideas and other information

When I can, I also write down the time. Usually when I started and stopped a task. Not only does this tell the IRS how much time I worked in a day, but more importantly it tells me how much time I worked. This acts as a feedback loop to let me know if I'm working too much (rare) or not enough (frequent).

Accounting

How much accounting do you need to do? Not as much as you fear, but probably more than what you're doing.

Accounting is keeping score, and there are writers who love being hands-on with numbers. Michael Anderle, a thriller writer who was also a software programmer, was comfortable with spreadsheets. In his interview with *The Author Biz* podcast, he could rattle off the number of clickthroughs and conversation rates for each day's advertising on Facebook.

This is useful data to know, but when you're starting out, stick with the basics. When you're more comfortable and have a procedure set up, add to it to suit your needs.

Since the numbers you're working with involve a lot of addition and subtraction, it's time to get comfortable using a spreadsheet program. Even if all you want to do is to add and subtract your income vs. expenses, it's best to let your computer do the math.

On my website, I have a basic Excel 2007 spreadsheet file you can adapt for your own use. It consists of four columns: date, description, income, and expense. It automatically does the math and even gives you the monthly and year-end balances.

> Writing history… Is similar to accounting: you enter facts into the accounting system you've devised in support each entry with a document delivered into the system from the real world. I was going to say writing history is more creative than that, but then we've all heard about how creative accounting can be.
> **Richard Rhodes**

This sales sheet lets us keep track of how many of each book we sell at an event. A copy of this is available in the resources section of our website. Look at the Resources chapter in the Appendix for the URL.

The other component to keep track of is book sales. This takes a little more work, and it doesn't seem like much of a result, but after a year or two, the benefits begin to show. Tracking your book sales each month shows you your hits and misses and how much you're earning on each platform. If you publish a wide variety of books, instead of a series, you'll be able to tell in which direction your sales are trending. At least you'll feel more comfortable with your decisions because they'll be backed by solid numbers.

After that, it's up to you. Here are some other things to track:

● **Tracking visitors to your website.** Your blogging software, such as WordPress, keeps track of how many visitors your site receives and which posts they read. Your website host has tools such as AWStats and Webalizer that track of a lot of statistics. So many, in fact, that it can be overwhelming. Hint: Keep it simple, and look only for the Visitors and Unique Visitors Columns.

● **Ad campaigns.** Feedback is a vital tool to making these work. Even if you're spending only $5 of $10 a day on an Amazon ad campaign, wouldn't you like to know how many visitors it is drawing? How many books were sold? Can you spend less and get the same results?

Taxes

I'm not versed in tax law. I only pay them. This section will focus only on how best to handle your dealings with the government. Specific tax strategies should be taken up by a qualified professional.

Are you a writer or merely someone who plays around with creating stories?

The answer may not matter to you, but it does to your family, your friends, your future financial health, and to the IRS. Particularly the IRS.

As you set up your business, you need to establish your ground rules to ensure that you're running it like a business and not a hobby. This is an important distinction to the IRS.

A business is something you devote money and time to on a regular basis, with the intention of earning money from it eventually.

A hobby is an indulgence, a pleasure, a plaything, a way to pass the time and express your creativity without the intention of making a profit.

The IRS cares about you only when the fruit of your labors creates income or expenses that you declare on your tax return. If you treat the money as part of a business — if you declare your losses as part of a business — then the IRS could audit you to seek proof that you are, indeed, operating a business.

If you do that, you should make sure that you have in place a plan to prove that you are operating a business.

Don't be afraid of the IRS. If you respect them, take them seriously, follow their rules, and don't take shortcuts or resolve to explore uncharted frontiers in tax law, you should be fine.*

What Becomes a Business Most?

> My books bring me in quite enough money — that is to say the bloodsuckers take most of it, and if I made more, they'd take more, so I don't overstrain myself.
>
> **Ariadne Oliver**

This is where regular recordkeeping pays off. Any records can be used to back up your claim that you are working regularly on creating and marketing your writing. It could be a calendar on which you keep track of your projects. It could be a notebook with a page devoted to each day, recording what you did as part of the business. It could be a database of your story submissions, rejections, and sales. It could be a business checking account that keeps business expenses firewalled from household expenses.

Another important thing to record is anything you've done to learn how to run a successful publishing business. Classes in advertising, courses in writing ad copy, consultations with book cover designers, hiring a website designer: All this will show the IRS that you're running a business and you're learning how to run it.

So there is no one set of records you have to keep but a lot of different things. For example, I have a notebook in which I keep track of each day's work. I also have a big year-at-a-glance calendar on the wall showing my business appointments. I have scads of files, images, printouts, and photographs which show how much work I've put into each book.

Fortunately, the IRS is open about the standards you need to meet. Visit *www.irs.gov/spanish/hobby-or-business-irs-offers-tips-to-decide* to get the latest information. For example, on the sheet published in 2007, the IRS asks these questions:

Does the time and effort put into the activity indicate an intention to make a profit?

Does the taxpayer depend on income from the activity?

If there are losses, are they due to circumstances beyond the taxpayer's control or did they occur in the start-up phase of the business?

Has the taxpayer changed methods of operation to improve profitability?

Does the taxpayer or his/her advisers have the knowledge needed to carry on the activity as a successful business?

Has the taxpayer made a profit in similar activities in the past?

Does the activity make a profit in some years?

Can the taxpayer expect to make a profit in the future from the appreciation of assets used in the activity?

There is another rule to keep in mind. If you've been in business for more

---

* Just remember that I'm not a tax attorney. Consult your tax adviser before doing anything with your financials.

than five years, the IRS will look at whether you made a profit. If you did in three of those years, that supports your claim that you're running a business.

Here are other ways you can support your claim that you're building a business:

1. Keep regular track of your income, expenses, and sales.
2. Keep track of your business-related phone calls.
3. Advertise your books.
4. Attend classes to improve your skills.
5. Keep a checking account solely for business use.
6. Have written plans to grow your business, such as a production schedule that covers several years.

The IRS pays particular attention to authors who deduct mileage for conventions and author appearances. The IRS allows filers to deduct a certain amount per mile of travel for business trips. If you want to use this deduction, keep a record of your travels, listing the mileage, dates, locations, and purpose of your trips. These have to be kept up throughout the year and they have to be detailed, including the names of people you visited. Again, consult the IRS's website for details.

They Fought the IRS and the IRS Won

Not every deduction passes the IRS sniff test. Here are three examples drawn from tax court records:

- For 17 years, an employee for the City of New York worked on his writing in his off hours. The sum total of his work was a single manuscript, which he failed to sell, and a biography of his mother, for which she paid him $700. In his 17th year, his attempt to deduct his office space was audited. When asked if he wrote for profit, he called the question "an insult;" it's obvious that writers write only to make money. The court looked over his collected works, the result of 17 years of labor, and ruled he wasn't trying hard enough.

- This couple went the wrong way in deducting their expenses. In 1959, they flew to Japan to visit their son, then flew around the world. They edited their diary into a manuscript that failed to find a publisher. The court disallowed their deduction of $6,487, worth about $60,000 today.

- Our nominee for the most dedicated researcher goes to Ralph Vitale, the federal government employee who went above and beyond in researching his novel about prostitution in Nevada. For two years, he visited Nevada's finest brothels, taking notes and interviewing the women about their profession. His novel, *Searchlight, Nevada,* earned him $2,600 in royalties, for which he claimed nearly $11,000 in deductions, including $3,480 in cash payments to the girls. The court allowed most of his expenses, but harrumphed that paying prostitutes in cash was "inherently personal" and disallowed those deductions.

The Race to File

When the last firework has popped after New Years Eve passes into New Years day, another clock quietly starts. A race is under way, even if you don't know it.

The deadline in the U.S. to file taxes is April 15. Depending on your situation, this is either fraught with peril or a pretty calm period. It's the latter for us.

I used to fill out the forms myself. I'd dig out the bills, tote up the expenses and charitable donations, grab the forms, figure out what new laws Congress changed to benefit their donors and screw us over, fill out the forms, double-check my math, stare bewildered at how much we owed, triple-check my math, correct the number I added when I should have subtracted, get new forms, fill everything out again and then file.

Adding and subtracting is not one of my talents.

Somehow, we managed year by year, but once I started Peschel Press, life became a lot simpler.

First, I earn a lot less money plus I have a lot more potential deductions.

Second, I keep track of my business expenses throughout the year.

Third, I hired a CPA.

Fourth, I try my best to take care of my CPA so he'll continue to be my CPA. This is probably the most important aspect of your job, because their job is really tough. Imagine doing nearly a year's work in three months. That's what CPAs who help people file their taxes do. From roughly February 1 (when you get all your 1099s) to April 15, the majority of their year's work is performed. They can file extensions for the dawdlers, but you don't want to be one of them. The time you spend preparing your taxes doesn't earn you a cent, so you want to spend as little as possible on it.

(Warning: What follows is a simplified discussion of how I do my taxes. It is not intended as tax advice, nor am I a tax attorney.)

Here's how:

1. Set up a file folder marked "Tax Year [YEAR]". Keep it near the desk where you pay your bills. Throw in it your paper receipts: office supply store, bookstore purchases, post office for books you ship to reviewers, the printer who did your flyers and banners. Everything.

2. Record your expenses on an Excel spreadsheet called "[YEAR] Balance Sheet." It's one I use every year and breaks down what we spend into categories my accountant uses. My expenses encompass anything bought for the business, including books, supplies, webhosting, post office box, vendor fees, marketing services, mileage to conventions and book signings, and printed materials. I also include my internet access, and the power and water needed to run the office. Since I work from home, I only deduct a percentage of what the house uses, the exact percentage determined on the advice of my CPA.

3. Record my income on another spreadsheet. That comes from three sources: direct sales, royalties, and interest income from our saving accounts.

That's for my use.

I wait for the online bookstores to send me my 1099 forms. This is the form they file with the IRS that reports how much they paid me. That's the amount I claim as income. I put together the income from our direct sales with those in the spreadsheet and send the files to my accountant.

He double-checks my claims and warns me of any changes in tax law that might affect my return. My instructions to my CPA are specific. I don't want to break new ground in tax law. Claim what I'm entitled to and pay the bill. The last place you want to be creative is in your finances. Unlike critical reviews, words from the IRS can hurt you.

Technology

> Any sufficiently advanced technology is indistinguishable from magic.
> **Arthur C. Clarke**

I'm not a Luddite.* Really. I love technology ... when it works and makes my life easier. Computers that hold millions of words, ebook readers, scanners, OCR software, email; I wouldn't be able to do the work I love without them.

But I dislike tech that complicates my life and invades my privacy. Apple's iPod is much harder to use for playing music than my Sansa Clip. ITunes 11 was so terrible that I rolled my copy back permanently to 10.7.0.21. Photoshop CS2 from 2005 does all that I need. The new MS Office 2010 charges a monthly fee; I already own the 2007 version and I'll keep using it so long as I have a computer to run it on.

So I'm smart about the tech I use. I let it into my life but I'm suspicious of anything unproven or that comes with strings attached. So should you. Whether it's software, your website, or your book, the goal is the same. Own it. Control it.

Nothing is permanent. If your website is built on someone else's site, it's there until the company goes out of business. If your blog's design is

---

* *Luddite:* Self-employed textile workers or weavers in 19th century Britain who smashed the newly introduced powered looms that threatened their livelihoods. Opposition to the money-saving and impoverishing machines grew so widespread it required military units to suppress the rebellion. The word possibly comes from Ned Ludd, a weaver who in a fit of rage broke a couple of knitting frames. He wasn't a revolutionary, however. Depending on the storyteller, he acted out of anger from either being whipped for idleness or taunted by the local boys. Either way, the word lives on to describe anyone who is reflexively against new technology, even if that person has a valid point.

controlled by someone else — a publisher or web designer for example — you don't have as much access to it. If your files are stored in the cloud, they're vulnerable to hackers or any fluctuations if you didn't make a backup.

Which leads to making copies of your files, which you should do regularly because anything can happen.

Regular Backups

How many backups should you make? As many as you're comfortable with. Some people are happy with one. Columnist James Lileks, however, makes multiple backups, stored at his home office and offsite. He even prints paper copies of his web pages.

Personally, I have three. I use two external hard drives, one to store copies of the files, the other as a system image using Windows' program. I also copy my writing projects to a CD every couple of months. When I finish a book, I copy everything associated with it to two DVDs and store them in a folder.

I admit that I'm pretty slapdash about my archives, but I've been working with my files for going on two decades, starting when I was storing my book projects on 3.5-inch discs. I'm comfortable with it.

Defending Your Computer

Your computer is the most important machine in your business. When it goes south, not only can it take your files with it, but it forces you to put writing on hold until you find a solution. Your books go unwritten, your emails go unanswered, and you can't react to anything crucial that happens in cyberspace, from an invitation to speak at an important event to slanderous attacks on your books online.

To lengthen the life of your computer:

● **Follow procedures.** Shut down the computer the way it wants you to. Don't turn it off by turning off your power source. Don't perform a "hard shutdown" by holding down the start button; use that method only if the software locks up and you have no other choice.

I am bored with the world I inhabit. I appreciate its technology and general wealth, but don't feel inspired to love it. For me, whether reading it or writing it, fiction is an escape.
Richard Blake

● **Keep the area around the computer clear of obstructions.** Computers create a lot of heat. That's why there are air vents on the box. Make sure air can circulate around it. Keep it away from heat. If the office temperature goes above 80 degrees regularly, invest in air conditioning.

● **Keep hair and dust away.** Build-up from animal hair and dust can heat up the hardware and shorten your computer's life. Vacuum the slots every few month. If you're comfortable working around cables and hardware, look inside the box once a year. Check for dust build-up. Use the vacuum cleaner with the gentlest brush attachment to suck it up. It doesn't have to be pristine, but you don't want dust dunes crawling across the motherboard.

"Honest, honey, I have no idea how cat hair could get inside the computer."

WARNING

- **Don't kick the computer.** The box to my computer is on the floor at my feet, and I have to take care not to run my chair or vacuum cleaner into it.
- **Vacuum the keyboard,** especially if you have cats. The keys on most keyboards will pop off if you run a knife blade underneath one edge and lever it up gently. It'll snap back if you push the key straight down. The larger keys such as the shift, enter, and delete keys might also be attached to the keyboard with a metal loop. They can be pried up, but do so very, very carefully. If you clear around all the single keys, the bigger keys need not be removed at all.

Every couple of years, depending on how much your kitties like sleeping on the keyboard, lift a key and look. If you see a carpet of hair, bust out the vacuum cleaner and get to work. You'll need to remove a lot of the keys to get most of it out.

- **Guard against viruses.** If you have a PC with Microsoft Security Essentials on it, keep it up to date and schedule a regular quick scan weekly. Run the full scan at least quarterly. It'll take several hours depending on the number of files you have. You can work while it's going on, but the computer will run slower. I try to run it early Sunday morning, while I'm eating breakfast and relaxing.

Need I say you shouldn't visit dodgy websites, or download files unless you're certain you know who they are from?

Never download a file from an email unless you're sure about it. Hackers like to send you an email with a familiar name on it, attached to a file that will do serious damage to your computer if you open it. I route my email through my Gmail account, and it takes out 98 percent of the spam.

Also, If you get an email warning of a security breach at a website, never take its suggestion to click on the link inside the email. Go directly to the website instead and investigate.

- **Defrag your hard drive** (Windows only). This applies to computers with hard drives that use a rotating disc to store its data.

Your computer stores each file as a continuous chain of data. If there's not enough room, it will scatter the data across the surface of the drive. The file works fine, but it creates a lot of fragmented information. As you add, rework, save, and delete files, the hard drive becomes more fragmented. It works harder. It does that very well; it was designed to do that.

It takes a long, long time for a hard drive to become so fragmented that it noticeably slows down. Depending on how many files you work with, it could take a year of daily use before a significant problem could arise.

Defragging your hard drive every quarter, or even every month, keeps that from happening. If you use Windows 10, it will defragment your hard drive for you, even while you're working on it.

The newer solid-state drives (called SSDs) do not need defragmenting, but they can be optimized.

Apple designed its hard drives to not need defragging.

The Best Defense: A Second Computer

If you want a writing computer that never needs upgrading and is protected against viruses, get one that isn't attached to the internet. Make sure it has only the programs you need for working. No cat videos, no solitaire games, and no music except what you need to write to.

A computer dedicated to writing is probably the best investment you can make in your career. Here's why. We are creatures of habit. We respond to patterns. We see food, we eat it. We lay down, we're inclined to sleep. We sit in front of the TV, we veg out for hours, longer than we intended to.

Twyla Tharp talked about this in her book on creativity *The Creative Habit*. When you sit at your desk and turn on the computer, are you in writing mode? Solitaire mode? Email mode? Check a few websites mode?

The task you do often is the one you will be habituated to do every time you sit down. It's like when I go downstairs in the morning, I turn on the WiiFit and exercise. When I open the fridge and see a six of Troeg's Java Head, I take a bottle.

A second computer can habituate you to writing. When you sit there, you'll have nothing else to do but your work. No matter how much you want to, you'll never access the internet. And your software will never go out of date and never fall prey to viruses.*

How Fast Is Your Computer?

If you have to be online a lot, the speed of your internet service will affect your productivity. Waiting for a webpage to load not only adds time to getting something done, it's wears down your mental focus and concentration. If you need to use the internet while you're working, consider paying more for faster service.

The same tip applies to your computer. If you turn on the computer, walk to the coffee machine, walk back, and you're still waiting to get to work, consider getting a newer, faster model.

---

* Unless you plug in a flash drive and it has a malware program on it. Remember to practice safe computing!

Chapter 25
Continuing Education

Key Points to Remember
- There are many different ways to learn; find the method that works best for you.
- Whatever book or class you choose, stick with it before moving on to another choice.
- Online classes let you learn at your own pace; some let you return for refresher courses.

There is no true expertise in the humanities without knowing all of the humanities. Art is a vast, ancient interconnected webwork, a fabricated tradition. Over-concentration on any one point is a distortion.

Camille Paglia

Successful writers are made, not born. Successful business owners don't arise out of nothing. They succeed through hard work and perseverance. That's the way of the world and to believe otherwise provides a convenient justification for not working hard and a shield against criticism.

An aversion to an honest assessment of your limitations is a very human reaction. No one wants to hear that they don't measure up, even if they know it in their heart of hearts.

But if you want to get better, you'll have to either harden your shell, or accept the blow, give yourself time to whine about the unfairness of life, and get back up and try again.

That's what continuing education is about. It's about taking a class, buying a book, watching a video series, or reading stories from better writers and learning from them.

That's the fun part about learning: The vast majority of what you need to know is out there, in the open. You can learn to write. You can learn about worldbuilding, character development, realistic dialog, descriptive settings, proper grammar. You can learn how to hire people to do specialized work like cover design, website building, and catchy book descriptions.

The one thing you can't learn is that divine force of creation, of inspiration, of that imaginative leap that results in iconic characters and worlds like Sherlock Holmes, Ankh-Morpork, Mandalay, the Orient Express, Middle-Earth, and Milliways, the restaurant at the end of the universe.

You can be taken to the edge of the creative lands. You can be advised to sit quietly, let the words flow, indulge your issues that leave you sweating and shaking, and exile the critical voice that would have whispered in Tolkien's ear "In a hole lived a hobbit? What kind of sentence is that. You mean like a vole? Or a mole? Or a groundhog?"

You can be shown the border, but you have to step across alone. Everything else, however, you can learn.

How We Learn

We learn how to learn in school, except that we were taught the wrong way.

You certainly see that in the way we were taught writing. I witnessed the American education system through my three children, and now that they're out, I see how little they learned.

Rather than bore you with a rant, I'll keep it simple: some methods of learning are more effective than others, one size does not fit all, and you have to learn for yourself what works for you.

In my case, it was by doing. Rather than buy a bunch of books and read them, I should have bought a few books and wrote stories using their suggestions, and gotten readers' feedback about what worked and what didn't. Although I read a lot, and I like reading, that's more for entertainment than education.

I also learned that not everyone who know their business are capable of teaching what they learned. That's especially true in the field of how-to-write books.

I read one recently from an author who wrote a few successful novels in the ancient military / fantasy genre. He came from a business background, and he confidently told us what to do (much like I'm doing).

His brief book was filled with business jargon but few details. He advised us to build our platform and author persona. He advised us to have a website (good) to display our books (right) and to blog frequently (ummm, not 100% right). He advised sending press releases, without saying why and how you can do so for maximum effectiveness. He even advised us to learn the demographics of readers in your genre, without following up on how you should do that. If he did that himself, he didn't tell us how to do that.

In short, his book was thick on the familiar generic advice, with few actionable details but plenty of exhortations to research your options.

Someone trying to follow his advice would quickly exhaust themselves putting his suggestions into play without doing the most important thing, which is to write more books.

So it's important not only to educate yourself, but to find the right teachers.

Options

Local Writers Groups

These groups can be formed through national or state organizations, universities, or libraries. They can meet anywhere from weekly to monthly, and their quality varies widely. It can be a good place to get general feedback on your writing, or terrible places where inexperienced writers abuse each other.

Writers Organizations

Groups have formed around the major genres and some have local chapters as well depending on where you live. One major advantage of joining one of these groups is that you'll meet writers in your genre at varying levels of skill and success, and it's easier to trade information and advice.

Writers Conferences

While writers organizations hold conferences, there are also many independent groups who meet annually. Best-selling authors are invited to attend and give speeches and seminars, and agents and editors are invited to hear pitches and give feedback. There's even an annual conference for indie writers in Las Vegas sponsored by the 20Booksto50K Facebook group. Even if you can't make it, they tape their sessions and make them available via YouTube.

Online Classes

Many writers and author service companies offer free and paid courses. Many of them are simply filmed sessions, but some offer a mix of film with real feedback on the assignments. As of 2020, you can check out these offerings that I've found worthwhile:

David Gaughran: This Irish writer with the amazing beard publishes historical fiction and nonfiction books on Amazon (*Decoding Amazon*) and book marketing (*Followers*). His free course "Starting from Zero" teaches how to build an audience for your books. (*courses.davidgaughran.com/courses/starting-from-zero*)

Kindlepreneur: Dave Chesson has done great work researching how Amazon markets books, and this free course is a good introduction into Amazon ads. (*courses.kindlepreneur.com/collections*)

Reedsy: This marketplace for editors, cover designers and marketers offers free marketing, plotting, genre writing, revision, and more. (*blog.reedsy.com/learning/courses/*)

Dean Wesley Smith: This longtime author offers not only filmed courses but regular monthly workshops. (*deanwesleysmith.com/online-workshops/*)

Iain Rob Wright: If you want to learn how to self-publish from coming up with an idea to publication, this free course offers more than 50 hours of instruction. No strings attached; he makes his money from affiliate links to services like ProWritingAid and Amazon affiliate links. (*azofselfpublishing.teachable.com/*)

> I think the best advice to writers attending a conference or beginning a writing class is to ascertain where you stand in relation to the other participants and learn from those who are a step or two ahead.
> **Betsy Lerner**

Mark Dawson: This best-selling thriller writer offers courses for the beginning author (Self Publishing 101); advertising on all the major platforms (Ads for Authors); cover design and more. They're expensive, but a purchase entitles you to return to them again and again (and he lets you download the videos and provides transcripts), and he updates the courses as the platforms change. They're expensive, however, so look into the free courses before deciding if you need these. (*selfpublishingformula.com/courses/*)

Gale Online Courses

Gale (or ed2go) online classes are widely available through public libraries. The class listing is huge, covering all kinds of subjects. We'll concentrate on those that would be most useful for indie authors. These courses last six weeks with two lessons per week. They are self-governing; if you don't do the work, you won't learn anything. The more you put into the class, the more you will get out of it.

If you haven't written even a postcard since leaving high school, start at the beginning with *Writing Essentials*. This is basic, basic, basic, but if you are unsure how to write a simple paragraph, start here.

If you have written Christmas letters and can sustain a narrative over a paragraph, start with *Beginning Writer's Workshop*. You'll get a better understanding of narrative structure. If you have a short story idea buzzing around in your head, you can use it as the basis of many of the exercises.

Next comes *Write Fiction Like a Pro*. Much more in-depth. You'll cover the three-act structure, scene and sequel, characterization; all sorts of topics. Begin this class with a firm idea of a novel and you'll finish the class with an outline and enough material to get it written.

After *Write Fiction Like a Pro* is its follow-on class, *Advanced Fiction Writing*. It covers some of the same ground but is much more focused on the mechanics of getting your idea into a coherent form. You'll be able to flesh out that novel in this class.

Follow up *Advanced Fiction Writing* with *The Keys to Effective Editing*. This should be self-explanatory. The more editing you can do in advance, the cleaner your finished manuscript will be. A clean manuscript is easier on your beta readers, your agent, and your editors. Don't pay someone to fix penny mistakes when you can fix them yourself. *The Keys to Effective Editing* also introduces the marvelous concept of style sheets. Also called a story bible, a style sheet keeps you from making mistakes with names, locations, and characters and can be expanded to cover your 23-volume series.

Next comes *Research Methods for Writers*. Whatever genre you write in, you need to know more than your reader does. Don't make mistakes such as having snowdrops and foxgloves blooming in the same garden at the same time. They don't and any gardener will know you didn't do your homework.

Gale has many other, more specialized writing classes, such as writing romance or mysteries. They won't all be useful to you; see which ones meet your requirements.

After the writing classes, focus on the business aspects. Start with getting your book in print so readers can find you. Gale offers two self-publishing courses. Both provide enough information to get you going. Try *Publish and Sell Your eBook* first. If you are interested in nonfiction, add *Write and Publish Your Nonfiction Book*.

Finish with a pair of general business courses. Being an indie writer means you are running a home-based business. First, take *Start and Operate Your Own Home-based Business*. Some of what's in this course doesn't necessarily apply to writing but most of it does. You'll be better educated when you deal with your accountant, your banker, your insurance agent, your neighbors, and your spouse. If you're running a business, you need a business plan. Gale offers *Creating a Successful Business Plan*. Do all the work in the 12 classes and you'll have a roadmap for where you want to go.

If your library doesn't carry the Gale courses, check to see if they carry other online classes. You'll get out of them what you put into them. Your library's resources can make you a better writer for less money.

What About a Master of Fine Arts Degree?

Short answer: No, with some qualifiers.

Medium-length answer: If your goal is to become a literary writer, yes. If you want to be an academic, teaching literature, no.

If you have money to burn and don't need an academic position and want the status of writing MFA and PhD after your name, why not?

If your goal is to be financially successful as a writer, absolutely not.

The reputation of MFA programs have been declining over the years. They've been criticized for turning out far more graduates than the education system needs. They train writers to write in a certain pattern, usually minimalist, by sanding off anything that creates a writer's unique voice, leaving you with an uber-voice that's the hallmark of MFA writing.

This situation worsened in 2020, when the government's overreaction to the Wuhan flu pandemic forced the closure of many universities. As of this writing, it appears that many of the smaller places won't survive the economic depression caused by the shutdowns, leading to an even smaller market for university-level professors. Worse, universities have been moving away from hiring tenure-track professors. Instead, you'll be working as an adjunct professor on year-to-year contracts, leaving you in a precarious position year in, year out.

> "
>
> You almost feel that any idiot with a nickel's worth of talent can emerge from writing class able to write a competent story. In fact, so many people can now write competent stories that the short story as a medium is in danger of dying of competence. We want competence, but competence by itself is deadly. What is needed is the vision to go with it, and you do not get this from a writing class.
>
> **Flannery O'Connor**

Do you really want to compete in that environment?

That's not counting the debt you'll incur. Four years of university, followed by a two-year MFA program, can leave you with an obligation that'll take a lifetime to pay off. All to make a precarious living at a university, writing books that few people will want to read.

There are some MFA alternatives. Seton Hill offers an MFA in genre fiction, while Kevin J. Anderson runs a publishing MFA at a Colorado university.

The question to consider there is the reward versus the expense. I'm not sure of the cost of either program, but let's say they're in the low five figures. Like, $10,000.

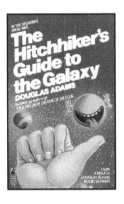

Which would benefit you more: spending $10,000 taking general courses in genre and publishing, or paying $3,000 to a good developmental editor — one you find on Reedsy who has edited best-selling novels for New York or London publishing houses — to go over your novel?

I know which direction I would choose.

Further Learning

The Resources chapter in the appendix lists products and services that'll help you on your author journey.

Whatever resources you choose, use them. Don't buy a book and put it on the shelf "for someday." I have a bookcase full of them, and the only thing I've learned is that no one learns by osmosis.

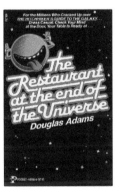

Another way to learn about writing good books is to read good books. And not only to read them, but tear them apart. Read with a pen at your side. When you come across an affecting scene, go back over it. How did the author set up the emotions? How far back in the story? How long are the sentences? How is the emotion stirred from sentence to sentence?

If you're looking for a place to start, let me recommend the whale and bowl of petunias scene in *The Hitchhiker's Guide to the Galaxy*. It's about a baby whale that suddenly appears above a planet, and what it thinks about as it falls to the surface.

Douglas Adams wrote the scene as a challenge to himself. He wanted to write about a character who suddenly appears out of nowhere and make you care about it.

It's brilliant. Funny and sad at the same time, because of the weird way the whale is introduced, its attempt to make sense of the world around him, the inevitability of its demise (known to the reader; not to the whale), and its last words, looking at the ground rushing toward it, and thinking *I wonder if it will be friends with me?*

I challenge you to read that scene, seriously, and not be affected by it.

PART V
Writing Life and Afterlife

If there's anything
you want to do,
do it now.
We shall all be
in little boxes
soon enough.

Josephine Tey

Chapter 26
Your Health

- -

Key Points to Remember

- Writing is a marathon, not a sprint. Maintaining your health is a day-by-day task as well.
- As you get older, your body cannot recover as easily from irregular sleep and poor nutrition.
- When you're too ill to write, try tasks that don't require much energy.

- -

The writer, like the priest, must be exempted from secular labor. His work needs a frolic health; he must be at the top of his condition.
Ralph Waldo Emerson

Founded in 705 A.D., the Keiunkan hotel is known as the oldest in the world.

There is one major difference between working for someone and working for yourself. It is a fact that, when understood, can be so terrifying that it can send people who dreamed of leaving the rat race to put on their track shoes and race back to the comfortable, dull corporate world.

Here it is:

You are the most valuable person in your company. You are irreplaceable.

That doesn't sound so scary, until you realize that in the corporate world, workers are interchangeable. We're cogs in a machine. We can be pulled out and replaced, sometimes at a whim, and the company will go on.

You can replace every person in the company, from the janitors to the CEO, and it still lives.

Well-managed businesses outlive the lives of their founders and beyond. How long? Centuries, even millennia. The family that runs the Nishiyama Onsen Keiunkan hotel in Japan has catered to travelers since 705.

That's right: the 8th century. The same family has run it for 52 generations.

Not you, the author. Your business lasts one lifetime. Yours. Even if your creations live on, you won't. Nobody can write a James Bond novel like Ian Fleming. No one can plot a Hercule Poirot mystery like Agatha Christie. There are writers penning official novels starring their creations, but they're not the same. They're not failures, and they can be a pleasure to read (some more than others). But no one will say they're as good as the originals. They can only be good in their own ways.

So when you hang out your shingle, keep in mind that no matter what genre you write in, you're the only person who can write like yourself. Your brain, your imagination, your experience, your endurance, your

"

[When a man must] abstain from nearly everything that his neighbours innocently and pleasurably use, and from the rubs and trials of human society itself into the bargain, we recognise that valetudinarian healthfulness which is more delicate than sickness itself.
Robert Louis Stevenson

ambition are the ingredients you'll use to bake your unique creations.

And that means taking care of the most important part of your business. You.

Health

I'll start with two general observations. One of them will be obvious, the other not so obvious until you experience it.

Eat healthy, get enough sleep, don't smoke, don't abuse your body too much, yada yada yada.

I won't rehash these old standbys; I'm not your father. You've heard this advice all your life. I'll only add that certain habits will affect your creativity and productivity. Too many late nights, and you risk coming to the desk hungover, spent, fatigued. You'll be tempted to ask your boss (you) to beg off work, and your boss will probably agree, because they're tired, too.

So let's agree that you should be aware of your vices, give you the agency to deal with them as you see fit, and move on to the unexpected pitfall trap you will still encounter.

The less physical work you do, the weaker you get.

After I graduated from college, I worked several physically demanding jobs. I was a temp employee, typing invoices one day, unloading trailers the next. I shipped bar-code scanners for a company. I delivered bread; a job that required me to get up at 3 or 4 a.m., be on the move all day, and finish at 3 p.m., ready to collapse into bed and do it again the next day.

Then I found my first desk job, editing copy at a newspaper. Instead of hustling all day, I sat behind a desk. I gained 10 pounds the first month.

The years passed. I got married, had kids, bought a house. I did yard work and home improvements. I worked in the yard, building stone walls and garden beds. I ate what I wanted and as much as I wanted. When I wasn't doing chores, I wrote novels in my home office.

By the time I reached 235 pounds, I was prediabetic and risking high blood pressure. I was also suffering from sleep apnea. I would have difficulty sleeping on my back. I'd snort and gasp, waking Teresa who would wake me so I'd turn on my side and go back to sleep.

All this, on top of a second-shift schedule — usually 4 p.m. to midnight, with some early and late shifts as well — really did a number on my health. I had to do something.

The turnaround began when Teresa bought a WiiFit for the kids. Since I loved playing video games, I started exploring what it could do. Sometimes I played the fun stuff like skiing, the driving range and running around Wuhu Island. Other times I tried out the exercises. I wasn't consistent, but it was a little better than doing nothing. At work, I bypassed the elevators and took

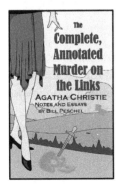

the stairs. During my lunch break I'd circle the parking lot several times.

It wasn't much exercise, but over the next few years, I dropped 35 pounds. I realized how much better I felt. I still had hypertension and was prediabetic, but my sleep apnea faded to where it was an occasional nuisance instead of a life-threatening condition.

Then I moved into my 50s, and it became clear that I might not remain at the newspaper until retirement. The chain that owns the newspaper had cut back on print production to three days a week, followed by layoffs. Since they needed reporters, and they certainly weren't going to lay off management, that left the copy desk as the most vulnerable low-hanging fruit.

In 2012, the staff won the Pulitzer Prize for its coverage of a scandal at Penn State involving a former coach who was convicted for pedophilia. It was the only major prize the paper had won, and Teresa and I breathed a sigh of relief. They surely wouldn't institute major layoffs at the newspaper so soon after we won the Pulitzer.

Eight months later, shortly after midnight on New Year's day 2013, I shared a glass of champagne with the survivors of the copy desk purge. That was the end of one career and the beginning of another.

It was a traumatic parting. Even though I had Peschel Press already running, even though I knew we had savings to tide us over, even though Teresa was thrilled that I would be home all the time (she still is; go figure); no matter how much I told myself we would be fine, my body was disagreeing the only way it knew how.

I had heart palpitations. I'd lay awake in bed and feel my heart pause, then thump hard, like it was trying to swallow something thick. Waves of panic would wash over me. I became extremely paranoid about my heart. I was obsessed with thoughts of dying.

This wasn't the first time anxiety washed over me. A decade before, when I started at the paper, I had a similar attack. The chest pains were so frightening that I walked into the ER and told them I thought I was having a heart attack. After an EKG and later a stress test, I was told I wasn't having heart problems at all. Anxiety.

Now, they were back, and harder than ever. More exams, more tests, and the results came back the same. Anxiety.

I was relieved, and I responded by throwing myself into my book projects. *The Complete, Annotated Mysterious Affair at Styles* came out in mid-2013. Six months later, the deluxe edition of *The Secret Adversary* appeared.

For the next 18 months, I stayed at my desk for 12 hours a day working on annotating books, setting up the business, learning how to market books, and building and improving my website.

During this time, however, big changes were occurring in my body. Not only was my weight going up — I was no longer walking in the parking lot and it was only one flight of stairs down to my desk — but I wasn't moving around nearly as much. Most of the home chores were finished, and my son had taken on tasks such as mowing the lawn and weeding the garden beds.

The day of reckoning came at a local mystery convention. The bookseller agreed to sell my stock in return for appearing on panels and helping out. On the day of the event, I loaded the car with three heavy boxes of books and brought them to the site.

That's when I discovered I had no muscle strength at all. Mind you, I was never a Schwarzenegger, but I had been capable of moving around boxes. What had happened was that my muscles had atrophied. Worse, my sleep apnea had returned.

That when you become an indie author and you're working from home, you have to make time for exercise. You have to get up and move.

I had to teach myself to pay attention to how much I eat and how much I exercise. It took a year to get into the habit of exercising every day, but now I know what I need to do to maintain my boyish 200-pound figure. It involves exercise in the morning, a 3-mile walk in the afternoon, and a 2-mile walk in the evening. I keep away from the carbs as much as I can and leave the sugar in the cabinet. When I do that, I've gotten close to 190 pounds. If I want to weigh less, I'll either have to eat less food with fewer calories, or kick the exercises up ten notches.

The Best Way to Keep Fit

Whether you walk, salsa dance, lift weights, garden, join a gym, or find a workout partner, the rule is the same: The best system for staying fit is the one you're willing to do.

The news media is full of contradictory advice. I call them the "you're doing it wrong" articles. For a long time, it was thought that a combination of aerobic and strength-training exercises were needed. Running, aerobics, jazzercise, along with lifting weights, either the barbells or the Nautilus machines.

The counter-argument, led by Mark Rippetoe with his "Starting Strength" program, pumps for weight-training alone, specifically a few basic exercises using barbells. As you get older, Rippetoe argues, you need muscle mass to help you maintain your balance and fitness, and weight training supplies you with all the benefits of aerobic exercise. He opposes running, because it weakens the joints, particularly the knees and ankles, and breaks down the muscle you're trying to build up.

Then there's disagreements over the body's ideal weight. The body-mass index known as BMI has been criticized as being an inaccurate measurement.

I admit I'm suspicious of it when I'm told my ideal weight, instead of the 190-200 pounds is 157 pounds. I haven't weighed that little since junior high school.

There's also another argument that says being a little overweight is actually better for you. In *The Obesity Paradox*, Carl J. Lavie points to studies that show slightly overweight (not obese) people survive serious diseases better than skinny people.

Again, I'm not going to argue for or against any of these positions. I just want to lay them out for you to investigate and decide. But it is important that you exercise regularly, avoid smoking, watch your weight, and that will keep you fit enough to let you create your magic on the page.

Health Insurance

Getting health insurance in the U.S. is fraught with peril, especially if you're an indie author without a spouse on a company health plan. If your income is low you can try to qualify for Medicaid through your state government. If you are a high-earner you can afford a policy.

If you're in between, you either go bare (live a healthy lifestyle if you do) and pay for treatment when you need it, or hunt for coverage.

As I was writing this, another option surfaced. Eleven writers organizations formed the Book Industry Health Insurance Partnership (BIHIP).* If you join one of the eleven organizations forming the Independent Book Publishers Association (*ibpa-online.org/*), you'll qualify to approach a broker with Lighthouse Insurance Group and see what policies are available to you in your state.

Unfortunately, I don't have much more information than that and a lot of unanswered questions. For one thing, you can approach Lighthouse directly through their website. Would it make any difference in your policy options? Don't know. How much would it cost? Don't know either.

That's the only option I know at this time.

Carpel-Tunnel Syndrome and Other Aches

Spend enough time at your desk writing, and your body will start complaining. It could take the form of muscle ache, swelling in the joints, a buzzing in your elbow, or a crippling pain as you curl the fingers to type your first words.

---

* Consisting of American Booksellers Association, American Society for Indexing, Authors Guild, Book Industry Study Group, Graphic Artists Guild, Horror Writers Association, Independent Book Publishers Association, Novelists Inc., Romance Writers of America, Science Fiction and Fantasy Writers of America, and Western Writers of America Inc.

It'll take several forms — carpel-tunnel syndrome, tennis elbow, bursitis, or arthritis — but it all means the same in the end: medical treatment or risk worse injury that could leave you crippled, unable to work, and risking a fall in revenue.

But you can do something about your body before it tells you that it's had enough.

• **Exercise:** The first and most important line of defense. Remember the phrase "use it or lose it?" It applies here. Your body is designed to be only as strong as it needs to be. If you were slinging boxes eight hours a day in a warehouse, you would build muscle and coordination. When you're sitting at a desk in an office, you'll be able to drive to work, walk up the stairs, get coffee and a bag of chips in the canteen, sit at your desk, and get home.

And that's a heavy workout compared to a full-time writer at home, where the longest trek you could make all day is to the kitchen for coffee and the bathroom for breaks.

Under those conditions, your body will grow slack and weak in a hurry.

• **Flexibility:** What can happen to your muscles will also happen to the flexibility in your hands, wrists, and joints. Just as exercise keeps your muscles toned, it can also keep your joints limber.

There are exercises that will gently stretch the tendons and keep them flexible.

1. Stretch your arms in front of you. Flex the wrists so the hands go up as far as they can go, then down. Up, down, up, down. Do this ten times.

2. Rotate your hands in one direction ten times, then in the other direction ten times.

3. Hold your palms level, fingers spread. Rotate them as far as they can go in one direction, then in the other direction. Ten times.

• **Ergonomics:** Make sure your desk and chair are adjusted for your height and your wrists are angled properly over the keyboard to keep you from getting the dreaded carpel-tunnel syndrome.

"What's so stressful about writing?" I can hear you ask. "It's not digging ditches."

Try this experiment. Stand up. In that position, lift one foot off the ground. Don't move it forward, just lift it off the ground, say, an inch.

Hold that position. If you're like me, after a few minutes, you'll start feeling the strain. Not much, but definitely there.

When you're typing, you're holding your hands in unnatural positions. They're raised slightly, angled slightly, kept in the air, resting lightly on the keys. They may be angled back from your wrists, which are resting (but not entirely) on one of those spongy rests.

If you've been writing for awhile, check the set of your shoulders, or have someone massage your shoulders a bit. Surprisingly stiff, aren't they?

That's what happens to your body day after day over several years. This is what you have to counter, with exercise, with flexibility training, with sitting properly, with frequent breaks, and with, if need be, compression gloves and braces.

Remember: I am not a doctor. I cannot diagnose your symptoms. I can't even give you guidelines. People have different tolerances for desk work. I spent more than two decades editing copy on computers. I have been typing since I learned to touch-type in junior high school. My hands are in good shape. Teresa took up writing seriously enough that within 18 months she had written several hundred thousand words, and she needs compression gloves and braces. There is no way of telling what will happen to you.

Gloves and Braces: If you're feeling pain in your hands on a regular basis, you may need to see a doctor.

If you developed problems with your hands and wrists, there are solutions to try. These are treatments that I've seen work with writers, but I can't say that they will work for you. Let your doctor or any other qualified medical professional examine you and recommend treatment.

That said, compression gloves give temporary, drug-free relief to sufferers of arthritis, and those who do a lot of fine handwork, such as sewing, quilting, and embroidering. These are gloves that slip snugly over your hands. They come in a variety of styles and sizes, from those that cover the hand to those that leave the fingertips free. They can be found in drugstores, orthopedic shops, and online.

Braces are used by those who suffer from carpel-tunnel syndrome. The carpel tunnel is an opening in your wrist through which nerves travel from the arm to the fingers. Those who type a lot, possibly in risky positions, inflame those nerves. Angling the wrist, such as when you're typing, compresses the tunnel and causes great pain.

The treatment is to keep the wrist straight, reducing the pressure on the tunnel and allowing the nerves to heal. Braces consist of stiff pieces of plastic sewn into a sleeve that is pulled over the hand and up the arm. They are anchored by a thumb loop. Because they cover the forearm, wrist, and part of the hand, they keep the wrist straight. Wearing them at night, while you sleep, gives your hands a chance to recover. You don't need to wear them during the day.

When You Get Sick

I'm talking about minor problems like a cold that lasts a week or longer.

Freelancers have a problem with illness that most workers don't have. If you don't work, you don't get paid. If the workers at your old job get sick, they

WARNING

Typing with compression gloves.

Typing with braces over the gloves.

can take a day or two off and still get a full paycheck.

(I know that's not always the case. When I delivered bread, I was told that if I didn't come in, a substitute would come in and he'd get that day's sales. There are jobs out there that come with no health benefits at all. Some business owners seem determined to squeeze as much out of you as they can, as if you're to blame for the crappy way they run their company into the ground.)

Getting sick at your writing job causes double the problems. Not only did you get sick, but so did your boss. You can't bring in a substitute. But that doesn't mean you have to write off the day, either.

Unless you're so dizzy you see two spouses before you asking, "Honey, are you all right?" you can push on and feel like you've gotten something accomplished, even if it wasn't moving forward on your next book.

Here are some ideas:

● **Reading:** Those articles you've set aside on your hard drive that you always meant to read; that friend's book by your bedside; books from your shelf that you hadn't touched since you bought them years ago; or short stories in your genre that are considered classics.

● **Editing your notes:** When I'm working on a book I'll leave notes everywhere: tucked in the manuscript, in files on the desktop, in my notebook. Going through my note collection refreshes my memory and reminds me of good stuff I had forgotten. Reorganizing them means one less thing for my brain to track and primes the pump for when I recover.

● **General maintenance:** A pile of emails that you meant to print out and file. Business expenses you meant to stick in your database. Your iTunes music that contains albums you no longer want to hear.

● **General computer maintenance:** Defragging the hard drive, running a deep scan of the system, or trawling through your file folders to trash the ones you no longer need.

● **Listening to podcasts:** If you have to stay in bed and reading hurts your eyes, listen to podcasts, particularly on writing and marketing.

● **Story ideas:** Lay in bed with a notebook computer, or a big pad of paper and pen. Free-associate ideas and write them down without judging them. Let the ideas flow. Some of them may spark a new direction, or a character, or a scene, or a joke. Let the muse enter you and surprise you.

● **Take care of yourself:** The key words are hydration (drink plenty of water), sanitation (wear fresh clothes and take a shower), and aeration (if the weather permits, open the windows; even in winter, five minutes will air out the room and leaving you feel chilly, but refreshed).

Chapter 27
Powering Up Your Work Habits

Key Points to Remember
- A habit can be created by linking an action you do regularly with the habit you want to form.
- Rewarding yourself occasionally encourages a habit to form, but don't do it regularly.
- Reminding yourself why you want to accomplish a goal motivates you to finish it.

> I never could have done what I have done without the habits of punctuality, order, and diligence, without the determination to concentrate myself on one subject at a time.
>
> **Charles Dickens**

> An often overlooked factor in one's writing success is discovering the conditions you need in order to write, and then managing to create those conditions.
>
> **Robert B. Parker**

Getting into the habit of writing regularly is probably the most effective tool in your arsenal. Develop this one habit, and you're on your way to a long-lasting career.

First, set aside time to write. If you think you can't, consider Robert Ferrigno. The future crime writer was a reporter when he interviewed Elmore Leonard. Afterwards, Ferrigno confessed he really wanted advice about how to become a full-time writer.

Leonard gave his standard answer: get up two hours early each day and write. Don't do anything else. After two hours, do your normal routine.

Ferrigno thanked Leonard and gave him a profile he wrote about an ex-CIA agent and asked him only to let him know if he thought he'd be better off selling shoes. Leonard wrote back, said he liked the article, and if Ferrigno got a book contract, he'd consider blurbing it.

A couple of years later, Ferrigno sent him the galley. Leonard liked it and blurbed it. When they talked over the phone, Ferrigno thanked him for the advice, but admitted that he lied to him when he said he would get up at 5 a.m.

"Yeah?" Ferrigno could hear the wariness in Leonard's voice.

"Yes sir, I got up at 4 a.m. every day for the last year and a half. You're a better writer than I am, so I figured I needed the extra hour."

(By the way, Leonard needed ten years of early rising before he broke out when Hollywood filmed his novel, *Hombre*, with Paul Newman.)

I don't necessarily recommend cutting back on sleep to allow time to write. If you have time to watch TV or surf the web for two hours every day, you have time to write. Give up the TV.

Setting aside a regular time for work is important for another reason that can alter your character. As I tell my children, over and over, "Character is what you do when no one's watching." Forming a positive habit creates in your mind the expectation that you will do that very thing.

It's a kind of circular logic. You have to do something habitually for the habit to be creative. When you do something regularly, your mind shifts into the habit mode. Sit down at the typewriter and write, and each time you sit down at the typewriter, your mind shifts into writing mode. It's a chicken-and-egg question in which the answer is "yes."

Make a ritual of it, and the work will follow. For choreographer Twyla Tharp, as she describes it in *The Creative Habit*, it's her morning cab ride to the gym. When she enters the dance studio, her body is warmed up and her mind is ready. For Toni Morrison, it's making a cup of coffee and sipping it while watching the sun come up. The softly growing light represents the transition from sleep to work.

So how can you build a habit? Cognitive scientists have found methods that work.

The Power of Small Goals

Humans resist change. We know what we like and like what we know. Change can be frightening, especially if we know it will change us in unexpected ways. It's why some creative people refuse to stop drinking and drugging, or get therapy for depression. They fear they'll lose the creativity that drives them. (As a former depressive, I know that's a lie. Sure, you may write fewer poems about decay and death, but you'll more than make up for it in the joy and energy and creativity of writing about other things.)

The way to change is to fool yourself. Start small. If you can't write for two hours, write for 25 minutes instead. Take a break, set a timer, and write for another 25 minutes. (Don't spend more than an hour at the desk however, before getting up and stretching.) If you still can't write, dare yourself to write 50 words. You can write 50, right? And if you can't write 50 words, consider a course in computer programming. You'll be happier.

For me, the first thing I do after waking up and getting my coffee is exercise on my WiiFit program. I've been doing this for years, and the pattern is so ingrained that when I go downstairs, I feel the urge to go to the TV, turn it on, and load the program. If I detour to the computer, I feel uneasy, like I'm missed something important.

The Power of Feedback

Establishing feedback tracks your progress and engrains in you the power of habit. Even if you're the only one giving feedback to yourself, it can still work.

William M. Gaines, the longtime publisher of *Mad* magazine, was fanatical about his to-do list. It was a simple list, with each item crossed off in its turn, but it was usually very long.

Gaines was fanatical about checking off his tasks. One staffer watched Gaines at work one day. One item on his list was to call one of the writers who contributed to the magazine. Early that morning, he called. No answer. An hour later, he tried again. No answer.

Throughout the day, Gaines worked through his checklist, and regularly called the contributor. By this time, the Mad man was curious about why Gaines needed to talk to the fellow so badly. Was it bad news? Was it something about the next issue, soon to go to press? It must be important.

Gaines kept it up, staying late at his desk and working through the pile of papers, manuscripts, and memos, and occasionally stopping to phone the guy.

It was late, well past quitting time. Gaines had lined out every item on that list, except the last one. Before giving up and going home, he tried one more time.

The guy picks up.

"George! How you doing? Great job on the article in the last issue."

That was it.

Now, I know some of you are asking, "Why didn't he put it on his next day's list? What was so important about that call that it had to be placed?"

I can't speak for Gaines, but I can guess. It's all about the habit that he had developed. He was the Boss. He had a magazine to publish, every four weeks. That was immovable. Most of his schedule was immovable.

If he got into the habit of shoving tasks off until tomorrow, where would it stop? If it was this phone call, why not another about a payment? Or about a bill?

We're creatures of habit. We're comfortable when we can indulge in our habits, and antsy if we're prevented. By succeeding in crossing everything off his list, Gaines could go home feeling fulfilled; he had done a day's work. If he hadn't, it would have bugged him. Not a lifelong-regret bug, but he would have been denied the pleasure of crossing that last item off his list.

(Lest you think William Gaines was a workaholic, he was also capable of relaxation. Every year, he would take contributors who had sold a certain number of pages to the magazine on a trip. China, Russia, the Caribbean, one week, all expenses paid.

This led to jealousy among those who hadn't succeeded. When Gaines' mother died, one artist asked if he was going to the funeral.

"I can't," he replied. "I didn't sell enough pages.")

The Power of Intermittent Reinforcement

Reward yourself. It can be a Godiva chocolate, a glass of wine, a TV show in the middle of the day. But not every time. Psychological experiments found that rats worked hardest at pressing the bar to receive a food pellet if they didn't get it each time. So don't be consistent with rewards.

The Power of Why

Being motivated can be difficult at times, especially when you're stuck.

Here's a trick I learned from Charles Duhigg's *Smarter Faster Better*, a book that, while I have problems with some of its assumptions and conclusions, contained sound advice I haven't seen elsewhere.

Duhigg described the changes the Marine Corps made in basic training to turn slackers into self-motivated, hard-charging jarheads. At the end of basic, they're put through the Crucible, a three-day challenge to their strength, stamina, and will to finish.

Duhigg focuses on the story of Eric Quintanilla, a young man from the streets who entered the Marine Corps because he had nowhere else to go. After passing through the Corps' new model for training, he and the rest of his platoon participated in the Crucible. On the second day, after long marches and little sleep, this tired, hungry, injured group of men must climb a steep hill. To motivate themselves, the recruits fall back on a technique taught by their drill instructors.

They ask each other: "Why are you doing this?"

Quintanilla's answer was "to become a Marine and build a better life for my family."

As Duhigg explains, "If you can link something hard to a choice you care about, it makes the task easier, Quintanilla's drill instructors had told him. That's why they asked each other questions starting with 'why.' Make a chore into a meaningful decision, and self-motivation will emerge."

Naturally, the platoon finished climbing the hill and the Crucible.

"To teach ourselves to self-motivate more easily," Duhigg concludes, "we need to learn to see our choices not just as expressions of control but also as affirmations of our values and goals. That's the reason recruits ask each other 'why' — because it shows them how to link small tasks to larger aspirations."

The Power of Minimizing Distractions

Source:
KnowYourMemes.com

To be productive, writers need more than Virginia Woolf's advice to have "money and a room of one's own." Today, she would add "and a way to keep one from spending the day on Twitter and Facebook."

Coping with distractions is challenging. The technological advances that let us be more productive also gave us the lures keeping us from accomplishing more.

Word processors make it easier to write, but they also encourage us to never stop writing. The internet opened new ways to reach all kinds of information as well as view galleries of Kitler photos. Smartphones keep us in

> The chains of habit are too weak to be felt until they are too strong to be broken.
> **Samuel Johnson**

Hemingway *Editor*

touch with people and distract us with games and bongs announcing new tweets.

No one is immune. We are easily distracted and find it difficult to tune out our surroundings and focus. But we're also an inventive species, so we have these tools to fight back:

● Browser plug-ins that let us block the internet, like StayFocusd for Chrome and Leechblock for Firefox. To block the entire internet, there's the subscription software Freedom for the Mac and PC, and SelfControl for the Mac.

● An alternative is to have two computers on hand, one connected to the internet, and one not. This has the added benefit of being able to use old software you're familiar with and not having to worry about viruses and malware.

● Distraction-free writing software is designed to have a simple interface and few distracting colors. Here are a few of them:

Typed *(Mac only, $29.99)*
Write! *(Win only, free)*
OmmWriter Dana II *(Win, Mac, iOS, $5.11)*
Writer *(Chrome, free)*
Hemingway Editor *(Win, Mac, web, free online)*
iA Writer *(Mac, iOS, Android, $4.99-$19.99)*
Byword *(Mac, iOS, $5.99-$11.99)*
Calmly Writer *(Chrome, free or $0.99)*
Ulysses *(Mac, iPad, $19.99-$44.99)*

The Power of Deadlines

There are many types of deadlines, depending on length: short (25 minutes or an hour); medium (longer than a day, either a week or a month); and long (a year, five years, or even longer).

A short deadline puts you under pressure to perform and you compete against a timer. The Pomodoro Method was created to encourage you to get the task done now.

A medium deadline is useful for finishing anything up to a short novel. It can't be forgotten; it'll stay on top of your brain and won't go away. If it's set on an easily remembered day, such as Friday (end of the workweek, right?) or the end of the month, it gains added power because it coordinates with the calendar. Pin the month to the wall, cross off each day, and you can see the time passing.

A long deadline is useful for planning purposes, but less so as motivation. It's too far into the future to put much pressure on you. But a long deadline can gain power when it's broken into shorter deadlines. For example, if you

The timer is tomato-shaped because *pomodoro* is Italian for tomato.

want a 60,000-word book within six months, take the 26 weeks and divide it into the word count. You'll need to write 2,307 words a week, or 461 words per day during a five-day work week.

TIP

Whatever your deadline, shorten it by ten to twenty percent. This builds in slippage caused by illness, holidays, and general laziness. If you're focused on meeting your deadline, you won't notice the difference, and finishing early gives you time to check the manuscript and make minor corrections.

Chapter 28
Spousal Support

Key Points to Remember

- Spousal support comes in different ways: emotional, financial, even taking on the chores.
- The author in return needs to be accountable for finishing the work and not be distracted.
- Good communication is key to avoid resentment.

The greatest service a wife can render her writer husband is not typing his manuscripts for him, but keeping people away from him. Of course, a husband might do the same, if his wife is the writer.

Patricia Highsmith

Love and marriage, as Sinatra sang, may go together like a horse and carriage, but love and writing can get along like a house on fire, with yelling and screaming.

Having your spouse on your side can boost your writing career. Providing moral support, keeping the books, editing your work, managing your website and ad campaigns. There's a reason why so many authors dedicate their books to their faithful spouses.

Unfortunately, sometimes love doesn't survive a spouse's foray into creating art. It happens so often that art should be added to the four A's — abandonment, adultery, addiction, and abuse — that can destroy a relationship.

Not surprisingly, history shows that it's mostly men who instigate these kinds of problems, either from jealousy or resentment toward their woman who writes, or by combining their art with one of the other A's to create a marriage made in hell:

• The great French writer Colette was 20 when she married an author and publisher who helped her write the four Claudine novels that launched her career. He also published them under his name, took their copyrights, and pocketed the royalties, so when they broke up later, he continued enriching himself from them while she fell into poverty.

• During the 1950s, Peg Bracken's *The I Hate to Cook Book* revealed to the male half of the human race that the distaff side did not have a natural gene for cooking. The male editors she approached rejected the book out of hand, and a woman editor finally bought the book. Nor did Peg have her husband's support; his reaction to the manuscript was a succinct "it stinks," a judgment that, not surprisingly, also doomed his marriage, but not before he saw the size of the first royalty check.

But there have been plenty of helpful spouses:

• Novelist and critic John Bayley nursed Iris Murdoch as she succumbed to Alzheimer's disease, and after her death memorialized her

> "
>
> Be ruthless about protecting writing days, i.e., do not cave in to endless requests to have "essential" and "long overdue" meetings on those days. The funny thing is that, although writing has been my actual job for several years now, I still seem to have to fight for time in which to do it. Some people do not seem to grasp that I still have to sit down in peace and write the books, apparently believing that they pop up like mushrooms without my connivance.
>
> **J.K. Rowling**

in *Elegy for Iris*.

• Novelists Hilary Mantel and Margaret Atwood have husbands who are renowned for their devotion. Mantel's husband, Gerald McEwen, handles her business affairs and gives her plenty of alone time to think and write. Atwood's spouse, author Graeme Gibson, is equally proud of his wife's greater success; she jokes it's because he's "six foot four and gets the tops off jars." One woman writer joked that "Every woman writer should be married to Graeme Gibson."

• A spouse's worth is not just limited to the emotional or business support. Stephen King's wife, Tabitha, literally rescued from the trash the opening pages of *Carrie* and convinced him to finish the book by offering to help him with the women characters. *Carrie* became his first best-seller, and the sale of the paperback rights enabled the family to escape poverty.

For better and for worse, your spouse affects your career. The question is how to get them on your side if they're not already there? If your partner is so opposed to you writing, you might have to choose, like Peg Bracken, between the marriage and your dream. Associating with toxic people or emotional vampires is emotionally and creatively draining. That's why siblings cut themselves off from their families over drug, alcohol, abuse, or severe money-management problems.

But if you're in a good relationship, there are steps to take that will keep your spouse on board with your dream and even be willing to help.

• **Communicate.** Include your partner in your dream. If they don't know you want to write a book, tell them (seems obvious, right? I'm sure it is to *your* spouse; I'm talking about those other writers). You need alone time to think and write, so you need to tell them when that is. Let them know what you're thinking, even if it sounds like you're oversharing.

• **Protect your work.** Communication does not mean talking to them about your work-in-progress unless you feel comfortable doing so. It doesn't mean letting them read your first draft. Your partner probably won't understand that, in Hemingway's immortal words, "all first drafts are shit" (a contestable point, but not here). Finished stories, on the other hand, they should read if they want to and if you trust their judgment.

• **Be accountable.** Some books take longer to write than others. Whether it's three days or three years, your spouse deserves to know about your progress. Set a deadline to finish the first draft. Don't be over-optimistic; be realistic about your abilities and how quickly you create finished work. If it'll take six months, say that (you may want to add a month, so if you finish on time you'll look even better). Break it down into the number of words a day you need to write to get there; setting short-term goals will help you reach your goal. Tell your partner how you're doing; it'll keep you up to the mark as well.

- **Admit failure.** It may seem better to suffer in silence the pain of a broken book, but your partner is going to notice that something is wrong. Now is the time for honesty and openness. Lay out the facts, but more importantly, say what you're going to do to fix it. You'll feel better by letting it out, and — who knows? — they may know ways to help.

Chapter 29
Your Will

- -

Key Points to Remember

- The life+70 copyright means your family could profit from your work for a long time.
- A will makes clear your intentions and establishes a structure where decisions can be made.
- Even your papers have potential value to a university after your death.

- -

Everyone must leave something behind when he dies, my grandfather said. A child or a book or a painting or a house or a wall built or a pair of shoes made. Or a garden planted. Something your hand touched some way so your soul has somewhere to go when you die, and when people look at that tree or that flower you planted, you're there.

Ray Bradbury

WARNING

When your work is published, it is copyrighted automatically. Congratulations. During your lifetime, and for 70 years after your death, you own that work, and you and your descendants have the right to profit from it.

That's the good news.

The bad news is that it's possible for your work to be stolen, lost, or orphaned.

How? By contracts and theft. Inattention to either could cost you dearly.

There's a small chance of that happening, but so is getting struck by lightning, and if it happens to you, the consequences can be devastating.

Here's how to protect yourself from bolts from the blue.

● **Read your contract.** This basic business principal applies to anything you sign, whether it's a book contract, a mortgage, or a wedding certificate.

Don't take anyone's word about what's in it. If an agent says his take is 15% and the contract says 25%, guess which one the judge will say you should follow. The one with your signature on it. If your publisher leaves you the movie rights, make sure it's in the contract.

Reading the contract will also inform you of issues that you won't expect. You may not realize that the publisher held the audio rights to your book, even if they don't intend to exercise it. You may not know that your agent gets the right to profit from your next book, even if she doesn't handle it, because you hired someone better.

If these issues bother you, the time to get them resolved is before you sign on the line that is dotted. Afterwards, you've lost all leverage.

So what does this have to do with copyright? If you sign a publishing contract, you want to make sure the company does not acquire the copyright (unless you agree to, such as in a work-for-hire job like ghostwriting). You want to make sure they don't perform a rights grab,

> Looking back, I imagine I was always writing. Twaddle it was, too. But better far write twaddle or anything, anything, than nothing at all.
>
> **Katherine Mansfield**

WARNING

getting the right to publish in a format they don't intend to exploit (such as audio, film, or foreign translation).

You want a clause in the contract to get the rights back in case the company goes bankrupt, or the book goes out of print.

"Why would they keep these rights?" you ask. Because companies are valued according to the rights they control. Intellectual property is worth money even if they aren't being exploited. If the company fails, those rights can be auctioned to the highest bidder.

- **Be wary of theft.** In 2014, Mormon romance novelist Rachel Ann Nunes was asked by a reader if she collaborated with Sam Taylor Mullens. The reader had noticed similarities between Nunes book *A Bid for Love* and Mullens' *The Auction Deal*. The reader had asked Mullens, and he told her that they were collaborators.

But Nunes never heard of Mullens, who had stolen her book, changed some of the details, and published it. When Nunes pushed back, she was harassed on Facebook and Goodreads by Mullens' supporters. Her books were given one-star ratings on Amazon. The attacks stressed her out, and she gained weight and couldn't sleep or write.

After an investigation, it was discovered that Sam Taylor Mullens wasn't a male author, but the pen name for a female teacher from Utah. Nunes sued her for copyright infringement, and although she won the case, it took four years and caused a lot of stress and money.

How to Protect Your Work

- **File a copyright notice with the Library of Congress.** Yes, your work is already copyrighted, but this step will allow you to collect punitive damages should your lawsuit win at trial.
- **Hunt for plagiarized books.** Set up a text search using unique lines from your books. Save it as a bookmark. Every quarter or six months, run a search (To speed things up if you're using Firefox or Chrome, store these bookmarks in a folder. Right-click on the folder and both browsers will let you open all the searches at once).

But beware: Some of these sites aren't worth pursuing because they're run by scammers who steal information from people seeking free ebooks. But there are sites out there selling stolen work. It's best to check with sources you trust. Join the Facebook group 20Booksto50K and ask there, or visit the Writer Beware site (*accrispin.blogspot.com*).

Wills

The most important story that you write is the one that's read after you die: your will.

> It is the deepest desire of every writer, the one we never admit or even dare to speak of: to write a book we can leave as a legacy. And although it is sometimes easy to forget, wanting to be a writer is not about reviews or advances or how many copies are printed or sold. It is much simpler than that and much more passionate. If you do it right, and if they publish it, you may actually leave something behind that can last forever.
>
> **Alice Hoffman**

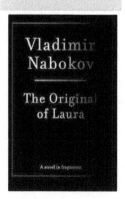

Writers leave behind something potentially more valuable than money, insurance policies, collectible Beanie Babies, and other valuables. We have intellectual property: books, unpublished works, and personal papers. Complete works that can be republished; incomplete works and ideas that can be finished. If you don't decide what will be done with them, someone else will do it for you, and perhaps in ways you did not intend. A will not only determines what happens to your literary legacy, but also who benefits from it.

Another major piece of information to leave behind are your passwords. No one knows completely what you do online. After you're gone, your executor should know how the money is coming in, where you made friends, and what accounts should be closed or ignored. They need to know both the login name and the password. These sites can be divided into four types:

• **Money critical:** Any site from which you get paid or which receives money from you. Ebook publishers, PayPal, bank accounts, government tax sites. Does your family know where your domains are parked and how they are paid for? Your executor should know in advance that AuthorName.Com needs to be paid every year.

• **Business sites:** Anything you used in the course of running your business. Your social media accounts where you posted frequently. Your YouTube channel. The site that handles your newsletter. Your executor may want to download and archive your posts, and let your friends know of your passing. Any online stores that saved your credit card info should be closed.

• **Low-priority sites:** These need attention but not immediately: alumni associations, library and newspaper sites, online courses.

• **Low-priority sites which can be ignored:** That Disney Movie Club account was never used. Social media accounts and posting services that went out of business.

Leaving behind a paper list of your passwords will help your family write "The End" to your life online.

Without a Will, There's No Way

Franz Kafka asked his friend Max Brod to destroy all his stories. He didn't. Vladimir Nabokov wanted his unfinished works destroyed. The note cards for his last unfinished novel, *The Original of Laura* appeared. John Steinbeck's children and his last wife have been in and out of court since his death in 1968 fighting over his royalties and the film and stage rights to his works; it might have finally reached the end after a half-century of litigation.

Not all wills are perfect, but dying without one, or one that does not follow the law, is a recipe for disaster. When Stieg Larsson, author of the *Girl with the Dragon Tattoo* series, died of a heart attack, he left his possessions to one of

Sweden's political parties. Sweden rejected that will because it was not witnessed, as well as competing claims from his unmarried partner of 30 years. His estate, including the rights and royalties to his series went to his father and brother, not his partner of three decades.

At least Larsson's family was interested in keeping his works in print. There are numerous instances of family members making decisions that would have horrified the author. They run the gamut of letting the author's works go out of print because they were embarrassed by their subject matter, to asking outrageous amounts for reprint rights.

Even a finished, legally binding will can cause problems if it's not updated. R.A. Lafferty, considered by many to be one of the great short-story writers of science-fiction, left his estate to his sister. He came down with Alzheimer's, and she died while he was in a nursing home. Because a secondary heir was not named in his will, his estate was divided among the surviving relatives, who all had to agree on any publishing deal. This proved so contentious that the family solved the problem by auctioning the rights to his works.

The best way to ensure that your wishes are known is to have a will. A good place to start is at Neil Gaiman's website. Moved by the plight of his friend John M. Ford, who died without a will, he posted a sample will created with the help of lawyer and author Les Klinger. It sets up a trust. You decide who will be the members and who will be in charge, and together they'll share the royalties and decide on the disposition of your intellectual property.

We used it as the basis of our wills. A lawyer looked it over and tweaked the provisions to conform to the State of Pennsylvania's laws. In addition, he also set up the procedures that will handle making medical decisions and other legal issues. For only a couple hundred dollars, we ensured that our family can financially benefit from our work after we're gone.

They don't know it now, but years from now, it'll probably be my children's favorite story.

A copy of the will can be found in the appendix. Neil Gaiman's post can be read at *journal.neilgaiman.com/2006/10/important-and-pass-it-on.html*

Life Insurance

So long as we're talking about money and death, another question that you should consider is life insurance.

Some people should have life insurance. If you're single, the answer is most likely no. If you're married and have children, you should consider providing for them if you're attacked by a fan or suffer a fatal mishap while on a book tour.

While insurance companies tout whole life policies as an investment tool, it's far less expensive to take out a term policy. A policy costing a couple

It matters not how a man dies, but how he lives. The act of dying is not of importance, it lasts so short a time.
Samuel Johnson

We live as nouns, but we'll be remembered as verbs.
Bill Peschel

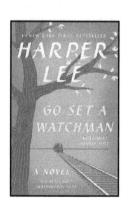

hundred dollars a year could provide a six-figure return, removing one major source of concern in the event of your death.

Your Archive

You've left a paper trail all your writing life. Do you want anyone to read them? What about the trunk novels, the ones you wrote early in your career that are so bad you buried them? Do you want them published?

It's worthy of thought because if the answer's yes, you'll want to create an archive to store your work and arrange for its disposition in your will.

If the answer's no, follow Terry Pratchett's example. When he finished a book, he destroyed everything associated with it: drafts, notes, and alternative texts. At a public ceremony after his death, his executor drove a bulldozer over his hard drives, ensuring that nothing escaped.

Destroying your papers has a long literary history. Thomas Hardy and Charles Dickens both made bonfires of their papers.

Telling a friend to destroy your works is a less-reliable method because it depends on someone else's decision. The dying poet Philip Larkin asked his secretary to destroy his diaries. She used a heavy-duty shredder to do the job. On the other hand, Franz Kafka ordered his best friend Max Brod to destroy all his manuscripts (to be fair, historians argue if Kafka meant it). Brod not only told the writer, "No!" but preserved everything from Franz's hand, including the unpublished novels that made his reputation. Vladimir Nabokov ordered his family to destroy the note cards for his last, unfinished novel. They were published.

It appears that the better the family relationship, the greater the chance your wishes will be carried out. Harper Lee wanted *To Kill A Mockingbird* to be her only published novel. Her literary executor, a lawyer, decided to publish *Mockingbird's* first draft, *Go Set a Watchman*.

Could a university want your archives? You might be surprised. Once the province of great historical figures, universities have opened the doors to lesser-known authors who have created noteworthy works in certain genres, explored new areas in nonfiction, or maintained longstanding ties to their alma mater.

• At the University of Texas at Austin, the Harry Ransom Center acquired a wide range of archives and papers from 20th century writers, artists, poets, and dramatists. Many major figures are represented in whole or in part, but they also have the papers of once-popular writers such as Kathleen Winsor and Leon Uris, TV writers such as Lee Blessing (*Picket Fences*, *Homicide*), and hypertext fiction pioneer Michael Joyce.

• Over his long career, Lev Raphael has published more than 25 books, including memoirs, mysteries, literary fiction, essays, historical fiction, and

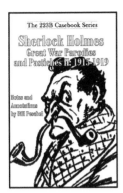

Some of Bill's books are available at the University of Minnesota's Sherlock Holmes collection.

literary criticism. He is an Edith Wharton scholar and has written about the children of Holocaust survivors. His papers were acquired by Michigan State University, where he attended and taught.

• If you write in a particular genre, there might be a place for you, too. Brown University created a Thriller Writers Archive in 2012.

If you write science-fiction/fantasy, the Science Fiction Writers of America maintains a list of libraries with archives in that field (*sfwa.org/2011/04/libraries-with-relatively-large-sf-collections/*), such as Science Fiction Collection at the California State University, the Bud Foote Science Fiction Collection at the Georgia Institute of Technology, and the SFWA Collection at Northern Illinois University. Their page of advice to SF/F authors on keeping their archives apply to writers in other fields as well (*sfwa.org/2011/04/what-sfwa-authors-need-to-know-about-archiving-their-literary-papers1/*).

The University of Minnesota's Sherlock Holmes collection contains material by Arthur Conan Doyle and Holmes-related material by other writers.

Appendix
Exegesis

On the first page of *Career Indie Author* is listed my ten commandments:

1. Thou shall write!
2. Thou shall read widely
3. Thou shall continue thy self-education
4. Thou shall organize thy paperwork
5. Thou shall not covet thy fellow authors' successes
6. Thou shall resist temptations of FOMO, Imposture syndrome, Perfection syndrome, and other mental storms
7. Thou shall engage socially with authors
8. Thou shall pay it forward
9. Thou shall chart thy progress
10. Thou shall be mindful to enjoy your creativity, whether in writing a story, an ad or an email

Here's what they mean.

Commandment 1 should be self-explanatory, but we desire instant success. First-time writers see their book published, and expect that within a few days there should be sales and reviews and why isn't it on the best-seller list yet?

But telling stories and making books isn't a sprint, it's a marathon. Those who don't recognize that spend time and money promoting their sole book, when what they should be doing is working on their next book.

Whether you have one or many books published, you should still write. The best publicity for your last book is your next book.

Commandments 2, 3, and 4 focus on what you can control: your personal habits. Set time aside to read; schedule this if you don't do it naturally and regularly. Reading keeps your head in fiction, opens yourself up to new ways of telling stories, and educates you on how other writers do it. Self-educating reminds you of important principles and exposes you to better ways of working. Remaining organized, while time-consuming and tedious, helps you save time finding needed papers and documents.

Commandments 5 and 6 confront the mental games that demoralize and depress us. Number 5 reminds us that their path is not your path. Their success is not your failure. Learn from their success. Celebrate their success, if only because it shows that you can achieve it as well.

Commandment 6 also teaches how the mind deceives you. There is within us a monkey mind that protects us from what it perceives as pain. Risk can create pain, so it distracts you from it by playing on the fear of missing out. It draws your attention to something new: a new product, a new form of social media, a new marketing technique or even a new story idea. Imposture syndrome is present in many people; even accomplished people such as P.G. Wodehouse believed that they were not successful writers. Perfection syndrome sets an arbitrarily high standard for your work that you'll never meet, so you'll never risk failure.

The mind will distract you from walking a risky path. Don't let it.

Commandment 7 is a reminder to keep positive people around you, and fellow authors are more likely to sympathize with your struggles than family and friends. Listening to their struggles can remind you that yours might not be as bad, and they can provide useful advice and insights, just as you might with them. Believe me, being praised for editorial advice that helped them is rewarding for you.

Commandment 8 is a tenet of the indie author community. Share what you know, answer questions, and share your problems and challenges. We're all in this together; your success does not affect theirs; and a rising tide lifts all boats.

Commandment 9 is vital in business. Record accurate data — sales, expenses, advertising and website visits — and review it. Learn from it, and apply that knowledge to future decisions. You will make mistakes; everyone does. But you can control whether you'll make those mistakes again and again. People who never learn never progress.

Commandment 10 can be annoying advice, but it is a reminder that the indie writing career is an *option.* If you're not enjoying some part of the process, it's time to reconsider doing this. Reminding yourself why you got into this crazy business can help you through the third rewrite of a chapter, or getting up at 5 a.m. to get to a book festival on time, or spending a sunny afternoon filing papers and recording expenses.

> If you're going to become a writer, you have to start introducing yourself to people. You have to know how to talk. People need to like you in this business, to remember you well.
>
> **Richard Rodriguez**

> Let me sum it up for you. Information is not knowledge. Knowledge is not wisdom. Wisdom is not truth. Truth is not beauty. Beauty is not love. Love is not music. Music is the best.
>
> **Frank Zappa**

> Finis to all the manuscripts I've penned,
> And to life's fitful fever here an end,
> An end to lime-white women golden-tressed,
> And in God's hand at Judgment be the rest.
>
> **Anonymous,** 16th century

Resources

To help you build your writing business, *Career Indie Author* comes with a package of resources. The One-Page Business Plan, publication and metadata checklists, and Excel spreadsheets for recording book sales and income / expenses are available at *careerindieauthor.com/resources*.

Career Indie Author was not written to be the sole authority on the business side of writing, so I'm going to list here the products, books, courses, and other material that I've found useful.

I'm the first to admit that what works for me might not work for you. We have different styles of thinking, planning, filing, and recovering information.

For example, I've read a lot of books about how to write well and how to market and sell your books. Some of them were highly regarded, but they didn't work for me.

As for writing fiction, despite reading a lot of books, it was a free Gale course offered through my library, taught by Steve Alcorn, that pounded home to me what scene and sequel was all about. A video course taught me the concept of character tags, a simple technique that's easy to use.

In short, we learn in different ways. Some people learn by doing or through watching videos or listening to podcasts. Sometimes, what goes over our head early in our career becomes stupidly obvious later in life. And some people just collect stuff but never use them.

So for those of you just starting out, here are a list of resources that represent my personal recommendations as of 2020. These are the tools that I've found useful that might help you as well. Don't feel that you should get them all, or get them just because I say so. Read the reviews, talk to other writers, and educate yourself.

Software

Writing tools: Microsoft Word is still the dominant word processor, but that doesn't mean you have to use it. Your computer probably came with a simple text editor like Notepad (Windows) or TextEdit or Notes (Mac).

I use Word 2007, but for big projects I also use Scrivener (*literatureandlatte.com/*) along with a free Dropbox (*dropbox.com*) account. Dropbox is a file hosting service that lets me store files on their cloud server and access them from another computer. No matter which computer I'm working from — the office computer downstairs or the laptop in the dining room — I can call up the latest version of a Scrivener file, work on it, and save it back to Dropbox. Once a week, I backup my Dropbox projects to my main computer.

In addition, about every quarter, I back up all my files to an external hard drive. This is a hard drive, just like the one in my computer, that sits on the desk.

Artwork tools: These are tools used to create or modify art: book covers, banners, memes, interior art, whatever. I use two very old programs: Fireworks 3.0 from 1995 and Photoshop PS2. I mention this only to demonstrate that you don't have to get the latest software, and you don't have to upgrade just because the company wants you to.

Unfortunately, unless you find these old versions at a garage sale, you'll have to find alternatives. Photoshop is available from Adobe on a subscription model, meaning you have to pay a monthly fee to use it. If it is not worth it, there's the open-source GIMP (*gimp.org*) which was designed as a Photoshop alternative. It has a high learning curve, but there's plenty of online tutorials, YouTube videos, and books to learn from.

Promotional image created using BookBrush. There was no option for using a non-standard sized book cover, hence the squashed look.

A British company called Affinity offers Affinity Photo (*affinity.serif.com/*) as part of their three-product suite. Reasonably priced ($50), it contains many of the same features as Photoshop and was designed from the ground up to work with Affinity Publisher and Illustrator. There are also online tools that offer to make images for websites and social media, such as Canva (*canva.com*) and BookBrush (*bookbrush.com*). Typically, their free tools offer limited choices, and you have to buy a subscription to unlock more features.

Ebook design: Kindle Create, Jutoh, Calibre, Draft2Digital

Trade paperback design: InDesign, Affinity Publisher, Word.

Recently, I bought Affinity Publisher (*affinity.serif.com/*). Affinity creates award-winning software that's cheaper than Photoshop and has many of the same features. Their suite includes Photo, Illustrator, and Designer, and they're designed to work together seamlessly. I put this book together using Affinity, and I highly recommend.

Universal Links: Draft2Digital, StoryOrigin, BKLNK

Distribution (Marketing): BookFunnel, StoryOrigin

Ebook Distribution (Direct): These sites offer direct access to their sites: Amazon, Apple, Kobo, and Nook (Barnes & Noble).

Ebook Distribution (Aggregates): Aggregate sites like Smashwords and Draft2Digital let you put up your ebook file, then choose where they distribute them too.

Smashwords and Draft2Digital both distribute to these sites: Amazon, Apple, Kobo, Nook (Barnes & Noble), Library Direct and Overdrive (which supplies libraries with ebooks), Baker & Taylor's Axis 360, Scribd.

Smashwords also distributes to: cloudLibrary, Gardners Extended Retail, Gardners Library, and Odilo.

Draft2Digital also distributes to: Tolino, 24Symbols, bibliotheca, Hoopla, and Vivlio

Courses

Self-Publishing Formula: (*selfpublishingformula.com/courses/*) For using Amazon Ads, I'm learning from Mark Dawson's Ads for Authors video course. It's expensive ($800+), but it's a lifetime membership so you can take the course as many times as you need. It's early days for me; I'm only about 25% into the Amazon ads module, but I've learned new things about Amazon ads (and other things, including how to use Excel to analyze my campaigns), and I'm going to apply my knowledge to the campaigns I already have up.

Reedsy Free Courses: (*blog.reedsy.com/learning/courses/*) Free ten-day courses by email with a little bit of information each day. Book design, distribution, writing, cover design and more.

Gale Online Courses: Public libraries offer a variety of online courses, often free or at a reduced cost. We found Gale, or ed2go, with its huge list of classes, covering all kinds of subjects. Courses last six weeks with two lessons per week.

Books and Websites

There are thousands of books out there on the craft of writing. If you spend enough time, you'll compile a small library of works. Some are by famous authors, some by excellent teachers, then there are those who think they know what they're talking about, and then there's the charlatans and what I think of as book preachers who are better at inspiring wannabe writers than educating them.

While many of these books are entertaining to read, the ones I've chosen provide value for money by covering important points about effective writing, but in a way that is engaging as well.

Amazon Decoded by David Gaughran. Like it or not, Amazon is a big part of a writer's life. Gaughran dives into how the bookstore side promotes books, runs Kindle Unlimited, and how you can use its algorithms to your advantage. He goes into detail about how to set up and run an ad campaign using your newsletter and social media accounts, Amazon's promotional tools, and recommendation services like BookBub to boost your books' sales.

Getting Things Done by David Allen. The best book for organizing my life, hands down. Even though I've fallen off the GTD wagon, I've returned to it and discovered all over again that I get more done with it than without it.

Self Editing for Fiction Writers by Renni Browne and Dave King. Here's how the pros do it. And by pros I mean F. Scott Fitzgerald and that crowd. What I like about Browne and King's approach is that they show you the stages a manuscript goes through, and how the changes are made. The book opens with a scene from an early draft of *The Great Gatsby,* followed by the published version. This way, you get to see authors struggling through figuring out what to say and how to say it. Always engaging and enlightening.

Make that Scene: A Writer's Guide to Setting, Mood and Atmosphere by William Noble. A lot of works by beginning writers sound alike. They describe the characters, deliver the steps of the plot, maybe tell a joke or two, and that's about it. They all sound alike because not enough effort was put into things like mood and atmosphere, characterization and description. It's these extra elements that lend flavor to the narrative, and helps you distinguish one author from another. *Make that Scene* is one of the few books I've found that focuses solely on this part of narrative. Noble describes the importance of setting and how it integrates with the plot, by adding drama, a counterpoint or ironic contrast to it.

Holly Lisle's One-Pass Revision (*hollylisle.com/one-pass-manuscript-revision-from-first-draft-to-last-in-one-cycle/*). Can you handle learning from a blog post? Lisle has written dozens of books using her one-pass revision technique, and while you may not want to go that far, she gives an effective step-by-step procedure that'll help you work your way through revising your novel.

Getting the Words Right by Theodore A. Rees Cheney. It's an old book, so you'll find it for sale in used book stores. Taking inspiration from thinking of revision as re-envisioning your work, Cheney walks you through the various stages, starting with the big picture and guiding you through revising sentences and even words. His section on handling transitions is worth the

price of the book alone.

Writing Novels that Sell by Jack M. Bickham and ***Techniques of the Selling Writer*** by Dwight V. Swain. Two classics that are still being read despite being published in 1981. Used copies are so expensive that you might as well spring for a new copy.

People's Guide to Publishing: Building a Successful, Sustainable, Meaningful Book Business From the Ground Up by Joe Biel. The owner of Microcosm Publishing in Portland, Ore., lays it all out about running a small publishing house. He details the publishing process from initial proposal to shipping the finished product. He explains the reasoning behind why he publishes some books and not others. He publishes only books he is proud of and he thinks he can sell. Absolutely vital for anyone who dreams of running their own publishing house.

Simple Will

(This is the simple will form from Neil Gaiman discussed in Chapter 29. Be sure to run this by your attorney to make it conform to your state's laws. Authors outside the U.S. can still take this to their legal advisors to use as a guideline.)

I declare that this is my Will. I hereby revoke all prior Wills.

1. I give [insert description of gifts of property, money, etc., or a simple gift (such as "my entire estate to ,if he/she survives me, or if not, to _____") or a fractional gift (such as "one-half of
my entire estate")].

2. I nominate _____ as executor of my Will, to serve without bond.

3. Notwithstanding any other provision of this Will, after my death, my executor shall not distribute any part of my estate consisting of (a) ideas, manuscripts, books, drawings, pictures, scripts, playscripts, treatments, stories, poetry, dramas, or any other fiction or nonfiction writings, whether published or unpublished, created in whole or in part by me (collectively "Writings"), (b) rights to proceeds from any Writings, rights to publish, exploit, license, or sell any Writings, contracts for the publication, exploitation, licensing, or sale of any Writings, and any derivative or secondary rights in or to the Writings or derived from the Writings, as well as (c) rights to any performances, recordings, readings, or dramatizations by me and my name and likeness (collectively "Creative Property"),but instead shall transfer all of the Creative Property to the special trustees named in this Will, to hold in trust in perpetuity (to be known as the "Creative Property Trust"), as follows:

A. The special trustees shall, in addition to those powers now or hereafter conferred by law or by the other terms of this Will, solely and exclusively have the following powers with respect to the Creative Property:

(1) To publish, exploit, license, and sell, in the special trustees' sole discretion, any Writings;

(2) To retain any Writings and refrain from publishing, exploiting, licensing, or selling such Writings for as long as the special trustees deem appropriate, at the risk of the trust estate, in the special trustees' discretion.

B. Notwithstanding any other designation of the trustee or trustees in this Will, after my death, _____, _____, and _____ shall serve as special trustees of the Creative Property Trust. If any of them fails to qualify or ceases to act as a special trustee, the remaining of them shall designate a successor trustee to serve in his or her place as a special trustee of the Creative Property Trust.

C. All income and principal of the Creative Property Trust (other than Creative Property) shall be distributed immediately upon receipt to _____.

Executed at _____, on _____, 20____.

_____

WITNESSED:

_____

Metadata Form

Metadata for [BOOK TITLE]

About the Book

Title:
Subtitle:
Series / Number:
Imprint:
ISBN:
ASIN:
Number of Pages:
Illustrations, Number of:
Trim Size:
Interior: (choose from white or cream)
Cover: (choose from matte or glossy)
Short description: Distributors like IngramSpark limit you to 350 characters.
Full description:
Author(s), illustrators and other contributors / Bio:
Prior work for each contributor:
Location (for each contributor):
Affiliations (for each contributor):

Prices

<u>GENERAL</u>

    Price: (print and/or ebook)

<u>INGRAMSPARK (price / discount / returns?)</u>

    US:
    UK:
    EU:
    CA:
    AUS:
    Global Connect:

Publication History and Notable Upgrades

Record what happened to this book during and after publication, including price changes, new editions, problems with uploading it, and any unusual situations worth recording. Repeat these headers for each bookstore (Kindle, Nook, Google Play, etc.).

First Published:
Latest Edition:

Discoverability

Amazon keywords should be completed before publishing your book, but the rest can be done during the process. Don't forget to write down your choices!

Amazon Keywords (limit 50 characters per line):
1.
2.
3.
4.
5.
6.
7.

Categories (Amazon):

BISAC codes:

Thema subjects:

Geographic region:
Audience:
Table of contents:
Review quotes:

Book Production Checklist

Title: _____

☐ Finish manuscript draft! Before you start; think. Did you revise everything you wanted? It's easier to do it now than after you create two Word files for the ebook and trade paperback editions.

☐ Copy edit manuscript

☐ Copyright page

☐ Chapter titles against table of contents

☐ Numbered chapters for correct sequence (1,2,3)

☐ Series of words for parallel structure

☐ Proper names for consistency, accuracy, checkmark as you go

☐ Parentheses to ensure they're paired

☐ Quote marks to ensure they're paired and no doubles w/in doubles

☐ Paragraph indents. First paragraph in chapter and after line space is not indented.

☐ Spellcheck manuscript

☐ Grammarcheck manuscript

☐ Get Bowker ISBN

☐ Contact Library of Congress Preassigned Control Number program (no closer than two weeks to publication) to receive number for copyright page.

☐ Proof manuscript file on Kindle before splitting into two formats.

☐ Fill out METADATA form

Create Trade Paperback

☐ Flow text into interior template file. Code original MS by finding italics and bold and coding them (like %%% or @@@). Save as text file, delete words in template file. Reopen text file into Word, cut and paste into interior template.

☐ Create EBOOK file. Delete MANUSCRIPT TPB file. Corrections made after this will be made to the TPB's interior template file and the ebook file.

☐ TABLE OF CONTENTS: To add leaders, either assign a leader to the first line, then update the TableOfContents style, or if you're using a previous template already modified, use the style.

☐ Format text using Styles

☐ Format poems, messages (telegrams, notes)

☐ Add back matter

☐ Add section breaks

☐ Style display heads.

☐ Add interior art. Greyscale if needed. Make sure final versions are kept in separate folder, and that all are the right size by adding horizontal and vertical resolution columns in windows explorer. Art must be 300dpi JPGs except for line art, which must be 600dpi BMPs.

☐ Add header

☐ Add page numbers. Make sure first page of each chapter does not have them.

Proof Trade Paperback

☐ PROOF START: Print PDF pages and cover and edit
☐ Proof cover, back cover text, spine
☐ Proof captions
☐ Check for widows and orphans (single words only)
☐ Check excessively tight or loose lines
☐ Paragraphs have ending punctuation
☐ Wrong-word errors
☐ Run Spellcheck and Pro Writing Aid PROOF FINISH
☐ Before making PDF, decompress all artwork (do not save)
☐ Print PDF using Save As PDF in Word or Nitro extension
☐ Check PDF to make sure chapter titles are at proper place
☐ Ensure styles are applied consistently
☐ Build cover / back cover

When TPB Is Finished

☐ Load onto KDP; set pages to CREAM
☐ When book appears at Amazon, claim on Author's Page Bibliography
☐ Update BookBub Author page
☐ Set up Goodreads page
☐ Send press release and b/w 300dpi of book cover to media outlets and groups that accept them (writers groups)
☐ Post to Facebook groups that accept them. DO NOT SPAM GROUPS.
☐ Copy book covers into "BUSINESS Book Cover" folder
☐ Create book page at your website

Prep IngramSpark TPB

☐ Update interior file before making a new PDF. Update copyright notice, check ads in the back of the book. Make sure that grayscale art is 300dpi saved JPG and line art is 600dpi saved BMP.
☐ Submit information to Ingram for cover template (bookmark in My Other Accounts folder). Get PDF.
☐ Visit https://pdf2jpg.net/ to convert PDF to JPG
☐ Resize cover art on template.
☐ Make sure document size is as stated in lower-left-hand-corner (for 6x9 it's 15x12).
☐ Save as CMYK. Make sure it's not compressed.
☐ Check file's horizontal and vertical dimensions in Windows Explorer.
☐ Post to IngramSpark.

When We Receive TPB

☐ File copyright with Library of Congress. Double-check spelling of title, author and other info. Send two copies to Library of Congress.

☐ Send one copy to satisfy the CIP program obligation to Library of Congress; US Programs, Law, and Literature Division; Cataloging in Publication Program; 101 Independence Ave., S.E.; Washington, D.C. 20540-4283

☐ Mail copies to friends / reviewers
☐ Note on Free Book List File
☐ Add book to Bookshop.org site
☐ Announce in newsletter.

Create Ebook

☐ Copy artwork into new folder
☐ Check artwork for size (79dpi, 600px wide); cover (300dpi, 600px wide); and type (RGB).
☐ Compare EBOOK file with TPB template file using the Word function.
☐ Add End Page — Newsletter solicitation with CTA
☐ Add catalog page, author photo, at end of main text and BEFORE footnotes
☐ Ensure publication names are italicized/non-italicized where appropriate
☐ Bold and underline footnote title
☐ Underline footnote link
☐ Add back copy text to front
☐ Move copyright to back.
☐ Add line: Ebook version by [company]
☐ Add ** links to artwork
☐ Modify Table of Contents as needed
☐ Proof captions
☐ Run Spellcheck
☐ Run Grammarcheck
☐ Create ebook, using Kindle Create for KDP, Jutoh for rest.

When Ebook Is Produced

☐ Proof ebook.
☐ Check footnote links by working back to front, front to back, then move down to next footnote and repeat.
☐ Check for correct placement of art and spelling/facts in captions.
☐ Check hyperlinks
☐ Load onto Kindle, Nook, Kobo, Google Play
☐ Load onto Smashwords (for iTunes and other sites)
☐ Announce on newsletter

When Ebook Has Appeared on Sites

☐ Update sales spreadsheet with new title
☐ Update website book page with links
☐ Update Amazon Author Page bibliography

☐ Update Goodreads
☐ Send announcement to groups
☐ Set up Google Alert for book's title

About the Authors

Teresa Peschel lives with her family in the Sweetest Place on Earth. She has long been interested in sustainability, resource depletion, and finding a balanced life, not too much and not too little. Why take more than you need when other people and animals need lives and space too? While growing up, she read plenty of science-fiction and fantasy and wondered what the authors hand-waved away about how difficult it really would be to terraform another planet. She read plenty of romances and wondered where the characters' relatives were and how they paid the bills. So as Odessa Moon, she also writes science-fiction romances set on a terraformed Mars.

Bill Peschel is a former journalist who shares a Pulitzer Prize with the staff of *The Patriot-News* in Harrisburg, Pa. He also is a mystery fan who runs the Wimsey Annotations at Planetpeschel.com. The author of *Writers Gone Wild* (Penguin), he publishes through Peschel Press the 223B Casebook Series of Sherlockian parodies and pastiches; a collection of Sherlock Holmes stories featuring Mark Twain; reprints of Victorian true crime books; and annotated editions of mysteries by Dorothy L. Sayers and Agatha Christie. Peschel lives with his family in Hershey, where the air really does smell like chocolate.

Lightning Source UK Ltd.
Milton Keynes UK
UKHW030948181122
412418UK00007B/796